[GONE]

Site-specific Works

by Dorothy Cross

Robin Lydenberg

McMullen Museum of Art

Boston College

DISTRIBUTED BY

UNIVERSITY OF CHICAGO PRESS

This publication is issued in conjunction with the exhibition *GONE: Site-specific Works by Dorothy Cross*, organized by the Charles S. and Isabella V. McMullen Museum of Art, Boston College.

Curator: Robin Lydenberg
Photographic prints: Stephen Vedder
April 14 – July 12, 2005

The exhibition and catalogue have been underwritten by Boston College with major support from the Patrons of the McMullen Museum. The exhibition also received generous support from the Cultural Division of the Department of Foreign Affairs of Ireland and from the Government of Ireland.

Library of Congress Control Number: 2005920580 ISBN: 1-892850-09-5
Distributed by University of Chicago Press

Exhibition Coordination by Naomi Blumberg and Stoney Conley
Editing by Vera Kreilkamp
Copyediting by Naomi Blumberg
Design and typography by Keith Ake, Office of Marketing Communications
The catalogue is composed in Melior and Minion. Printed by Dynagraf,
Cover: Dorothy Cross, *Ghost Ship*, 1999, photo: Ronan McCrea
Back cover: Dorothy Cross, *Chiasm,* 1999, still from performance video, courtesy of the artist

Photography Credits:
Caught in a State: Dorothy Cross; black and white photo of Kilmainham Gaol courtesy of Kilmainham Gaol Museum
La Primera Cena: Dorothy Cross
Attendant: Dorothy Cross; *Urinals,* John Kellett
Snake: video stills from *Untitled* provided by Dorothy Cross; *Albino Python,* John Kellett
Slippery Slope: process photos, Dorothy Cross and Loring McAlpin
Chiasm: process photos, Dorothy Cross; video stills from performance provided by Dorothy Cross
Strangers on a Train: Dorothy Cross; *Kiss* by John Kellett
CRY: Dorothy Cross
Opening of the Sixth Seal, courtesy National Gallery of Ireland
Ghost Ship: black and white photo of "Daunt," T. Fergus Cross; process photos, Dorothy Cross; final large format photo and cover, Ronan McCrea
Lover Snakes/Virgin Shroud/Amazon: John Kellett
Eclipse: Todd Burgermeister
Shark.Cow.Bath: Dorothy Cross
Eyemaker: video stills of Mr. Haas, ocularist, provided by Dorothy Cross
Midges: still from video provided by Dorothy Cross
Stabat Mater: photo of cave, Loring McAlpin
All reproduced images scanned by Stephen Vedder

Table of Contents

Director's Foreword

This exhibition and accompanying book are the brainchild of Robin Lydenberg, a renowned scholar, literary and cultural critic, and professor of English at Boston College. Over a decade ago, our late colleague Professor Adele Dalsimer, co-founder of the University's Irish Studies Program, introduced many of us at Boston College to the work of Dorothy Cross, who has gone on to become one of Ireland's most celebrated contemporary artists. Since that time, Lydenberg has lectured and published widely on Cross. The Museum's chief curator, Alston Conley, and I exhibited several of her sculptures and videos in two group exhibitions at the McMullen: *Irish Art Now* (1999) organized by the Irish Museum of Modern Art in Dublin and *Eire/Land* (2003), an historically wide-ranging show that focused on the political, cultural, and aesthetic particularities of Irish land and landscape that we organized in conjunction with professors from Irish Studies. Seeing clearly Cross's importance as an international as well as an Irish artist, the Museum proposed devoting a solo exhibition to her work that would serve as a launching pad for a new study of the artist's work written by Lydenberg and would coincide with, complement, and complete a major retrospective of Cross's sculpture, photography, and video works at Dublin's Irish Museum of Modern Art to open in June 2005. The collaboration between scholar and artist throughout this project was inspiring to witness. Both are so passionately engaged in exploring the space inhabited by the cerebral, the sensual, and the aesthetic; both so generously exchanged their ideas so that the product could be much more than the sum of its parts. Both are due our deepest appreciation and gratitude.

Given Lydenberg's particular interest in the site-specific projects, we arrived at the bold decision to organize a show and catalogue devoted to a body of work no longer in existence. Without attempting to recreate or simulate these projects, our chief curator Alston Conley designed an exhibition that enables viewers to imagine, from the traces left behind, the dynamic experience of audiences present at the original events. Stephen Vedder, Assistant Director of Photography in the University's Media and Technology Services, refined the original documentary slides with advanced scanning techniques to arrive at the high quality images in the exhibition and catalogue. He also provided invaluable technical and artistic advice on image selection and formatting. Generous loans of objects from the artist, Loring McAlpin, and David Fitzgerald and Brid McCarthy at the Kerlin Gallery in Dublin have allowed us to complete the picture.

We are grateful as well to Naomi Blumberg who coordinated this project from beginning to end, from copyediting the manuscript and wall text to advising on the selection of images. She was aided in these tasks by intern Jamisen Jenkins, who worked with her from Robin Lydenberg's manuscript to compose the wall text. John McCoy designed the website and wall texts; Keith Ake has crafted a stunningly beautiful book befitting Cross's inspired work, and Vera Kreilkamp provided extraordinarily discerning editing and research advice on the text of the catalogue.

As with all projects of this type, *GONE* could not have been undertaken without the support of Boston College, especially President William P. Leahy, S.J., Academic Vice-President John Neuhauser, Associate Academic Vice-President Patricia Deleeuw, Graduate Dean of Arts and Sciences Michael Smyer, and Dean of Arts and Sciences Joseph Quinn. The Lowell Humanities Series under the direction of Paul Doherty enabled Dorothy Cross to lecture at the exhibition's opening. We also extend thanks to the Honorable Isolde Moylan, Consul General of Ireland in Boston for her assistance in numerous ways and enduring interest in the project, and to Mary Lou Crane and Catherine Concannon of our Development Office for structuring our funding efforts. Major support for the exhibition and catalogue was provided by the Patrons of the McMullen Museum with generous contributions from the Cultural Division of the Department of Foreign Affairs of Ireland and from the Government of Ireland. Without their help, much of the work on the following pages, both textual and visual, would simply be gone.

Nancy Netzer
Professor of Art History
Director, McMullen Museum of Art

CURATOR'S PREFACE

Regained as Gone

"The world must be regained every day, in repetition, regained as gone."
—Stanley Cavell, *In Quest of the Ordinary* (1988)

This volume, published in conjunction with the exhibition *GONE: Site-specific Works by Dorothy Cross* at Boston College's McMullen Museum (April 14–July 12, 2005), brings together for the first time a particular body of Dorothy Cross's work conceived and executed during the 1990s in different locations around the globe. Because many of these projects were presented in remote places, and all of them for short periods of time, they have been viewed by relatively small audiences. This exhibition and accompanying catalogue, therefore, provide valuable photographic documentation and an extended commentary on Cross's contribution to the genre of temporary site-specific art.

I have been following and writing about Cross's art since 1998, when Prof. Adele Dalsimer, the late co-founder and co-director of the Irish Studies Program at Boston College, introduced me to her work. A literary interest in international avant-garde writers from Lautréamont to William Burroughs, an engagement with the interdisciplinary manifestations of Dada and Surrealism, and an interest in the theoretical frames of post-structuralism, psychoanalysis, and gender studies—all of these personal predilections found resonance in my encounters with Cross's work. Although this intellectual common ground first drew me to Cross's conceptual art, the striking visual qualities of her work and her subtle attentiveness to the life of matter have revealed new territories of unexpected beauty.

In all of her art, Cross explores the local particularities of time and place, even as she inclines toward the psychic commonality of our anxieties and desires. She brings this dual perspective to bear on three interrelated themes: the return of the repressed, the impossibility of desire, and the inevitability of loss. In ongoing conversations and correspondence with the artist, I found myself drawn to how these topics were animated in what we began to refer to as her "gone" works.

The nine site-specific projects presented in *GONE* were created in locations as varied as a Byzantine church in Turkey and an abandoned handball alley in Ireland. These works evoke the return of repressed histories (*Caught in a State*, *La Primera Cena*, *Attendant*, and *Snake*); the complexities and limits of desire (*Slippery Slope*, *Chiasm*, *Strangers on a Train*); and the haunting traces of absence and loss (*CRY* and *Ghost Ship*). Cross did not set out to preserve or recreate the sites and objects used in these installations, but to collaborate with them, and to release them, transformed, into circulation. Remarking on the fate of personal family objects used in some of her works, she explains, "I am passing them away from me, breaking the line of inheritance."[1] By breaking this line of personal inheritance, Cross transmits to viewers the collective inheritance of a "common mortality, common love and common struggle" (Cross qtd. in Bonaventura 19).

The artist's model of transmission is not the didactic passing on of fixed meanings or rigid directives. On the contrary, Cross describes the weight of cultural, social, and moral conventions as a burden she has always resisted: "I didn't want to continue that inheritance [of the trappings of bourgeois civility] in a regular way.... I was interested in obliterating or transforming it." Transmission, in her work, is always an opportunity for transformation and change.

An early piece entitled *Shark.Cow.Bath*, executed for Artscape Nordland in 1993, is unique among Cross's site-specific works in that it was designed to be permanent. Even in this work, however, Cross allows mutability to unsettle permanence. The elements indicated in the title—a cow's upturned udder carved on a boulder of local pink granite, a bronze cast of a blue shark adorned with breasts, and a reproduction of her father's cast iron bath—were left exposed at a coastal site. The bath was placed halfway between low and high tide, and Cross was aware that this "domestic" element of the work, filled and emptied daily by the tide, would eventually be swept away by storms, leaving only the represented "natural" elements of cow and shark. *Bath* now lies submerged like some foundered craft in the North Sea waters, dispossessed. Whether it is the result of active choice or of natural evolution, such dispossession paradoxically keeps the individual elements of the work in circulation, open to future transformations.

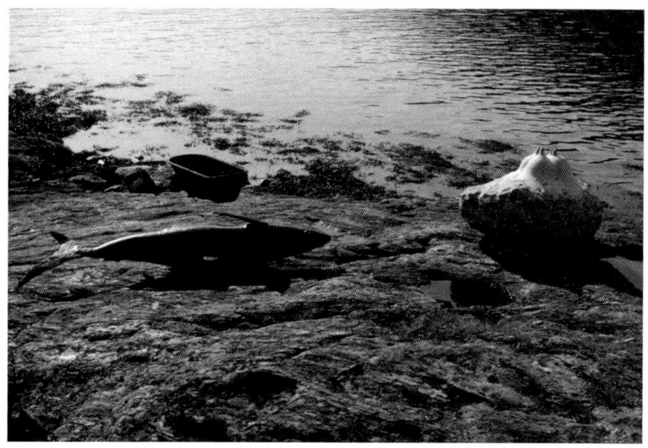

Shark.Cow.Bath, 1993

A liberating sense of letting go permeates Cross's site-specific art, in which she often abdicates personal history, cultural conventions, and even the autonomy of the individual subject. Cross's work also reflects the postmodern orientation in which the "privileged position" of the viewer, as the center or "origin of the coordinates" of vision, is deconstructed. Only when artist and viewer alike are "dispossessed and dispersed," do they actually "enter the picture" (Krauss 1993, 184). For Cross, such dispossession and the absence it leaves behind are generative. Dispossession, the choosing of that fertile void, clears a space for new creation.

In Cross's work, dispossession or loss is a not a termination but a beginning, or a beginning again. It has its part to play in the dialectical sequence of avant-garde practice described by Hal Foster as "ruination, recovery, and resistance" (1993, 166). For Cross, as for the Surrealists, this process is animating rather than melancholic. *Ruination* destabilizes the fixed meanings that contain and limit a given site, object, or image. The *recovery* that follows involves not an archaeological work of restoration and completion, but rather the reactivation of those repressed elements that defy order, hierarchy, and fixed identity.[2] Finally, *resistance* insures against the deadly memorializing of an irrecoverable past or the substitution of a new fixed meaning and order that merely replaces the old. Cross's method of dispossession and re-circulation in her site-specific projects constitutes such a strategy of resistance. This effect is enhanced by the impermanence of the installations and by the structural gap or hole built into each piece, maintaining it in a state of permanent incompletion.

Classifying an artist like Dorothy Cross is difficult; the only categories that seem appropriate to her work are those based on the transgression of definitive categories. Cross could be included in that group of artists Rosalind Krauss describes as "artists of the 'optical unconscious'" (1993, 206), artists whose works reveal how "human vision can be thought to be less than a master of all it surveys" (1993, 180).[3] Like the artists singled out by Krauss, Cross simultaneously makes and unmakes site, identity, form, and classification. She also has affinities with those we might call "artists of absence" or "artists of the trace"; her work, however conceptual, never evaporates into abstraction, but rather achieves, paradoxically, the materialization of absence and loss.[4]

Materialized, but never commodified, the temporary site-specific works Cross has produced since 1991 involve both production and performance, the simultaneous enactment of memorializing and dispersing. Perhaps all art, all representation, is memorial in that it points toward something that persists *in absentia*.[5] Cross's sited works escape the immobility of the monument and the austere sterility of the relic because they do not memorialize a single past event or lost object, but rather illuminate the ongoing process of disappearance and loss. A performative element runs throughout Cross's art, from early gallery installations such as *Ebb*, which the artist describes as a kind of "theatre piece," to her most recent and most theatrical site-specific projects, *Chiasm*, *Ghost Ship,* and *Stabat Mater*.

Performance theorist Peggy Phelan suggests that the "enactment of invocation and disappearance undertaken by performance and theatre is precisely the drama of corporeality itself. At once a consolidated fleshly form and an eroding, decomposing formlessness" (4). This drama of bodies that die and performances that disappear provokes the critic's effort to "preserve and represent" such mutability in the detailed, documented immobility of a text. Although Phelan cautions against this analytical desire as "a desire we should resist" (3), I have succumbed in this study to that conservationist's dream. The documentary images and critical analyses offered in this catalogue will fix, in an artificial way, the final form of these works. In Cross's contribution to this volume, however, a more dynamic temporality is restored by her visual and textual narratives of the process of construction of *Chiasm* and *Ghost Ship*. Ultimately, the McMullen Museum exhibition, which will come and go, offers a more truthful representation of the ephemerality of these projects.

The status of Dorothy Cross's temporary site-specific works as "gone" makes documentation and interpretation a necessity. Because her work continues to evolve in surprising and provocative ways, any study of it must be acknowledged, in Marcel Duchamp's phrase, as "definitively unfinished" (qtd. in Tomkins 3). The resistance of the nine works discussed here to any final analysis, their persistent elusiveness, their *GONE*-ness, is a tribute to Dorothy Cross's subtle realization of the entanglements of repression, desire, and loss.

Robin Lydenberg
Professor of English

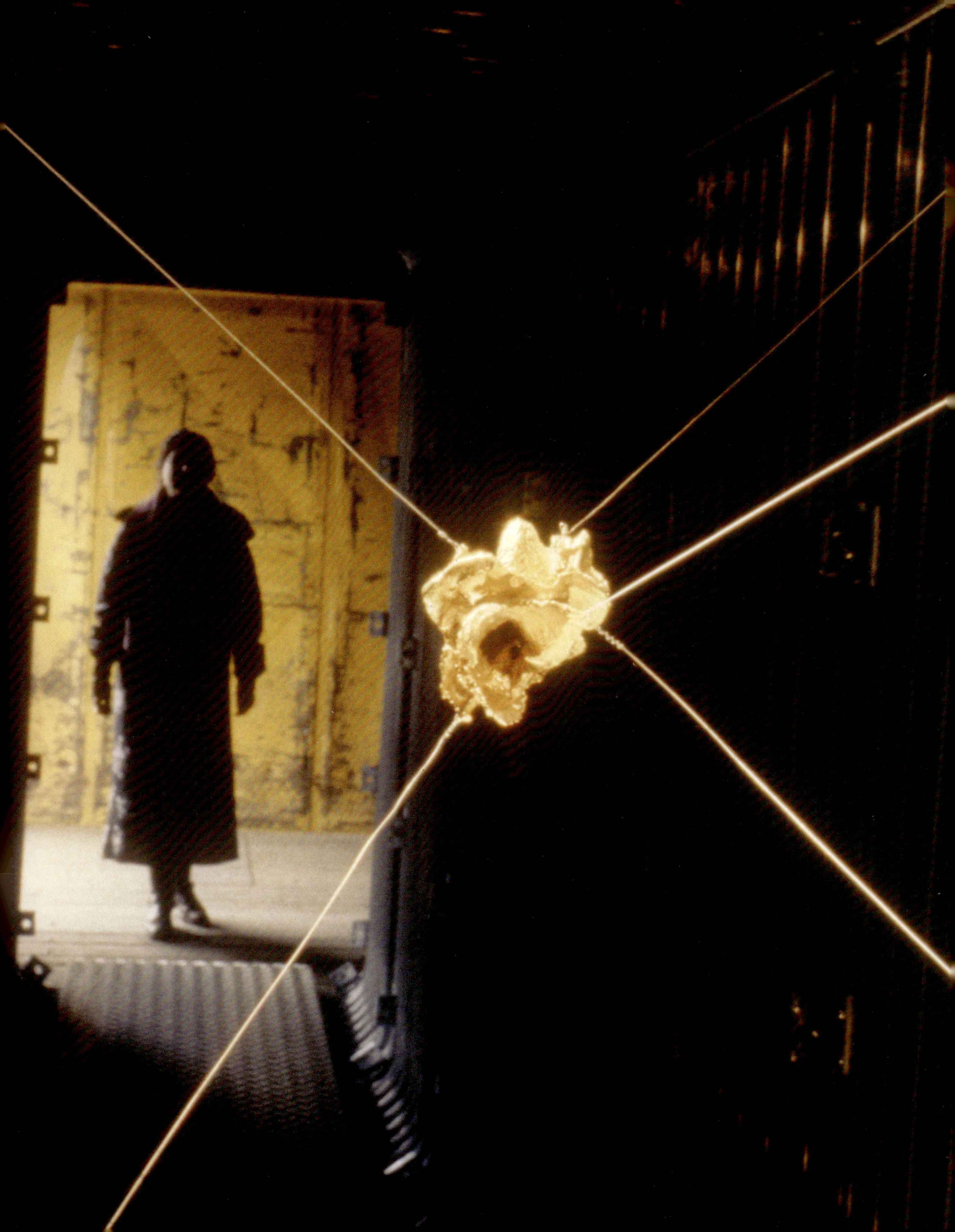

CHAPTER ONE

Dorothy Cross in Context

Dorothy Cross was born in Cork, Ireland in 1956 and pursued her early technical and artistic training in Ireland, England, and the United States. Many varied influences, including international travel and eclectic reading in literature, philosophy, and psychoanalysis, continue to broaden her conceptual range. Cross's work also reflects her interest in scientific exploration of the natural world. Since the early 1980s, she has worked in a range of genres, including jewelry design, printmaking, sculpture and assemblage, stage and costume design, photography, video, and site-specific installation. Her first solo exhibitions were in Ireland and by 1991 she was exhibiting internationally, with solo shows in major galleries in Philadelphia, New York, and London. Representing Ireland at the Venice Biennale in 1993, Cross gained wide recognition as an artist whose work is both local and global in its range of concerns as well as in its reception.[6]

FACING PAGE:
Strangers on a Train,
1996

Some of Cross's earliest sculptural work, produced while she was living outside of Ireland, deals with Irish cultural and political history and with the contemporary persistence of stereotypes of Irishness. With the insight that comes from distance and with a characteristic satirical wit, she exposes, mimics, and undermines the oppressive institutions and ideologies still shaping the daily life and imagination of Irish people at home and abroad. The most common representations of Irish cultural identity are framed self-consciously and critically in these early works in which Cross deconstructs images of a pre-Christian Mother Ireland (in the *Matriarchal* series and *Ireland Boxes* of 1982-3) and of a repressive patriarchal Catholic Ireland (in works from the *Chairs*, *Spires*, and *Contraptions* series of 1983-6). These sculptures embody a return of the repressed founding fantasies of Irish national identity. Ironically, when Cross returned to live in Ireland, her emphasis shifted from a concern with Irish culture and identity to broader explorations of gender identity and the workings of the unconscious.

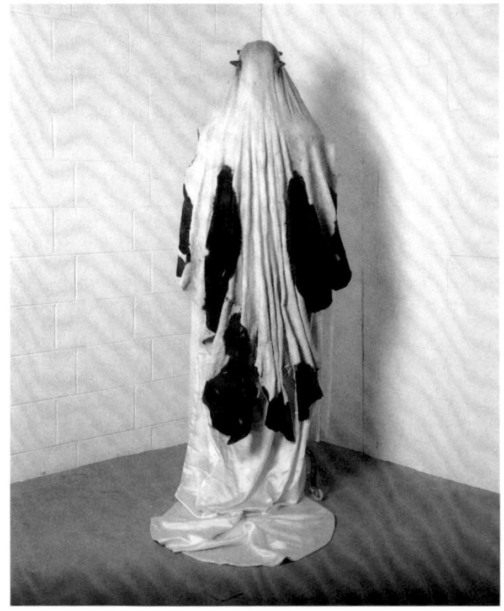

Virgin Shroud, 1993
Tate Gallery, London
Photo: John Kellett

Influenced by Carl Jung's theory that each individual contains a heterogeneous mixture of masculine animus and feminine anima, Cross began to explore gender ambiguity in a series of works that established her as one of the "Bad Girls" of the contemporary art scene.[7] In her solo exhibitions *Ebb* (1988) and *Power House* (1991), and most notably in the "udder" works produced throughout the 1990s, Cross destabilizes gender stereotypes and reveals her commitment to an art that "generate[s] interest in life, [because] it confirms uncertainty" (qtd. in Anson 20).

In many of the "udder" works, Cross reproduces essentialist stereotypes about women—including both feminist and misogynist images—in order to exaggerate and confuse these identities. In *Virgin Shroud* and *Amazon*, for example, she features two conventional trappings of femininity: the bridal gown as emblem of marriage, and the dressmaker's dummy as implement of "feminine" domestic labor and fashion. The *Virgin Shroud* is a tall figure, draped head to toe in cowhide, with four teats positioned like a crown at the head. Extending from below the cowhide is a white silk train from the artist's grandmother's wedding gown, trailing gracefully onto the floor. The convergence of wedding train and shroud suggests the deadening effect of marriage, the shrouding of individuality, of sight, of bodily freedom and mobility. The "udder" function of maternity seems to displace any intellectual function. Yet in a Magritte-like confusion of inside and outside, veiling and revealing, the cloak of cowhide asserts the return of the animal body traditionally contained and covered up by that white silk symbol of refinement and purity.

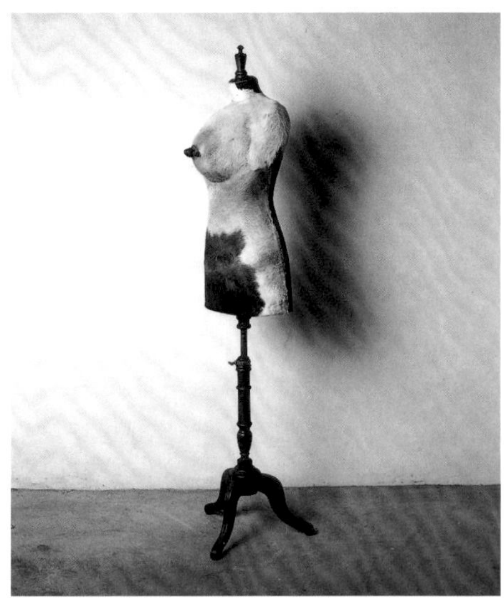

Amazon, 1992
Private collection
Photo: John Kellett

The cult of the Virgin Mary, the feminine ideal that Marina Warner and others have read as oppressing women's individuality, sexuality, and intellect,[8] is superseded in *Virgin Shroud* by the return of the repressed figure of the horned virgin goddess in her most powerful aspect. This looming form is described by one critic as having a "commanding, oracular, sexually ambiguous presence with clear connections to nature" (Cotter B44), and conveys to another the message that the "flesh will rise up, however much we, or those under whose power we live our lives, try to constrain it" (Macritchie 61).

Hilary Robinson analyzes the ambiguity of the udder works in general, and *Amazon* in particular, as they "negotiate the abyss between abusive or derogatory representations and those which honour or respect … and engage with the possibility of essentialism"(171).[9]

In *Amazon* the artist presents her variation on the figure of the virgin warrior and huntress known for having removed one breast in order to facilitate the use of bow and arrow. Cross's *Amazon* is fashioned here from a tailor's dummy covered with cowhide, a single swollen breast with erect teat at the center of her proud chest. One critic interprets *Amazon* simultaneously as a dissection of the "reliability, gentleness, infinite patience and mindlessness" of the cow, emblem of maternity, and as a surgical transformation of the "soft pendulous" udder into an armor-like phallic emblem of female power (Malbert 94).

Although many reviewers and critics focus on the way these works deal with female stereotypes, there are pieces in the "udder" series that perform the same liberating, subversive operation on stereotypes of masculinity: the workman's boots with teats sewn on to the heels, and a variety of masculine sports and entertainment equipment—the saddle, the gymnastic "horse," the dart board (with teat bull's-eye), and even the Guinness bottle—all are refashioned in relation to the udder. The cowboy's adventurousness, the gymnast's skill, the drinker's bravado are returned to a dependence on and affinity with the nipple, in a transformation that unmans, infantilizes, and makes vulnerable. Cross goes beyond the mere reversal of gender stereotypes to dismantle such binary oppositions at their very core.

When an interviewer remarks that Cross's early work seems to avoid the pitfalls of the "binary difference between men and women," the artist responds: "I am not remotely interested in determining difference. I would rather exaggerate the confusion" (qtd. in Colpitt). In the confusion generated by *Amazon*'s phallic teat or the Guinness bottle's nursing nipple, Cross subverts sexual dualism, allowing the return of the repressed "other"/"udder" gender to emerge where it is least expected. Although Cross recognizes the "animus/anima in any one person's head, and the desire that they be in perfect balance," her works demonstrate that such harmonious unity is "almost an impossibility" (Cross qtd. in Fowler 13).

The impossible desire for the convergence of opposites—whether within an individual's psyche or in an erotic encounter with another—is the basis for a body of work through which Cross explores the dangers and limitations of human passion. Often in these pieces, private or domestic enclosures designed to control and contain unruly desires are exposed to view, their explosive contents revealed. Lockers stand serenely with their doors ajar, while metal cut-outs of deadly sharks stream out their backs (*Locker Beds*); in a *Passion Bed* woven of metal wire, fragile glasses are precariously suspended, each one etched through with the image of a man-eating shark; a domestic *Dresser*, with generic male and female symbols cut out of its two doors, opens to reveal shelves on which delicate glasses bearing the same gendered figures are dangerously juxtaposed with heavy metal machine parts. In *Double Bed*, a wire mattress, interwoven with fragments of scientific glass instruments, sprouts female breasts and a giant phallus that seem to erupt and overflow the frame. In Cross's art, desire always leads to such impossible pairings, to a dangerous closeness that is never far from the threat of annihilation.

Cross propels the forces of desire and death into motion and into time in video works such as *Teacup*, *figure*, and *Eyemaker*, where the viewer's object of interest is alternately lost and found and lost again. In her first experiment with video, Cross set a film loop into a china teacup; the image shows a small boat in a storm as it struggles, capsizes, and then reappears to repeat the cycle. A similar pattern of loss and renewal was produced in the unannounced public projection of Cross's video, entitled *figure*, on a wall in the Temple Bar area of Dublin. The video was shot in front of the Dublin Customs House, and was originally meant to be projected onto the building's facade. Passersby saw the image of a naked male diver who plunged into the River Liffy and then reappeared to repeat his mysterious, and possibly suicidal, act.[10] Bureaucratic complications forced the removal of the project to Temple Bar.

In the stunning twenty-minute video entitled *Eyemaker*, a glassblower meticulously constructs a perfect glass eye, only to shatter it in the final seconds of the sequence. This work captures the delicacy and loving precision of an artist exercizing his nearly obsolete craft. The image of the glassblower is classically composed, perhaps reflecting Cross's admiration for Jean-Baptiste-Siméon Chardin. However, the camera's steady gaze is unsettled by what it records: the uncertain metamorphosis of molten glass as it passes from formlessness to suggest the shape of some mysterious planet or the nipple of a translucent breast. *Eyemaker* maintains an intimate connection to the material body, lingering over the proximity of the glassblower's fingertips to the glowing eye and steady flame. When the glass eye is completed and then shattered like a bubble, the viewer is reminded that the perfect desired eye is always one breath away from annihilation. In her video works, in particular, it is clear that desire for Cross, as for Freud, is not just sexual desire, but the desire to create, to know, to see, and to die.

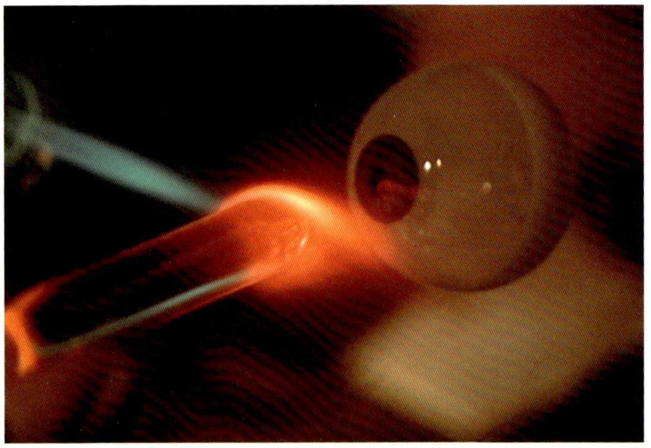

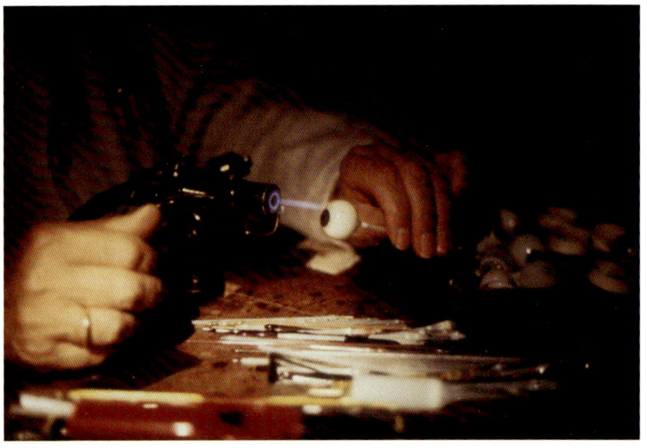

Stills from *Eyemaker*, 2000

Cross's nine-minute video *Midges* brings us deep into the terrain of Freud's *Beyond the Pleasure Principle*, into that imagined primordial moment when desire and death, the life instinct and the death instinct, first converge. A nervous camera eye scans an alien landscape of primeval looking trees and mysterious ruined wall, jumping forward to fix on one strange tree trunk growing horizontally, and then withdrawing to retrace its journey. This pulsation of the camera mechanism suggests what Rosalind Krauss has called the "specific beat of desire" characteristic of early film techniques (1993, 216). *Midges* surprises the viewer with one of those moments when "the real appears to burst into life from the shards of the … deathly still" (222). The camera unexpectedly discovers in this landscape of death and deformity a nude woman, draped limply over that horizontal trunk, from which she eventually rises up, absently embraces herself, then slowly and smoothly returns to immobility. The figure has been animated not by the camera's Pygmalion-like desiring eye, but by the barely perceptible but sufficient irritation of a swarm of midges (tiny gnat-like insects). The Surrealist dream of a chance encounter with a naked woman in a forest is rewritten here as the discovery of something far more primary than sex or gender—the death drive that comes into being, Freud speculates, simultaneous with the first stirrings of life.[11] For Cross, the dead and abandoned always have this potential for resurrection and metamorphosis.

These themes of repression, desire, and loss that appear in all of Cross's work find particularly powerful expression in her temporary site-specific art. Like her video work, the site-specific projects bring to the foreground the element of temporality. "Good art," Cross argues, "should make you consider yourself in relation to time, which means in relation to birth, life and death" (qtd. in Bonaventura 13). In her sited works, the experience of time and the effects of the unconscious go public, and place is transformed into a staging ground where viewers are engaged at the level of memory, desire, and anxiety.

Cross's contribution to site-specific art practice can best be appreciated in the context of the history of that genre's re-conceptualizations of production and reception over the past three decades. In the 1960s, many artists began to move out of the museums and galleries, creating sited works that challenged the ideological principles and economic forces dominating the art world. Their goal was, in part, to "democratize art" by bringing it into the public sphere (Jacob 15). Some works were constructed for permanent installation in a particular place (Richard Serra's *Tilted Arc,* 1981), others were designed to be dismantled after a given time or to disappear gradually through erosion and decay (Robert Smithson's *Partially Buried Woodshed,* 1970).[12] Whether asserting their permanence or their ephemerality, these works resisted what some artists saw as a deadly commodification of art. By the mid-1970s, the oppositional practice of site-specific art had become an international phenomenon and a frequent topic in art criticism.[13]

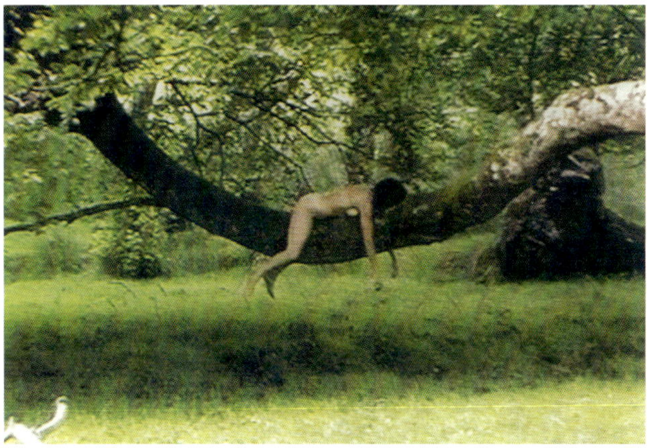

Still from *Midges,* 2000

Some critics herald the site-specific genre as an important shift away from the primacy of the object and the personality of the individual artist, and toward a dynamic interaction between art object, site, and viewer. These works encourage us to participate in the creative act not as detached, rational observers, but as bodies moving through space in real time. Encouraged to encounter art as an integral part of lived experience, the audience becomes a collaborator in the creative process. For an artist like Richard Serra, the elimination of the pedestal constitutes the "biggest break in the history of sculpture," because it shifts the focus toward the "behavioral space of the viewer" (Serra 141). This "expanded field" of site-specific sculpture, to borrow Rosalind Krauss's phrase (1985, 284), increasingly draws attention to the ways in which the experience of the art audience (which now includes the community surrounding the art site) is influenced by local institutions and discourses. Many site-specific works reveal the entanglement of the local with the global, of the "little tactics" of local institutions with the "great strategies of geopolitics" (Foucault 228).

One early and still influential current of site-specific work addresses the complicity of the allegedly neutral space of the museum with those larger geopolitical systems of power; artists like Hans Haacke, Marcel Broodthaers, and others interrogate the museum as a site with its own complex history.[14] While Cross has been included in several of these interventions in the museum, notably in Dublin and Zagreb, her engagement has been more participatory than oppositional, or as she describes it, "infiltration" rather than overt critique.[15] For the 1998 Dublin project, "Art into Art," several artists were asked to select and respond to one work in the collection of the National Gallery in Ireland. Cross chose "The Wounded Poacher"(1881) by Harry Jones Thadeus. Working on a reproduction of the painting, she blacked out all but two details: the poacher's head dramatically thrown back in pain as his wound is ministered to, and his hand resting in his lap. The details appear within two circles, as if seen through peepholes or lenses; their highlighted isolation and juxtaposition bring out an overlooked eroticism in this familiar genre painting. In the Mimara Museum in Zagreb (2000), Leonida Kovac of the

Museum of Contemporary Art curated an exhibition under the title *A way a lone a last a loved a long the.* Cross was invited to place several of her own works (such as *Teacup,* and *Mantegna and Crucifix*) in relation to selected artworks in the museum's permanent collection. Placed in unexpected relation to each other, art works old and new, religious and secular, were temporarily transformed.

In the nine site-specific works included in *GONE,* Cross looks beyond the particular issues related to art institutions and markets to explore a broader range of themes. Like many artists working in the genre, she challenges structures of binary opposition, transgressing the boundaries separating local and global, public and private, formalist and political, nostalgic and utopian. Writing about site-specific art, some critics invoke the theories of Gilles Deleuze and Félix Guattari to describe such projects as "deterritorializing" the organizational principles of a given space, disrupting hierarchies, opening borders, and multiplying identities. The resulting liberated space takes on a fluid and dynamic character.[16] Cross's work consistently achieves this double movement of the deconstruction and reactivation of a given site.

Contemporary site-specific art has transformed our sense of place, reflecting the effects of a postmodern theoretical skepticism that also reveals language as a field of power rather than a transparent medium. Like others working in this genre, Cross recognizes that no site is neutral, that our perception of space is always shaped by ideological forces.[17] Her site-specific projects often render that process visible and explicit, revealing each selected location as an intersection of multiple and even conflicting systems of knowledge and authority.

Art historian Miwon Kwon maintains that although the concept of the contemporary art site has become abstract and discursive, much site-specific art has remained resolutely anchored to concrete reality: "Despite the proliferation of discursive sites and fictional selves ... the phantom of a site as an actual place remains.... This persistent, perhaps secret adherence to the actuality of places (in memory, in longing) may not be a lack of theoretical sophistication but a means of survival" (2002, 165). In her site-specific projects Cross always combines a respect for the actuality of place with a desire to incorporate the physical presence and psychic engagement of the viewer into the artwork's lived materiality.

In addition to providing a real encounter with space, site-specific art provokes in the viewer an awareness of temporality as lived duration. Early minimalist earthwork artists of the 1970s reacted against what they saw as the traditional museum's deadly fixing of history in the interest of preservation and periodization. Abandoning the museums and galleries for the landscape, they incorporated the slow and continuous evolution of nature into their artistic process. Whereas these earthworks often attempted to produce the effects of a "prehistoric monumentality" (Owens 55), more recent installations in urban and industrial environments engage with the faster pace of modern history. Frequently located in marginalized neighborhoods or abandoned buildings, urban site-specific projects contradict modernity's narrative of progress. These spaces—charged with the nostalgia and melancholy of the outmoded, of cultural practices or institutions on the verge of obliteration—offer fertile ground for artistic transformation. Cross's sited works incorporate both the slow transformations of natural evolution and the artificially induced speed of modern obsolescence. In a complex work such as *Chiasm*, she creates a palimpsest of these two temporalities.

Working with locations rich in historical and cultural associations, site-specific artists like Dorothy Cross face some difficult challenges. Can they call up buried histories without replicating the deadening effects that originally drove them from the museum-as-mausoleum of artifacts? Can they resist the lure of heritage industry reenactments that often turn history into empty spectacle? Can they redirect the powerful backward pull of sentimentality toward a transformed future? Some critics write optimistically about an art that could make nostalgia productive, that could resurrect and transform cultural detritus. Hal Foster's imagined "dialectic of ruination, recovery, and resistance"(1993, 166) can be found in much contemporary site-specific art; it is realized with particular elegance and wit in Cross's work.

Cross explores the uncertainties and potentialities offered by the site-specific genre with a sensuality and ironic humor that set her apart from the austere pedagogical thrust often found in such work. Although some of her early sculptures and assemblages are explicitly political, the driving force of her art, as one reviewer notes, remains metaphorical and enigmatic rather than pedagogical (Murphy 5). In Cross's work the political and local incline toward the mythic and universal, and consciousness is disrupted by the effects of the unconscious. Deviating from a recent tendency in site-specific art toward dematerialized and deaestheticized effects, Cross never abandons the actuality of place, the materiality of the object, or her eye for unexpected beauty.

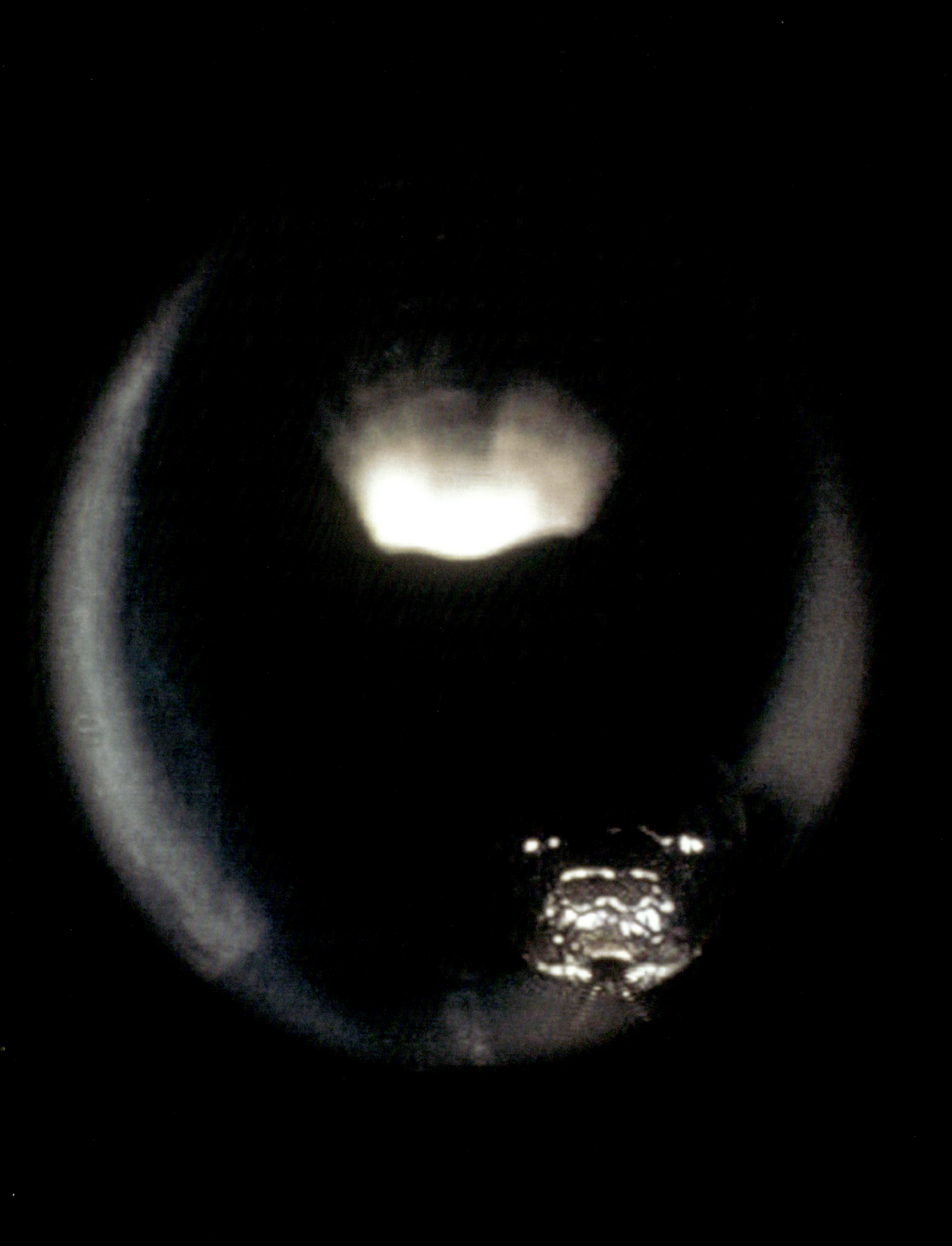

CHAPTER TWO

The Return of the Repressed

The complexity of Dorothy Cross's site-specific art derives in part from her understanding that every place is sedimented with unconscious as well as ideological and historical elements.[18] In the first constellation of works assembled here, she explores the political, cultural, and personal unconscious of several architectural sites, opening up hidden or abandoned spaces in which the artist activates the return of the repressed. These sited works bring viewers into the hidden recesses of a decommissioned jail in Ireland (*Caught in a State*), a convent residence in Spain (*La Primera Cena*), an underground men's lavatory in England (*Attendant*), and a Byzantine church in Turkey (*Snake*). Cross's art lays bare the constraints imposed by these specific secular and religious institutions and their accompanying ideologies. These constraints are loosened, in part, by the ironic wit that distinguishes Cross's work in this genre.

FACING PAGE:
Still from *Untitled*, detail from *Snake*, 1996

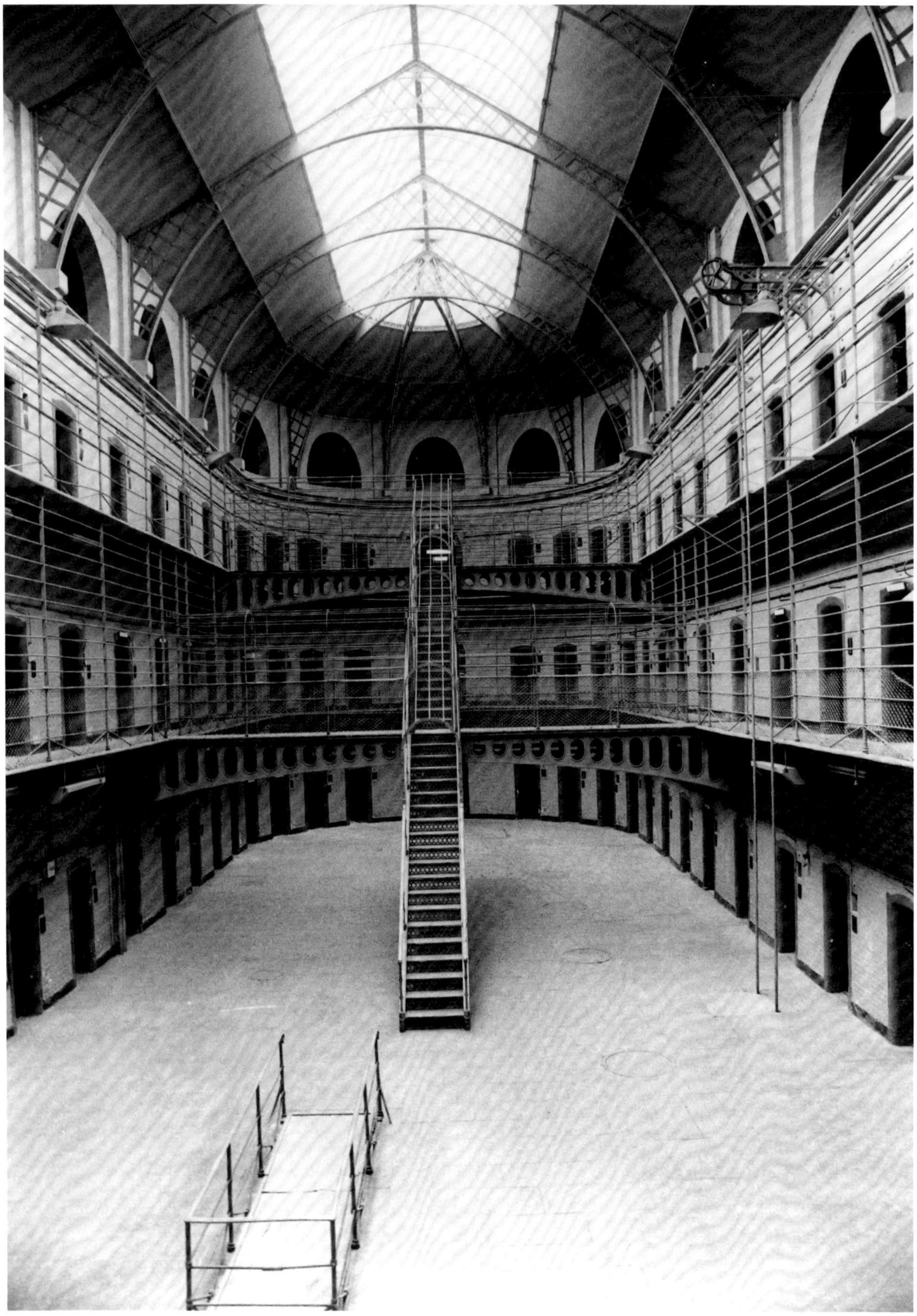

Kilmainham Gaol,
The Great Hall,
Dublin, Ireland

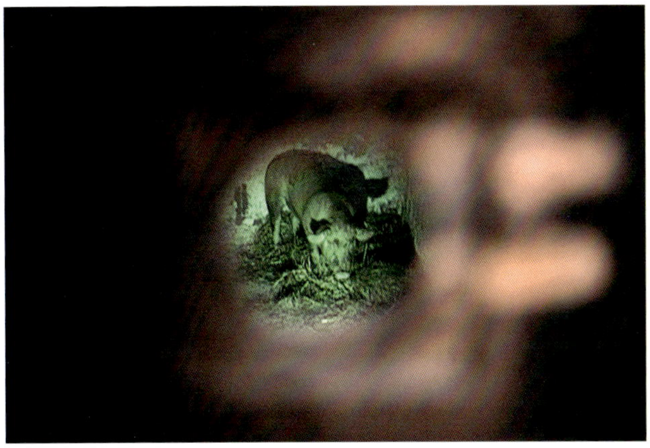 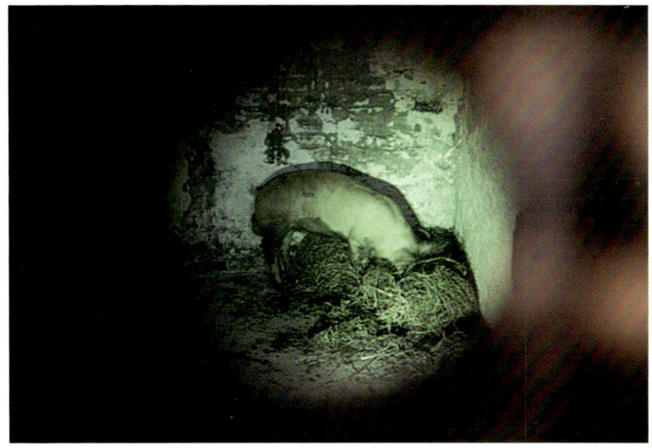

Caught in a State, details from illustrated calendar

The Stereotype Returns: *Caught in a State (1991)*

The first of the four pieces grouped together here was executed in 1991 as part of a group show entitled *In a State.* Works by twenty-one invited artists were installed in the lowest tier of cells surrounding the Great Hall of Dublin's Kilmainham Gaol. With a curatorial focus on national identity, the exhibition invited artists to reconsider Kilmainham Gaol's role in Ireland's historical memory. As a venue for art installations, prison architecture functions powerfully as both an abstract concept and a highly charged, historical site (Tyler 11).[19]

Cross's contribution to the exhibition was entitled *Caught in a State*, a piece consisting of a fetal pig curled up on a bed of straw, visible to viewers through the open door of its little cell. On the wall nearby, the artist hung an illustrated calendar displaying the image of a live adult pig inhabiting the same cell, photographed through the peephole of its *closed* door. Cross's original plan was to have a live pig occupy the cell, a witty gesture that would have given this colonial stereotype of the Irish as "pigs" a life of its own, an undeniable, irrepressible presence. In a compromise that ironically reveals the hostility of state bureaucracy and traditional museum culture to a living reality, city officials, citing health code restrictions, would only allow the artist to install a dead pig in the cell.

In his preface to the catalogue of *In a State,* Fintan O'Toole remarks that Kilmainham Gaol simultaneously evokes an "impulse to remember [and] an awareness of forgetfulness" (13). O'Toole witnesses in the exhibit a potentially transformative return of the repressed, of a "past [that] is refusing to stay in the past and insisting on re-emerging with undiminished force" (11). The Irish public imagination is haunted by generations of rebels who fought for Irish independence, were incarcerated and, in some cases, executed in Kilmainham Gaol by the British. During the Civil War following the 1916 Easter Rebellion, the same facility was used by the new Free State for the imprisonment and execution of its opposition. For several decades, Kilmainham and its ghosts succumbed to what one critic calls a "systematically induced amne-

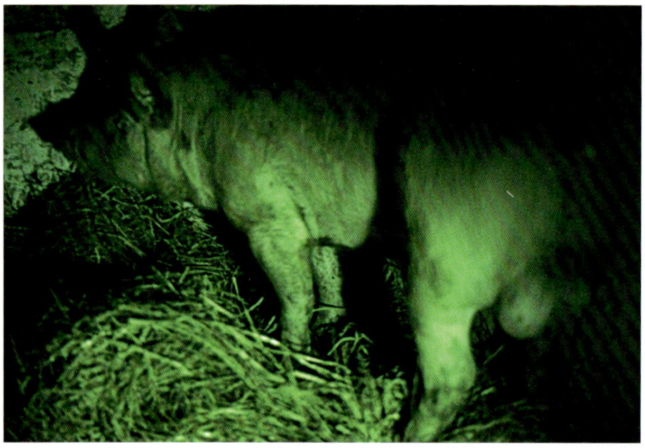

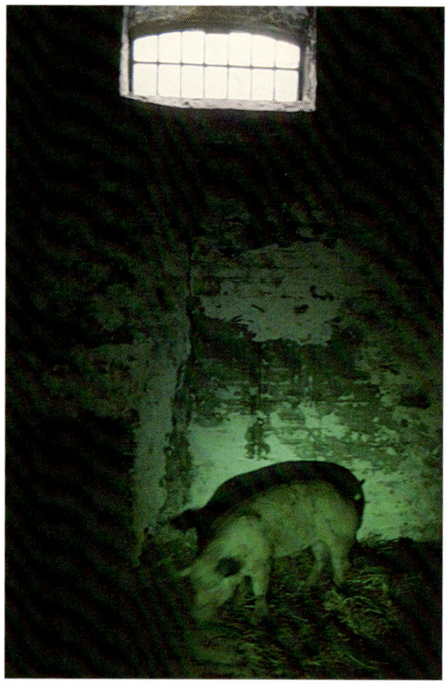

sia" (Maxton 45). Under the impetus of a renewed nationalism in the 1960s, the prison was restored as a heritage museum and national monument. Framed by what has been described, perhaps unfairly, as the "unrelieved nationalist litany" of the museum tour and video (Maxton 46), the renovations of Kilmainham Gaol transformed it into a truly "discursive" site.

Patrick Cooke, appointed curator of the museum in the 1980s, dedicated his tenure to recasting the nationalist explication of the prison's history into a more critical exploration of the issues.[20] He recognized the crucial role of artistic interventions, such as *In a State*, in the transformation of the prison from "a heritage institution [to] a cultural space" of debate (O'Toole 14). The artists engaged in the 1991 exhibition, including Cross, responded not only to the prison and its history, but also to its re-institutionalization as a national monument.[21]

The exhibition's ambiguous title, *In a State,* is a verbal play on the contradictory connotations of being situated within a particular political place and at the same time being out of control, uncontainable within those boundaries (O'Toole 14). The title of Cross's piece, *Caught in a State,* further complicates this rhetorical ambiguity, suggesting that national and cultural identity constitute a form of entrapment. One might also read into her title an allusion to the potential constraints of the museum's ideological narrative, and of the curator's conceptual framing of the art exhibit.

The heritage industry is often criticized for producing sentimentalized versions of history, commodified for tourism and popular consumption. Some site-specific artists work against these distortions, engaging the viewer in a confrontational pedagogy. Cross's conceptual and witty approach avoids the extremes of sentimentality on the one hand and didacticism on the other, by focusing self-reflexively on the installation's presentation, representation, and reception. Her work makes us aware that one "state" in which we are always "caught" is the word and image system that consciously and unconsciously determines, obstructs, and distorts our ways of seeing and knowing. *Caught in a State* exposes the limitations and exploits the potentialities of all sign systems, making visible and conscious the inability of representation to capture reality, but giving us productive and pleasurable ways to read the traces of its failure.

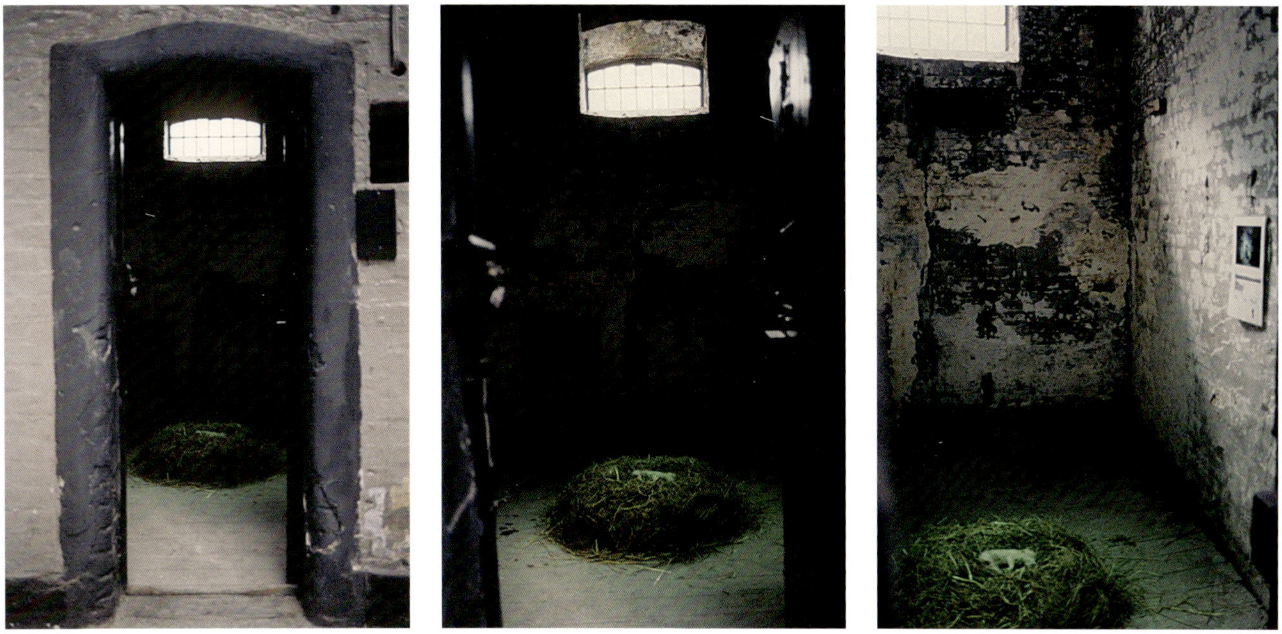

Caught in a State, views of the installation

Theatrically illuminated by a green light (perhaps an ironic nod to the nationalist light shed on Irish history by the museum's tour and video), *Caught in a State* makes no claim to historical accuracy; it is aggressively artificial, staged, and constructed. The green glow reveals not the heroic version of Irish martyrdom featured in the museum's narrative, but the degrading cartoon image of the Irish as they appeared in the British press: the "pigs in the parlor," fit only for internment or for exile in the rural territories "beyond the pale"—a more spacious but often no less oppressive imprisonment. Cross's piece reminds viewers that national character is never constructed autonomously from the inside, but is equally determined by those defining it from the outside as inhuman and abject. Kilmainham Gaol is one site where the brutal effects of those externally imposed political fantasies of the "other" were played out on real bodies.

At once literal and figurative, the visual elements in *Caught in a State* multiply uncertainties. Whereas the literal prison cell with its open door becomes a metaphor for freedom, the metaphor of the Irish as pigs is given literal, although sympathetic, embodiment. (Some prisoners were actually forced to sleep on straw, housed as animals—a reminder that rhetorical figures often achieve concrete manifestations.) This confusion of literal and figurative is repeated in the confusion of living and dead: is the glistening fetal pig dead or newly born? And is the abusive stereotype it embodies outdated or made ready for renewed circulation? Even the status of presence and absence become uncertain here: the fetus is present, but its preserved body is a mere simulation of life; the adult pig, on the other hand, is absent, but its lived experience is "caught" and fixed in the memorial photographs of the calendar.

Ultimately Cross's piece stages a double stillbirth: literally in the fetal pig's dead body and figuratively in the calendar "stills." Dramatizing the potential violence of seeing, this work shows how even in death the fetus is vulnerable to the viewer's gaze through the open door, and the living pig photographed through the guard's peephole is subject to the dehumanizing mechanism of surveillance that invades the inmates' privacy. The peephole images document not only the lived experience of the imprisoned, but also the distorting fantasy of the imprisoner: the guard's vision proves to be as limited by the prison's architecture as is the captive's mobility.

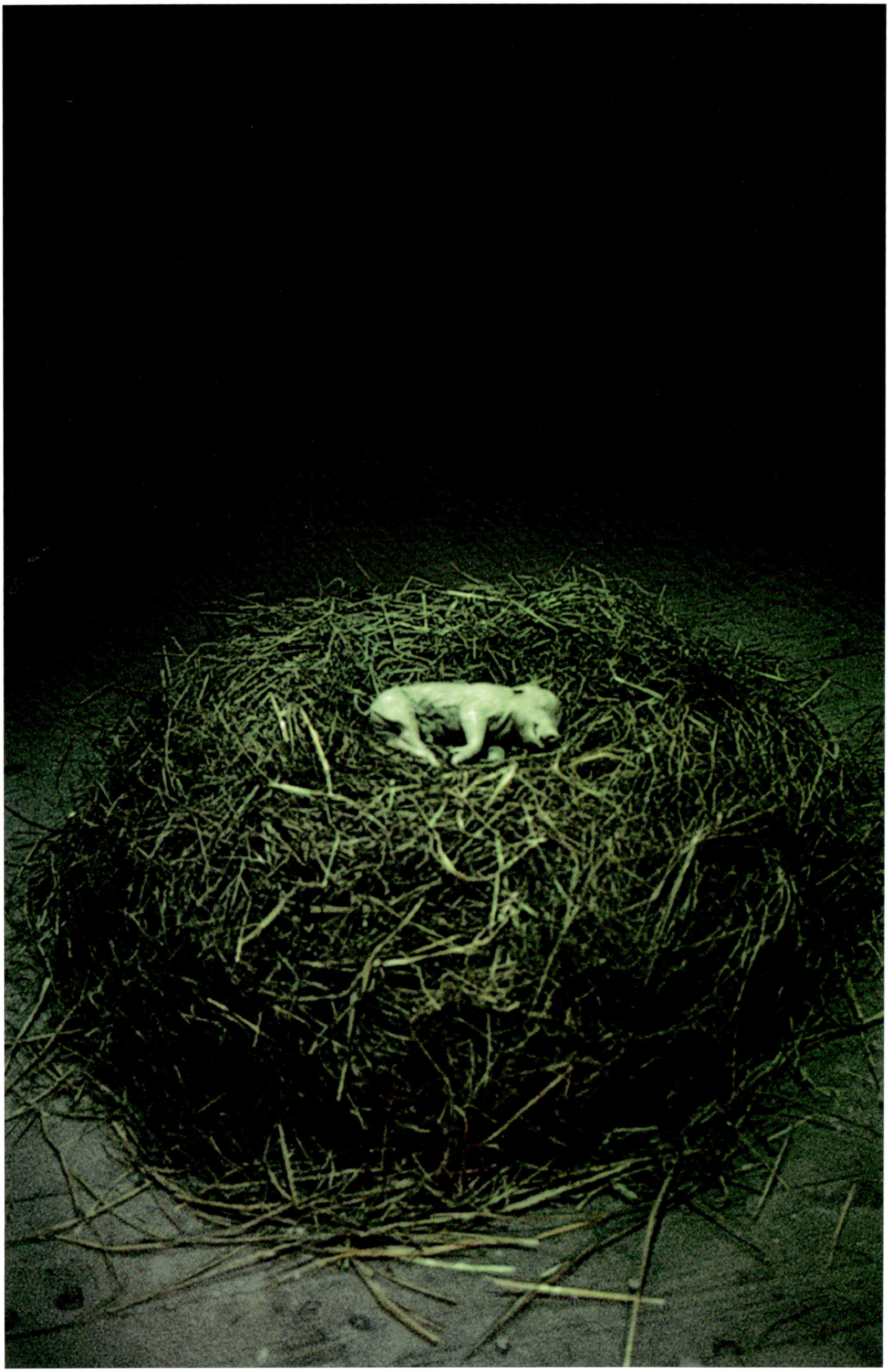

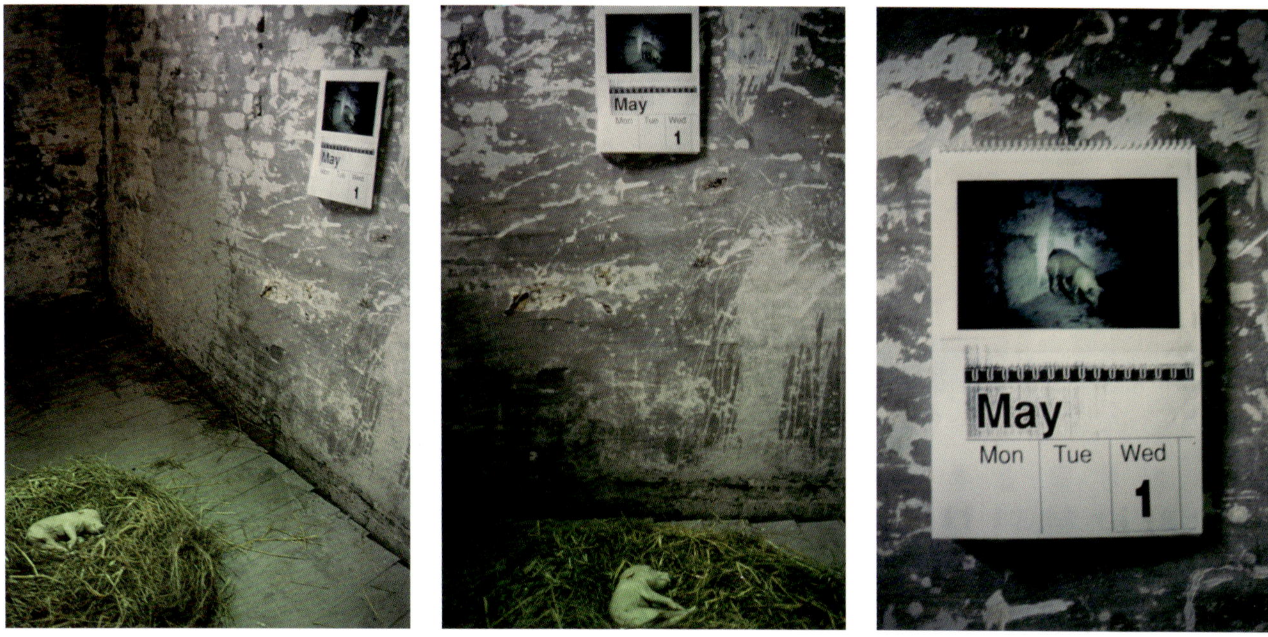

Caught in a State, fetal pig and calendar

The most powerful ambiguity of *Caught in a State* persists in the implied question: who is the pig here, prisoner or warden?

Innovations in prison architecture in the nineteenth century were based on a belief that moral rehabilitation could be fostered most successfully in a living structure that favored silence, isolation, and surveillance. Site-specific exhibitions in older prison facilities have interrogated the hypocrisy that allowed dehumanizing conditions to prevail in the name of religious and moral instruction.[22] Several installations in the Kilmainham exhibit explicitly address the oppressive and restrictive function of religion in the construction of Irish national identity; Cross's piece alludes indirectly to Christian iconography, but it focuses more on nationalist myths and media stereotypes. For example, the illuminated fetus in the straw seems to parody the traditional Christian nativity scene, but that scene is re-fashioned to enact the simultaneous "birth" and degradation (by the British) of Irish national identity. By exaggerating the green "colorized" view of nationalist history and by giving body to the degrading stereotype of the Irish as pigs, Cross exposes both as ideological constructions.

Caught in a State creates a complex temporality that simultaneously evokes abuses committed in the past and in the present. Cross describes the discontinuity between the live adult pig and the fetus as a "breaking of the line of inheritance"; but the piece also signals a complicitous continuity of present and past. Actual signatures and dated messages inscribed on the walls by inmates have been preserved in the prison's renovations. In contrast, the cell housing *Caught in a State* is adorned by Cross with a calendar lacking specific dates or events, an indeterminacy that suggests the timeless repetition of old brutalities and oppressions. The stillborn embryo is "still born," still coming into being; the same cycle of physical and representational violence always seems ready to begin again. In her collaboration with the site of Kilmainham Gaol, Cross suggests that this cycle can be broken only if its operations are made conscious and visible. In this work, as in others discussed in this chapter, Cross opens up a space and time in which the return of the repressed constitutes not a repetition of the same, but a critical transformation.

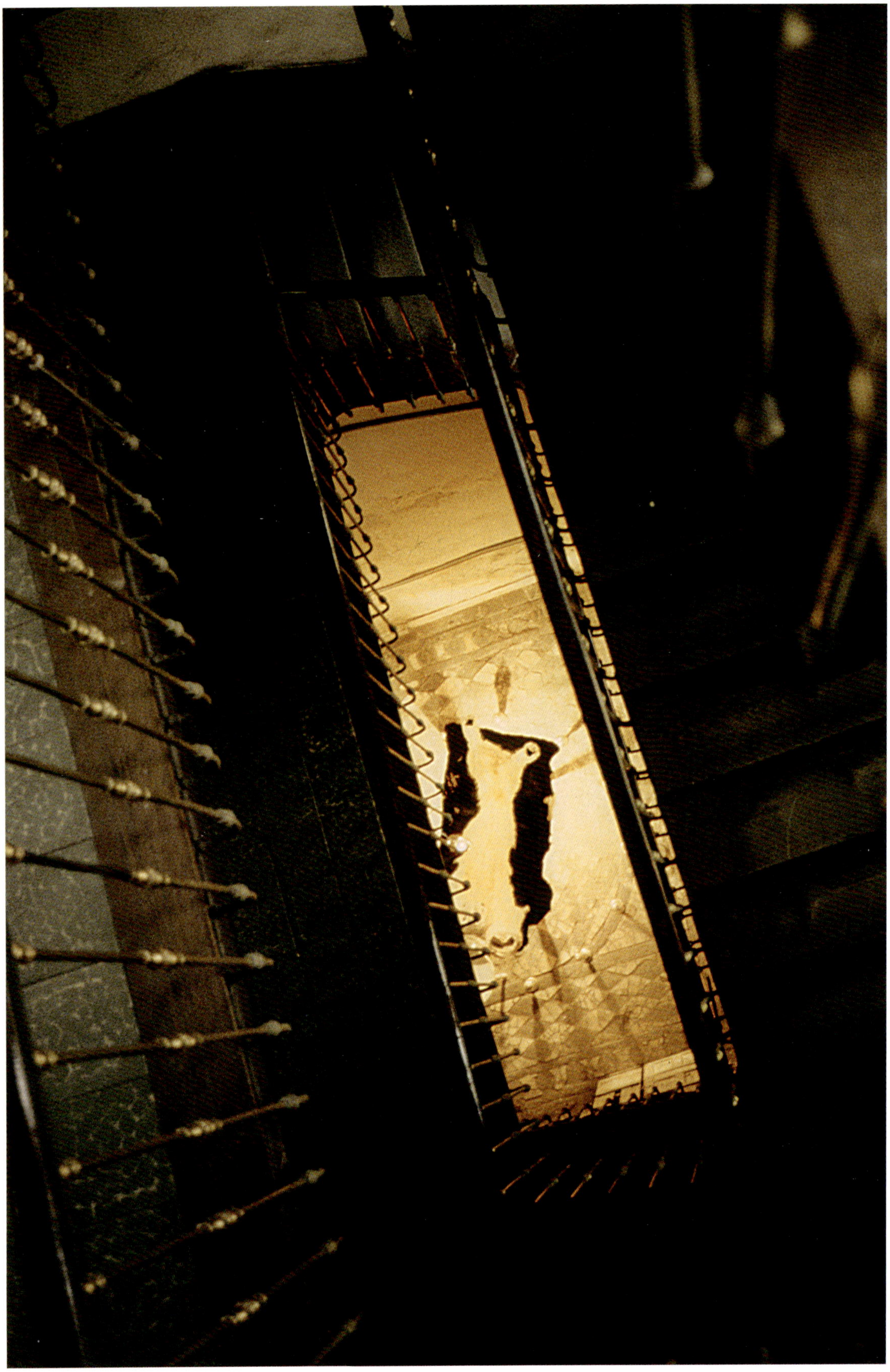

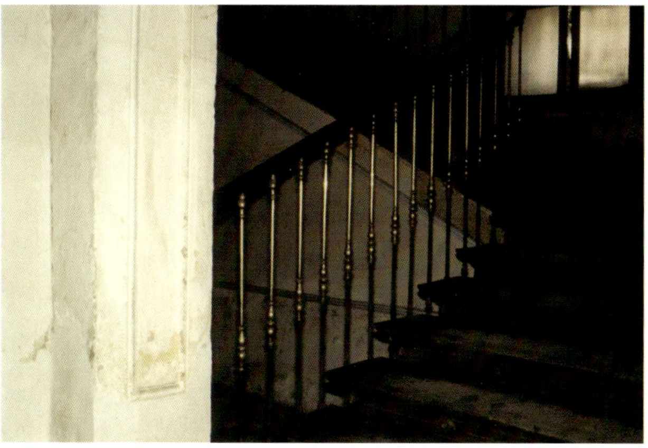

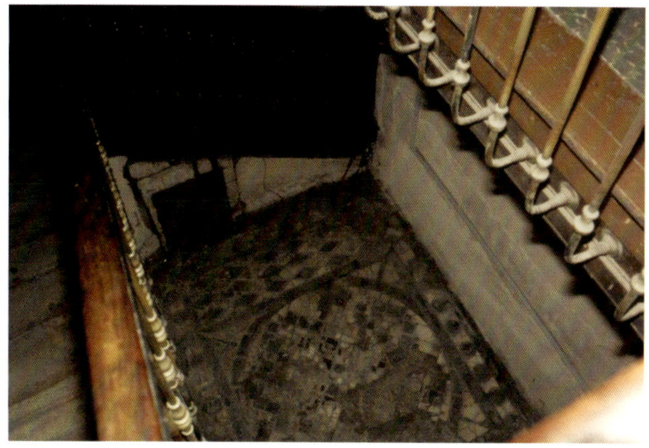

La Primera Cena, descent into the installation space

The Return of the Body:
La Primera Cena [The First Supper] (1992)

In 1992, Cross participated in another group exhibition, the Edge Biennial, for which each artist selected two sites: one in Madrid and one in London. She sought out in each of these world capitals some hidden or abandoned territory where the culture's repressed but constitutive fantasies lay buried. Working creatively across two disparate spaces—a nun's residence in Madrid and an abandoned men's public urinal in London—Cross brings together the territories of church and state, private and public, spiritual and corporeal, female and male. As she bridges the geographical and ideological distance separating the two sites, the artist also discovers a breach deep within each one, where everything designated as "other" has made its secret habitation.

Cross's Madrid site is a functioning twelfth-century convent providing a group of nuns with a refuge from the secular modernity of this dynamic city. Viewers enter the enclosed space of the convent and approach an area beneath an inner stairway that Cross describes as a "trapped little well of space." The work, entitled *La Primera Cena* or *The First Supper*, consists of a small rectangular table draped with a cow's skin, udders uppermost and central. Twelve blown-glass chalices covered with a thin layer of silver are arranged on the floor around the table, forming a circle that corresponds to the ornate pattern of the tile work. Some of the chalices are elongated and others rounded; each includes a small hole through which its contents might be sucked. A single chair is pulled up to the table beside the upturned udders, and the whole scene is illuminated from above and below.

Cross's intervention in the convent sets the stage for the return of the repressed prehistory of the church, and for the viewer's encounter with an archaic, pre-Christian, maternal fantasy. *La Primera Cena* achieves an uncanny convergence of pagan, secular, and sacred in this evocation of our common origins. Rather than contaminating the pristine territory of the convent, this piece brings within its walls a physicality, humor, and theatricality that animate the overlooked interior space of the stairwell with a scene of surprising beauty.

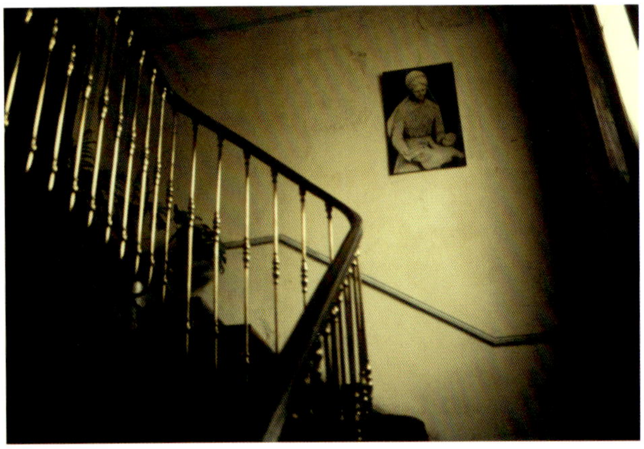

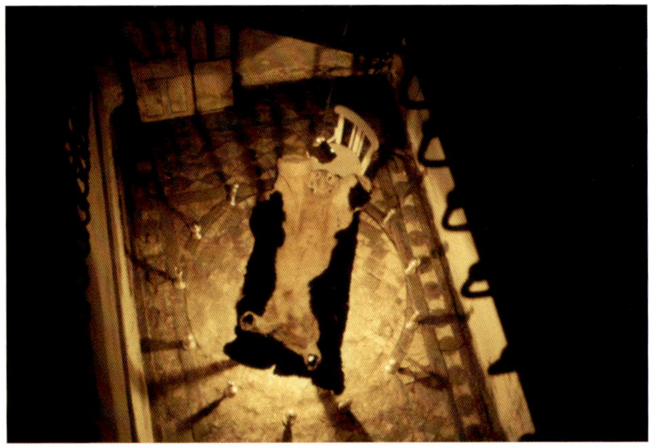

In the early 1990s, Cross produced several works in which she attempts to restore to Christian myth and iconography the powerful presence of the material body and desire. In one piece she drills a perfect hole through her family's illustrated Bible, making tangible the absence that can be created when passion is lost, the body denied or transcended. Although *Bible* makes visible the lack at the center of all systems of representation, where signs take the place of bodies, the effect of the artist's transformation is to intensify the material presence of the book as an object, thus bringing the body and embodiment back into play. In the subterranean alcove of the convent stairwell, Cross introduces the body, not in the artificial elegance of that "perfect void" she drilled through her family Bible, but in the cruder natural form of the cow's udder and teats.[23] *La Primera Cena* inaugurates the series of "udder" sculptures for which Cross has become widely known.[24]

These "udder" works celebrate hybridity, transformation, and metamorphosis; the cow takes on new life and functions, and in one piece (*Amazon*, p. 12) even humorously reclaims a pre-patriarchal female power. In the context of *La Primera Cena*, however, the hide suggests slaughter more than reincarnation; the skin is ragged, showing rough holes where it was cut away from the legs. The effect is at once gruesome and absurd, a scene of pagan sacrifice incongruously hidden within the convent walls. In the flattened-out hide that survives as a remnant of the absent living body one can still read the story of that body's history: the teats appear shrivelled and dry, bearing the marks of years of use and abandonment.

Tanners normally cut a cow skin on the underside, discarding the udders as useless. For her "udder" works Cross had this procedure reversed; the hide was skinned upside down, the udders preserved intact, their value restored. The small table used in the Madrid installation was similarly rescued by the artist, salvaged from the trash on a nearby street. With both hide and table Cross introduces those cast off or abjected elements of the secular world into the protective confines of the convent retreat. Both skin and table remind us of the passage of time and the materiality of loss that may be forgotten, at times, in the pursuit of the spiritual and eternal or in the blind acceleration of modern life. Cross is attentive to the convent's lived history, and

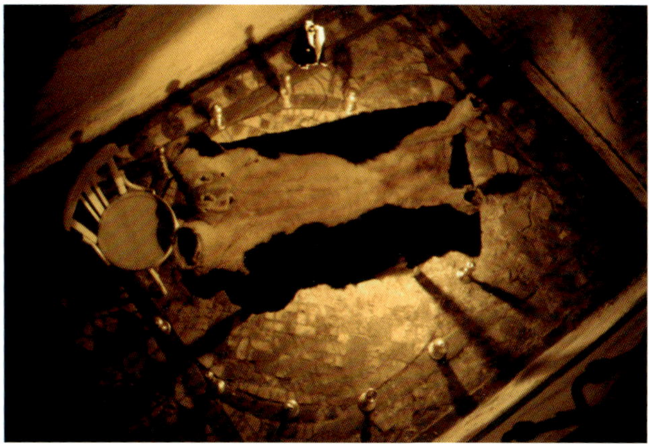

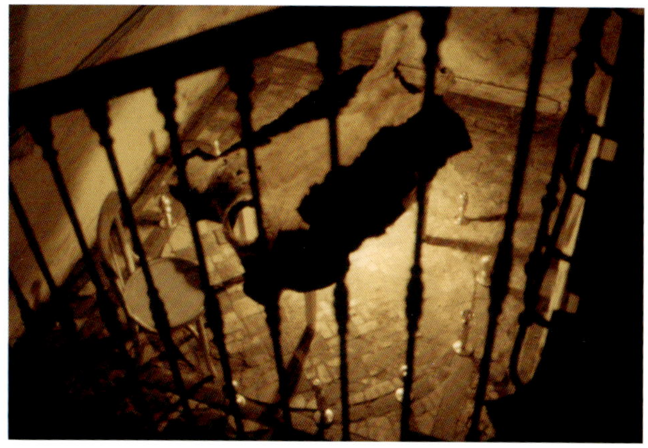

part of the appeal of the site for her is the evidence of age and use, the cracks and stains that mark its finely crafted interior with a dignified and melancholy beauty. Thus the worn table and cowskin that seem at first so incongruous in the space of the convent are also at home there. In *La Primera Cena* history and the body are sanctified by the convent site in a peculiar below-stairs ritual. Cross's piece lends this internal space the atmosphere of a crypt where something cherished, but long lost, has quietly come to light.

The title of this installation makes playful reference to the religious as well as to the art historical tradition of the Last Supper, transforming this potentially melancholy crypt into a witty tableau. Although she is not alone in addressing the challenge of revisiting this powerful myth—one thinks of Andy Warhol's persistent return to the image—Cross's variation on the theme is unique. Representations of the Last Supper are readily recognized, even in Western secular culture, as establishing the foundation from which the Church's authority proceeds. While the earliest painted versions of the scene feature a circular or horseshoe-shaped table, modern viewers are more familiar with later versions depicting the guests at the Last Supper posed frontally at a long rectangular table, balancing the central figure of Christ. These formal characteristics reinforce a tradition based on hierarchy and symbolic ritual. The narrative and iconography of the Last Supper inaugurate the linear salvation narrative of the Church and the eucharistic ritual dominated by the symbolic body and blood of Christ.

The convent residence is a female space set apart from, but still framed by, this tradition. Within that space *La Primera Cena* takes viewers back to the territory of the archaic maternal body and to a time before structures of hierarchy and difference were established, before the Church instituted a symbolic order guaranteed by a symbolic body. The circular arrangement of the chalices beneath the table evokes a pre-Christian mythical time of cycles and repetition that precedes the linear time of eschatology. The udder and teats recall our more intimate connection to nature and to what French feminist Luce Irigaray calls our ancient "maternal genealogy."[25] Cross's piece, however, is not a mere recasting of the Last Supper as a pagan instead of a Christian rite, with female instead of male protagonists. Rather, the elements of the work drama-

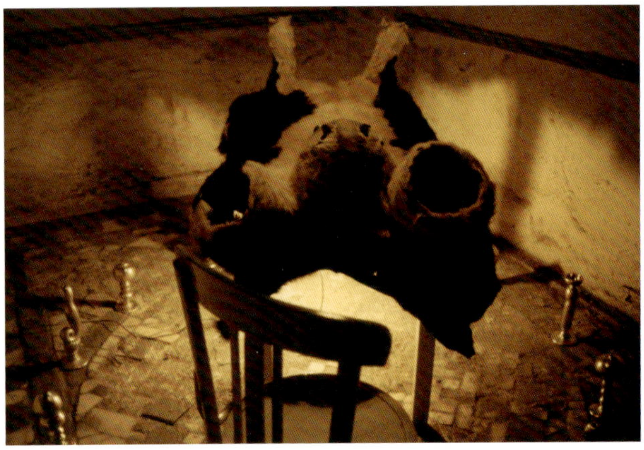

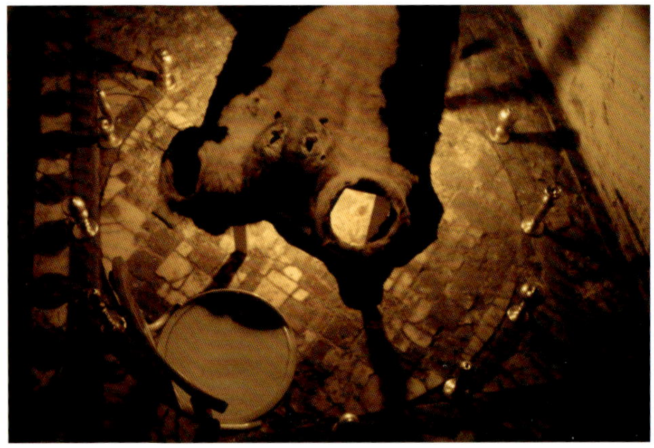

tize a more ambiguous transitional moment: the empty hide reminds us that the maternal body is always already lost. The scene of *La Primera Cena* is poised between the animal udder and the symbolic chalice. Not yet presiding over the table, but illuminated and rising up from below it, the twelve chalices prefigure the twelve apostles of the Last Supper. The rococo elegance of the goblets' silver-covered glass appears in sharp contrast to the rough materiality of the udder, yet the tiny hole in each chalice wittily imitates the teats' function, offering a new manner of "nursing." Thus these two opposing realms of nature and artifice, body and symbol, female and male, seem to join together in a common function of nurture and sacrifice.

In *La Primera Cena*, the new tradition about to rise up from beneath the primal animal body is still in its infancy. Although the church apostles are all male, Cross's transitional chalices are ambiguously gendered, their forms vaguely suggestive of phallus or breast. Responding to classic psychoanalytic theories about psychic development and the unconscious, Cross's piece prefigures the developmental imperative requiring each individual to give up the state of fluid and androgynous identities and to enter the fixed boundaries and differential categories of the symbolic order. This first meal, then, is designed to offer each diner a temporary return to that repressed pre-history in a Jungian smorgasbord of male and female sources of identification and desire. *La Primera Cena* creates a space within the convent where all boundaries are temporarily dissolved, our earliest bodily life acknowledged and even revered. The circle of chalices holds out the promise of the beauty and power of the symbolic realm, but also signifies its weakness—each goblet's precious metal patina conceals the fragility of glass.[26]

Like *Caught in a State*, *La Primera Cena* displays a certain stylized theatricality. Illuminated and viewed from above, the body appears in its material as well as in its symbolic incarnations. Also illuminated from below, however, the scene casts its own light, disrupting the detached and encompassing gaze of the audience. The single modest chair positioned next to the table invites more direct and individual participation. It may be that fantasies of that lost intimate connection to nature, the body, or the maternal breast are accessible only through the mediations of the symbolic work of art.

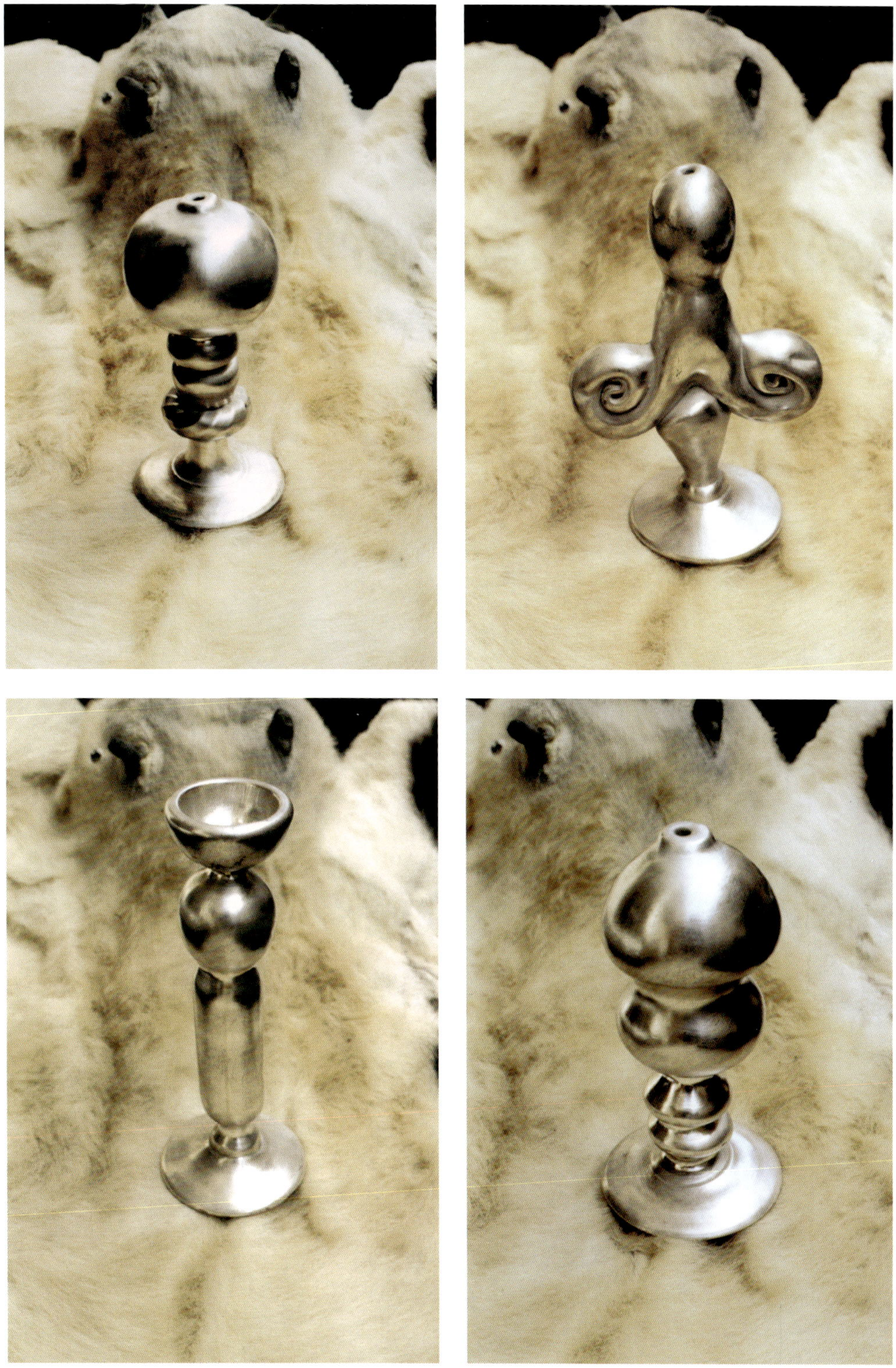

La Primera Cena,
Portraits of Chalices

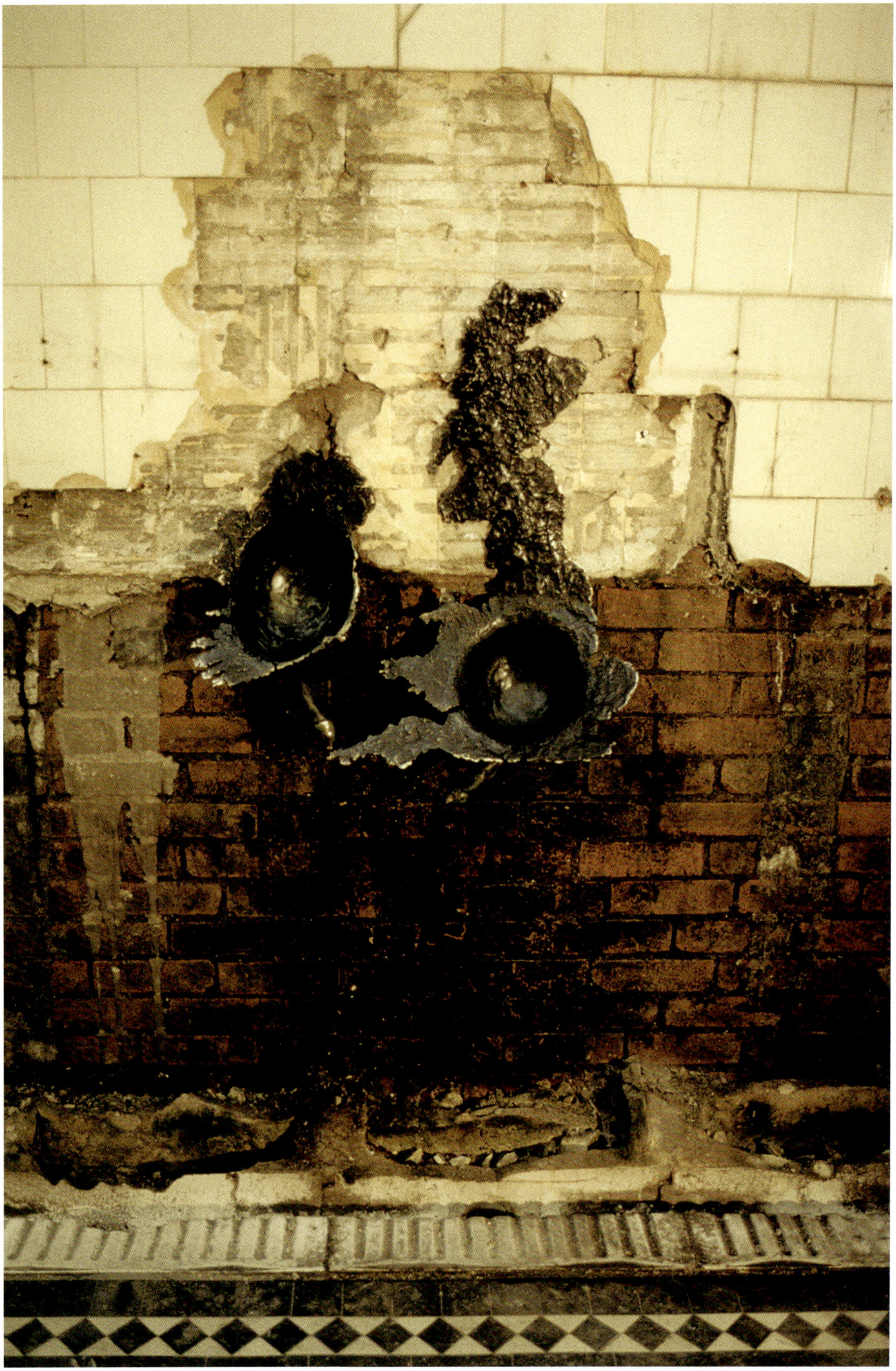

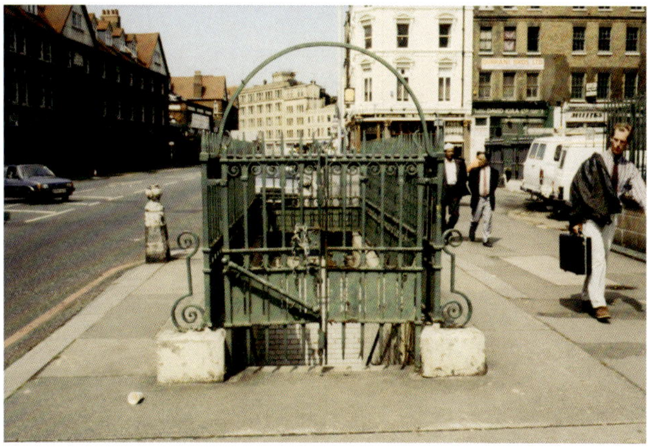

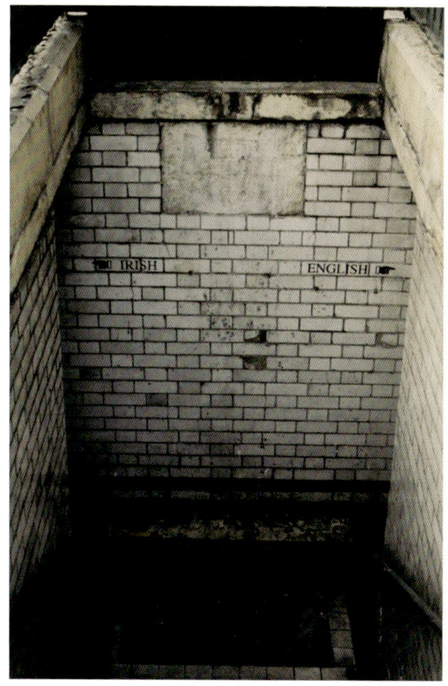

Attendant, entrance to the underground installation

Notes from the Underground: *Attendant (1992)*

The symbolic order that can be seen just emerging from beneath *La Primera Cena* in Madrid operates at full force in Cross's companion piece for the Edge Biennial in London, *Attendant.* Like the convent, this site invites the viewer into a subterranean space where the repressed underside of dominant systems of authority and knowledge lies hidden. Moving from private convent to public urinal, Cross takes us from a primal territory of the maternal, where male and female are still inchoate, to a male preserve where rigid definitions of masculinity, power, and aggression are simultaneously fixed and unsettled by the return of repressed desires and fears.

Cross chose for her London site an abandoned Victorian underground *pissoir* in a mixed immigrant neighborhood in the East End. Like the convent, the urinal's stained and cracked decorative tile work has the aesthetic appeal of the outmoded to which Cross is often attracted. The Victorian style of the facility calls up that era's repressive attitudes toward the body and bodily functions, an attitude reinforced architecturally by its underground placement. Visitors to the site descend the stairs to a landing where two painted signs direct them to proceed to the left or to the right. Instead of the usual lavatory choice of "Ladies" or "Gentlemen," the visitor must choose to descend as "English" or "Irish." Both choices, however, lead to the same lower area where the original fixtures, long gone, have been replaced by Cross's sculpture. Two bronze urinals, one in the shape of England, the other in the shape of Ireland, are mounted on the tiled wall; each map/bowl tapers below into an anatomically correct penis-shaped pipe. The two bronze organs incline toward each other and aim at a single drain hole in the floor.

Political and cultural specificity, both past and present, play an important part in the associations called up by this installation. Working in England, Cross explains, she felt more acutely aware of being perceived and positioned as Irish. The title of the installation, *Attendant,*

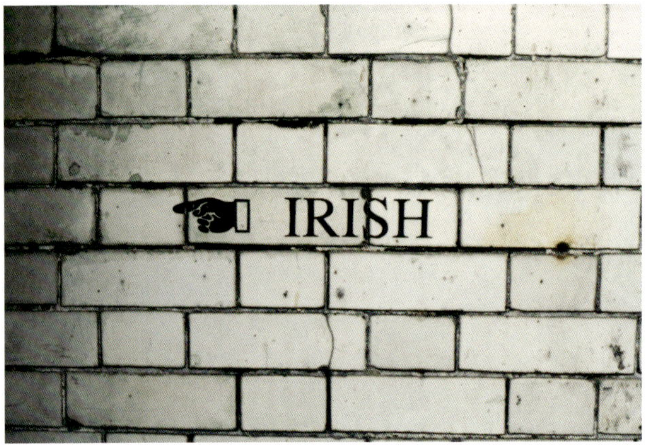

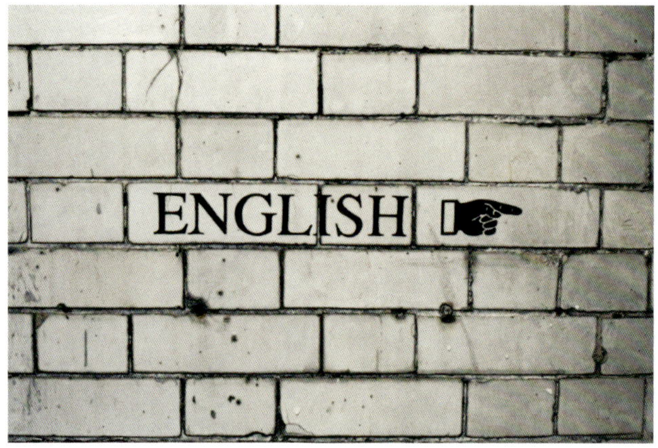

recalls the not so distant past when Irish immigrants were often employed in that capacity in public facilities. Cross gestures toward this history by inscribing the word "Attendant" on the door to the worker's alcove and installing a green light bulb inside. On their way to encounter this work, viewers pass through a marginalized neighborhood that houses some of London's more recent immigrant populations, as well as those who have been in residence for generations but are still designated as "other." This itinerary allows the current political context in Britain to reverberate with the site's buried past.

In Cross's transformation of the site, markers of class and ethnic difference are dissolved as soon as they arise, everything ultimately running together down the common drain. Viewers might be reminded of James Joyce's witticism describing the urinals outside Dublin's Trinity College as a "meeting of the waters," parodying Thomas Moore's sentimental lyric about the Irish "vallee so sweet . . . in whose bosom the wide waters meet."[27] Cross complicates this allusion in the London installation by adapting it to a meeting of Irish and English waters. The history of British efforts to segregate the Irish, even within Ireland, in prisons like Kilmainham Gaol or "beyond the pale," is mockingly reversed in this staging of an intimate confluence of the two peoples deep within the underground of Britain's own national capital. This meeting of the two nations is designed to suggest curiosity and desire rather than aggression. The penises incline toward each other in what appears to be a natural and spontaneous response that might only occur below ground. In the context of the encounter Cross orchestrates in *Attendant*, the punning title of the piece suggests both servitude and hopeful expectancy.

THE TROPE OF THE TOILET

Attendant indirectly alludes to the particularities of a political past, present, and future, but it also addresses the more general psychic structures of a collective unconscious. By choosing the toilet as her site, Cross forces this most private realm of bodily functions to go public. As a repository of buried psychic as well as bodily energies, the toilet becomes a place where the return of repressed and conflicting desires breaks through defensive structures of containment

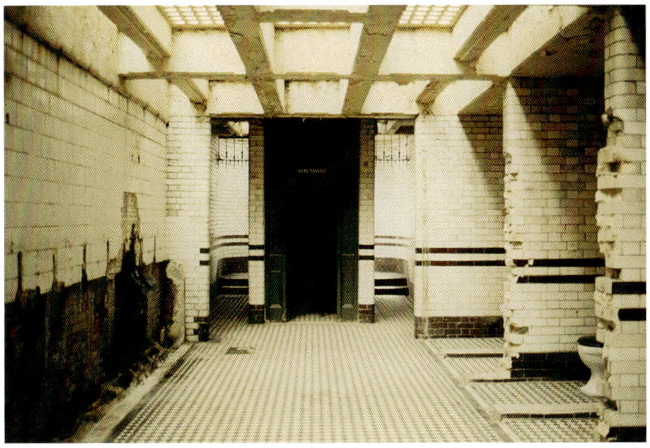

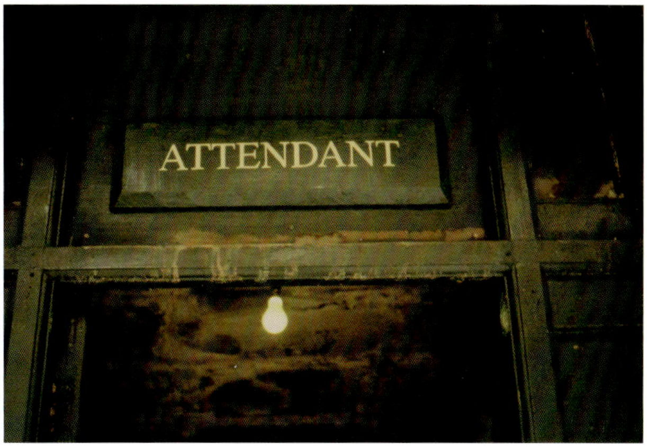

Attendant, underground installation site

and denial. Cross's London installation belongs to the venerable history of the toilet as artistic trope, and a brief reminder of that counter-tradition may illuminate some of the subtleties of this artwork.

In his sixteenth-century carnivalesque masterpiece about a family of giants, *The Histories of Gargantua and Pantagruel*, François Rabelais celebrates the excessive fertility of the body even in its most lowly functions, and associates that corporeal excess with the fertility of vernacular languages in their sensual, rhythmic, and nonsensical effects. In a stylistic *tour de force,* an entire chapter ("How Grandgousier realized Gargantua's marvellous intelligence by his invention of an Arse-wipe") is devoted to a potentially endless list of innovative "arse-wipes"—a litany of polymorphous perversity that is both physical and rhetorical. Deploying a comedy of degradation in which all that is high is brought low, writers like Rabelais use the lower bodily functions to subvert the sanctity of high culture and the sober and oppressive authority of church and state.[28] As this tradition continues through the eighteenth and nineteenth centuries, the joyously transgressive giant's body is replaced by a modern body of more modest proportions: vulnerable, mortal, and plagued by fears and desires. One striking example of this more modern body emerges at the end of the nineteenth century, in the fierce satire of Alfred Jarry's *King Ubu*. Jarry subjects his audience to abuse by an absolute ruler whose authority cannot be undone by scatology because he is already installed on its beshitted throne.

Scatology and the toilet also came to the fore in the collective work of Dadaist artists responding to the brutalities of World War I. Visitors to the 1920 Dada Exhibition in Cologne had to pass through a public toilet to the back room of a café, where the "gallery" was presided over by a stuffed pig in a military uniform suspended from the ceiling. The archetypal Dadaist gesture in this counter-tradition is, of course, Marcel Duchamp's *Fountain* (1917), a "readymade" or found sculpture consisting of a commercially produced ceramic urinal "signed" by its alleged creator, R. Mutt. Ironically, Duchamp's effort to resist "esthetic delectation" (Duchamp 141) in this and other works has subsequently been defeated by critical recuperations of *Fountain* as an object of formalistic aesthetic value.

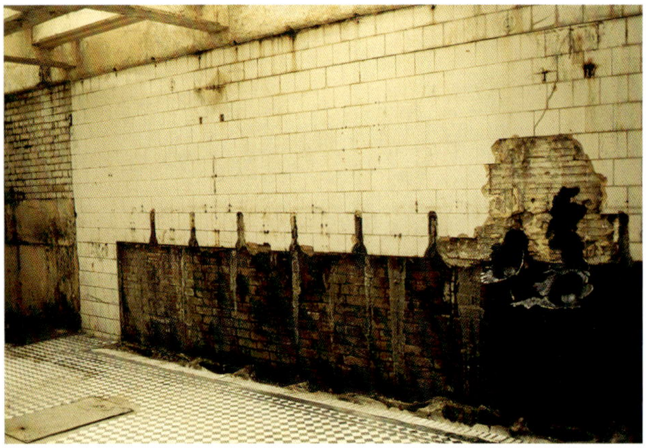
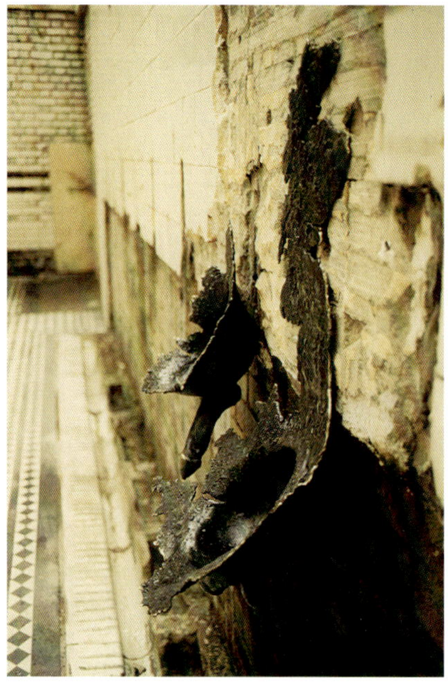

Attendant, Urinals in situ

Cross herself has no such fear of "esthetic delectation," and her meticulously, even tenderly, crafted bronze urinals have a very different impact from Duchamp's piece of commercial plumbing. While Duchamp's urinal is detached from its normal use, upended and rendered useless, Cross's urinals are incorporated into their social site, made anthropomorphic and functional. The pipes below each bowl and the drain in the floor suggest a good-humored Rabelaisian system of circulations and flows, rather than the cerebral chill of Duchamp's conceptualist joke. In conscious deviation from Duchamp, Cross fabricated her urinals in bronze rather than porcelain, creating a witty discontinuity between this most revered material and the lowly site and function to which it is devoted. In the traditional site-specific genre of public monuments, sculptures in bronze are most commonly installed on a high pedestal in the center of a public square or in front of a public institution. Cross's underground monument, in contrast, is mounted on the wall at a more human level, directing our gaze below rather than above. More critical than celebratory, this installation teasingly invites the most crude and familiar use instead of idealizing veneration.

FOLLOWING THE SIGNS

Although *Attendant* is linked by the trope of the toilet to this rich history of aesthetic transgression, it also leads viewers toward the more abstract problematics of the act of representation. In following that path, I will pass, with some trepidation, by way of psychoanalyst Jacques Lacan's "The agency of the letter in the unconscious or reason since Freud" (1966). Lacan's essay, like Cross's installation, pivots around the point of convergence of toilets and signs. Any reader familiar with this dense and tortuous essay may well doubt its usefulness as a road map, but I hope to show how Cross's site-specific piece gives Lacan's argument an unexpected clarity, and how the analyst's theory, in turn, illuminates the complexity of the artist's work.

Whereas Rabelais gives bodily materiality to the word, Lacan posits the body, or at least our perception of it, as a linguistic construction. The essay begins with an equation familiar to structural linguistics—the word TREE (the "signifier") is set over the image of a tree (the "signi-

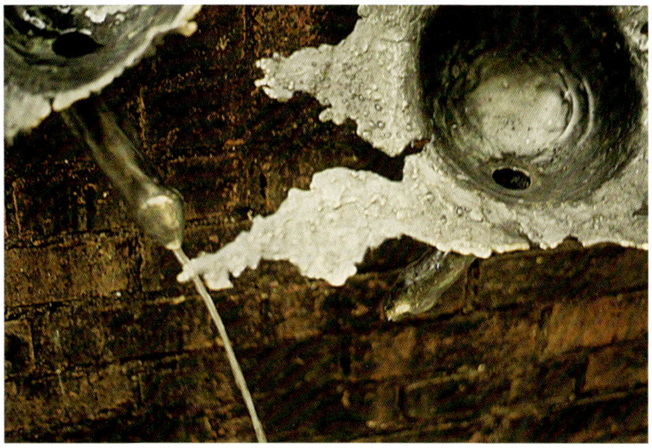

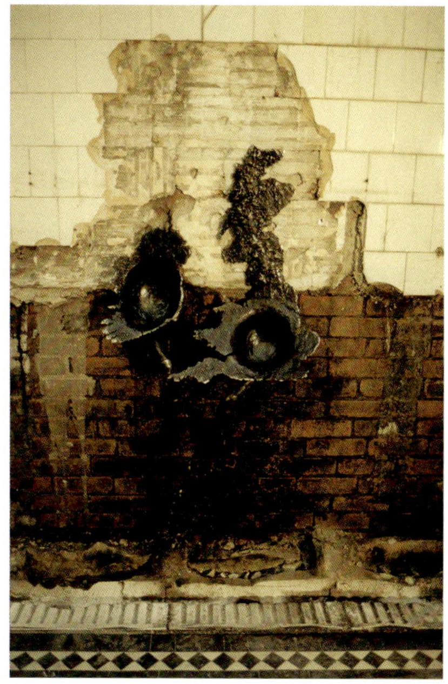

fied"), and the two combine to produce the composite and communicable "sign." To emphasize the arbitrariness of such an equation, Lacan substitutes another example: images of two identical doors are labeled with the different signifiers, "LADIES" and "GENTLEMEN"(151). Lacan provocatively suggests that what we perceive as the natural given of sexual difference is nothing but an arbitrary cultural and linguistic construction.

Lacan undercuts the high seriousness of psychoanalysis and linguistics with his own bit of toilet humor, but he is also in earnest about this exposé of sexual difference and of the constitutive structures of binary opposition that uphold the symbolic order. To show this funda-

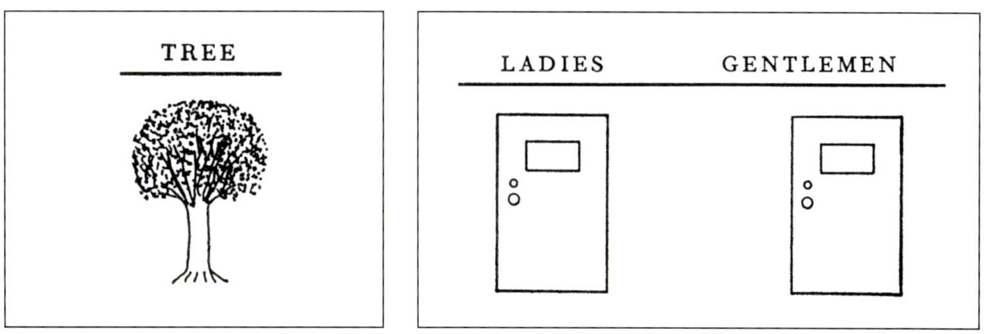

Figures from Lacan (151)

mental *méconnaissance* at work, Lacan puts these troublesome lavatory doors into an anecdote about a brother and sister sitting opposite each other on a train. As the train pulls into the station, the brother's angle of vision prompts him to say, "'Look … we're at Ladies,'' to which the sister responds, from her different perspective, "'Idiot! …Can't you see we're at Gentlemen'" (152). Lacan and Cross have both used the similarity between the "little enamel signs" on bathroom doors and in railway stations to raise questions about identity and place. In *Attendant*, the implied invitation to viewers to piss in one or the other bowl simply reenacts on a bodily level a linguistic choice already made on the landing above: to identify with and follow the directional signs for either "English" or "Irish" users of the facility. In both cases, representation and identification are shown to be illusory; these nationally segregated stairways lead to the same space below, and both nationally distinct urinal-maps are positioned to drain into the same hole in the floor. As one critic puts it, "inevitably, as with all such neat divisions, these signs lead you astray" (Isaak 26).

Lacan is pessimistic about the repercussions of this artificial production of difference: "For these children, Ladies and Gentlemen henceforth will be two countries toward which each of their souls will strive on divergent wings, and between which a truce will be the more impossible since they are actually the same country" (152). Lacan argues that the illusion of sexual difference and the impossibility of any unmediated relation, sexual or otherwise, is repeated in every cultural and political encounter, reducing to absurdity all forms of factionalism.

Cross is more optimistic than Lacan about the possibility of a productive encounter of self and other. The divisive, pointing index fingers of the signs on the landing are replaced below by the penises inclining tentatively toward one another. If Lacan's little travelers are forever "caught in the rails" of desire (167), Cross's cultural travelers go below ground where parallel lines may meet, and where a different set of rules, or lack of rules, may apply. The sly hint at homoeroticism in this underground meeting place is only one aspect of Cross's broader exploration of masculine identity, nationalism, and power.

THE TROPE OF THE MAP

Lacan's essay unsettles any certainty the reader may have about linguistic signs; Cross's work extends that destabilizing effect to visual sign systems such as mapping. Whereas Lacan mocks the "laws of urinary segregation" (151) that regulate the body and sexual identity through words ("LADIES" and "GENTLEMEN"), Cross appropriates and transforms the laws of property, political power, and even the laws of logic and grammar as they are manifested in the conventions of mapping.[29]

The trope of the map has become a familiar component in contemporary art (particularly politically oriented art), and a frequent focus of international exhibitions.[30] In her analysis of cartography in contemporary art, Irit Rogoff identifies the end of the twentieth century as a transitional moment in which "traditional geography [becomes] a sign system in crisis" (8). The exposure of its strategies of distortion and control have weakened the map's traditional claims to legibility, detachment, and neutrality. Some contemporary artists, as well as theorists like Deleuze and Guattari, have begun to imagine counter-cartographies that would transform the process of mapping. This new cartography creates what Rogoff calls "zones" of "disidentification," interstitial spaces in which fluid and multiple identities circulate freely (120).

Cross uses the map as an iconic and symbolic sign in some of her earliest sculptural works, where she incorporates an outline of Ireland into various dysfunctional "seats" of power (*Irish Coronation Chair,* 1984). No longer convincing as signifiers of power, these maps survive only as repositories of stereotypes of Irishness. Mapping has a particularly charged history in Ireland—from William Petty's seventeenth-century "Down Survey" that recorded the Cromwellian confiscations, to the nineteenth-century Ordnance Survey, in which Irish territories were linguistically as well as politically occupied. The dual English/Irish maps in Cross's London installation level that playing field. Both maps are left in silhouette, their surfaces without any inscription; anything written there will be written only in "water." In the underground site of *Attendant*, the map is no longer a system of knowledge and legal authority, an exercise in the power of dividing and naming; the map becomes literally an empty receptacle, its three-dimensionality opening it up to the instability of multiple, arbitrary, and temporary meanings.

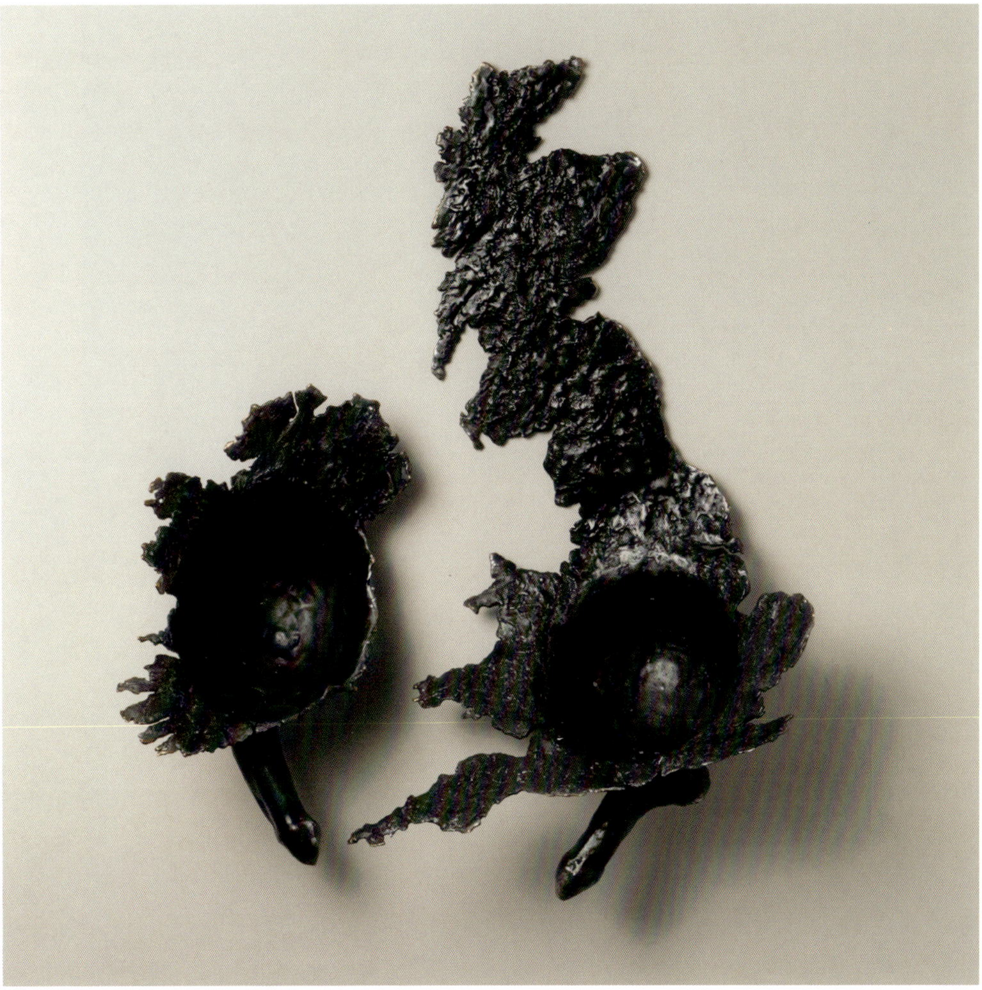

Urinals, 1992
Photo: John Kellett

Cross's use of the map silhouettes of England and Ireland in *Attendant* is a witty exercise in alternative mapping. Confronted with the two urinals, the participant "can both assert a national identity and lay claim to another country in the simple and satisfying manner of a dog staking out his territory" (Isaak 26). *Attendant* reduces nationalist and colonialist territorial claims to the level of an adolescent pissing contest or a canine compulsion.[31]

One distinction between traditional and contemporary sited sculpture is that the former tends to be work fixed to a single place and meaning, while the latter follows a more performative and nomadic itinerary. Cross's *Attendant* shows how counter-cartography can make a map into an ongoing journey. The new mapping achieved in this piece is already at work even before the viewer enters the installation, for the path to the site leads through areas off the conventional cultural map of the city. Following this uncertain path, the viewer is thrown into a more immediate experience of mapping—of the body, desire, fantasy, and anxiety. In Cross's counter-cartography, mapping is not imposed, but participatory, an open pathway to chance encounters above as well as below ground.

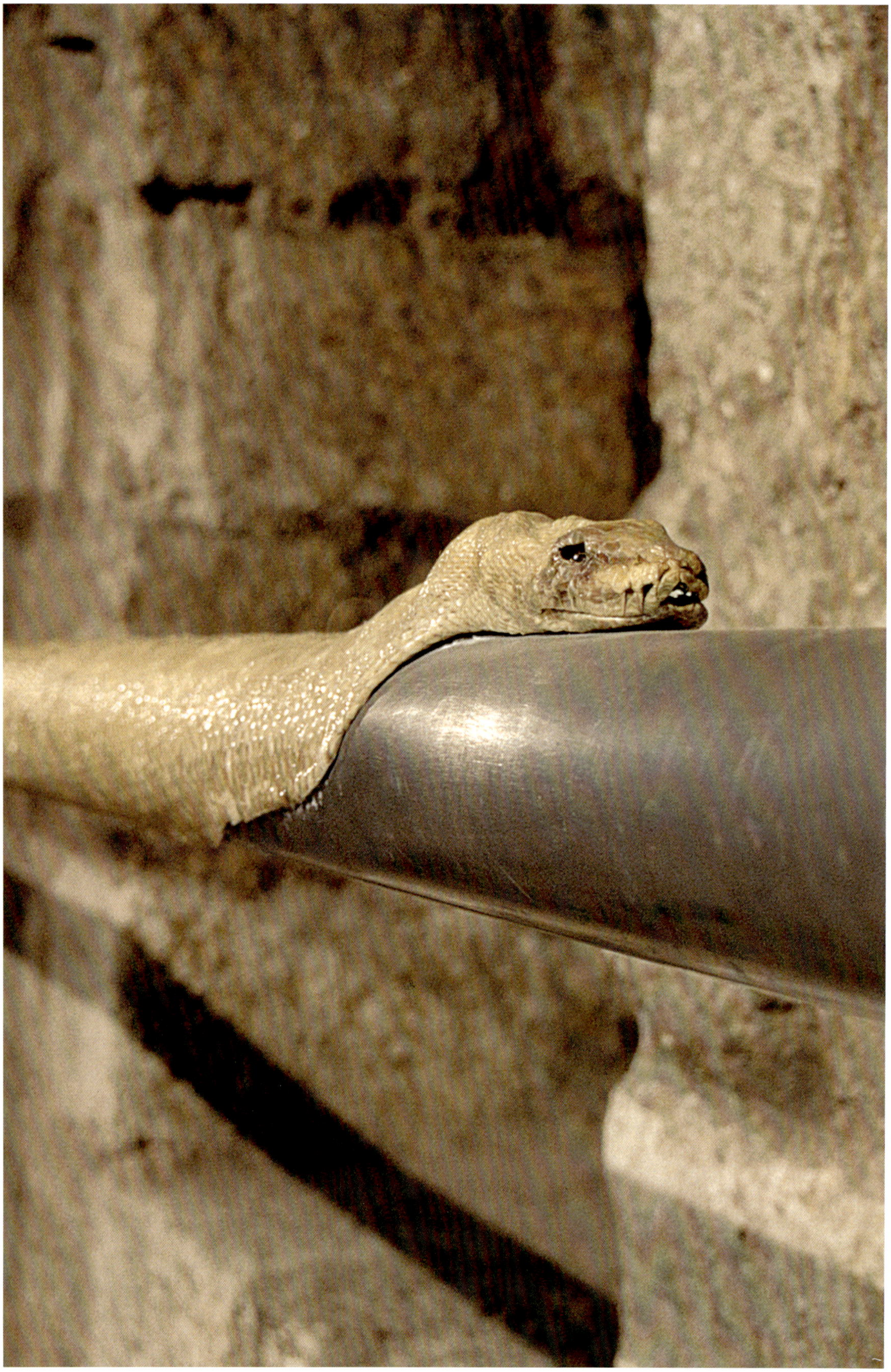

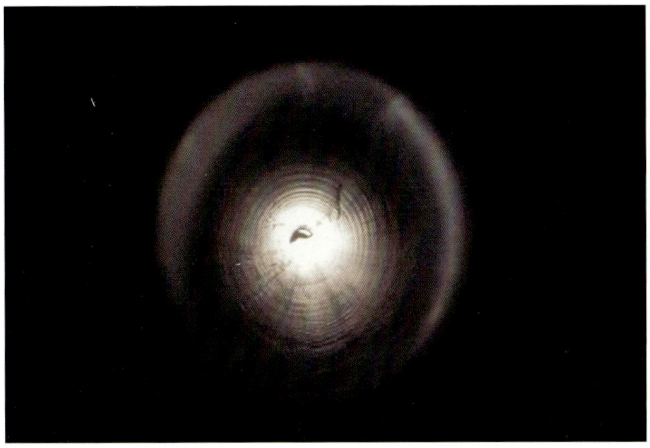
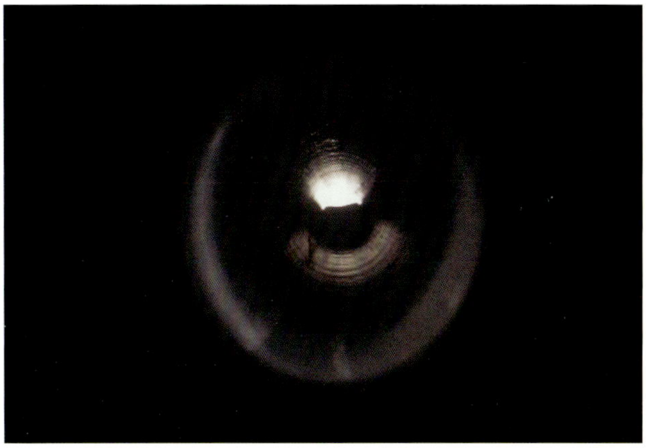

Snake, stills from *Untitled* video

The Eternal Advent of the Repressed: *Snake (1997)*

The final piece in this group of works that explore the return of the repressed in the architectural unconscious was executed in 1997 for the Fifth Istanbul Biennial. As in the prison, the convent, and the underground urinal, the repressed is uncovered here not as something alien that returns, but as something deeply embedded within the very structures designed to exclude it. *Snake* was installed in the early Byzantine church, Hagia Eireni, originally erected by the Emperor Constantine and now used as a museum and concert venue. Cross locates her work in a small enclosure next to the altar, where the viewer, seated in a low chair, looks through a hole in a small door to watch a video image of a black snake that appears to be advancing from the building's deepest recesses. On the wall next to the altar, in counterpoint to the approaching black snake, the artist has mounted a long horizontal pipe over which the skin of a nine-foot albino snake has been stretched.

Caught in a State, *La Primera Cena*, and *Attendant* are works that present individual signs in a static tableau; in the installation *Snake*, the artist adds the animating effect of narrative. Cross discovered in the lore surrounding the city of Istanbul an archetypal story about one man's dramatic attempt and inevitable failure to repress body, desire, and mortality. A Turkish legend tells of a princess confined by her father to a tower in the middle of the Bosphorous because of a prophecy that she will die of a snake-bite. Despite the father's precautions, a snake finds its way into the tower in a cluster of grapes and the prophecy is fulfilled. A surviving structure in Istanbul, built in the twelfth century by a Byzantine emperor, is identified as the "Maiden's Tower" of the legend; Cross initially selected this site for her installation. The artist's original plan was to drill a hole in the floor of the highest room in the tower through which the viewer would watch the video of the black snake gradually climbing toward the opening. Cross's proposal for the tower, however, never made it past city officials, and the piece was redesigned for Hagia Eireni.

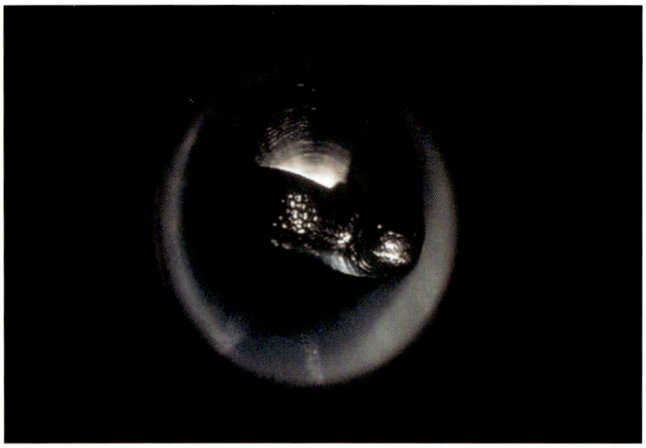

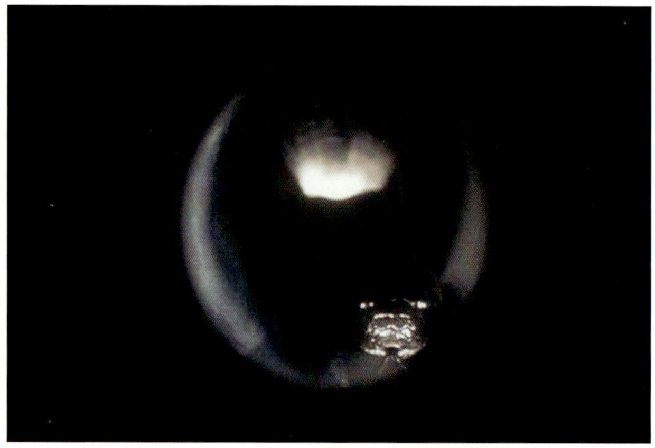

If *Snake* had been sited where originally planned, it would have woven together the tower's legendary use as a forced enclosure of safety for the princess with its historical function of defending the city against "foreign" influence. The architectural structure known as the "Maiden's Tower" has passed through several incarnations over the centuries: as a defensive structure to close off the Bosphorous against enemies, as a customs post to control incoming goods, and as a lighthouse to safeguard vessels. Its current use as a tourist gift shop and restaurant, welcoming rather than resisting the invasion of the foreign, would seem to be a dramatic reversal of its historically exclusionary function.

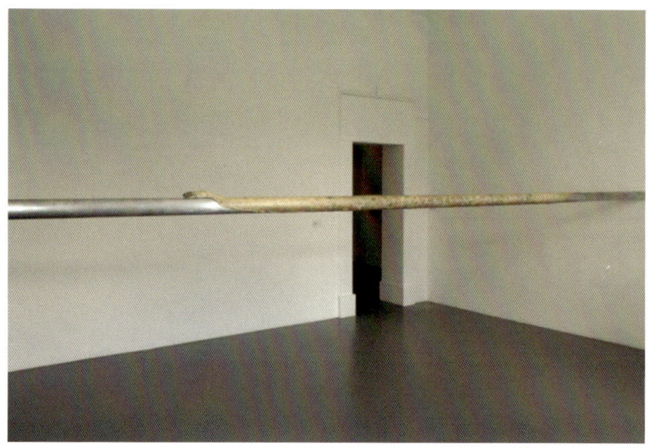

Albino Python, 1997, installed in Irish Museum of Modern Art
Photo: John Kellett

The tower site might have served as a reminder of how paternal and state power are exerted to police the body, family, and state against invasion. In its final installation in Hagia Eireni, the piece resonates with a different architectural space and generates a different set of associations. At the very heart of the church, unseen by most of its visitors, the snake—that most demonized figure in Christian mythology—perpetually approaches. As in *La Primera Cena* and *Attendant,* the excluded other seems to make its way through the very structure and ideology designed to repress it.

This excluded other, furthermore, appears as a double apparition: the live black snake recorded inside one pipe, and the dead albino snake fitted over the outside of another. Inside and outside, living and dead, black and white are joined in intimate relation here. In a later version of this sculpture installed in the Irish Museum of Modern Art, Cross positions the second pipe so that it pierces the facing walls of a room, as if exposing the inner structures on which the building depends. Mounted in the museum, Cross suggests, *Snake* exposes how nature is often sacrificed to institutional practices such as preservation and display. Whether

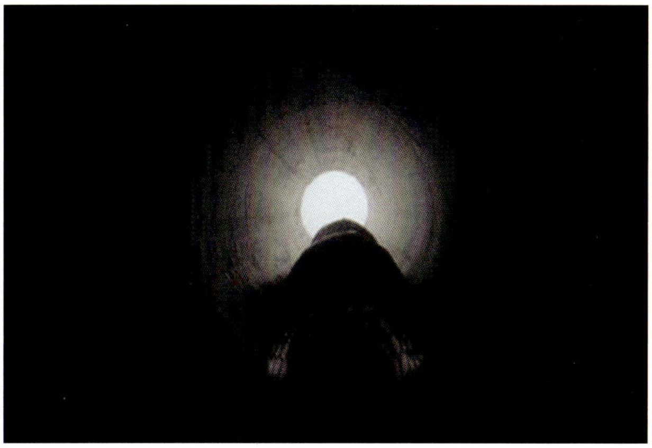

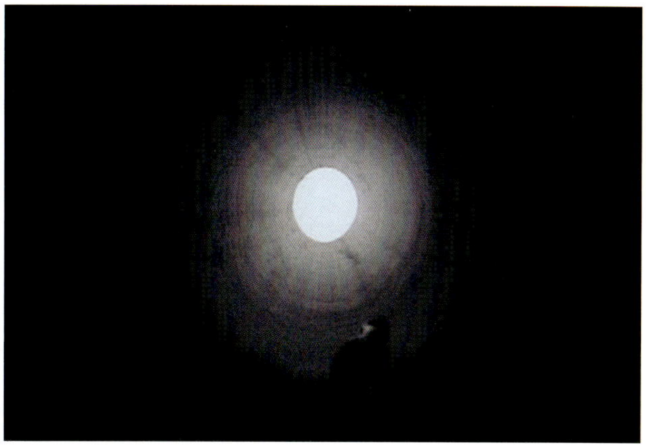

shown in the church or the museum, the beautiful skin of the albino snake impaled on its pipe can be read as an allegory of representation itself, of the ways in which representation commits violence against living reality. However, Cross's piece implies that the revenge of living nature is never far behind, and both the gallery and church are subverted by this hidden inner life. Like the two pigs in the jail cell, these two snakes reverberate with each other in a dynamic tension: no matter how thoroughly and violently the one snake is contained by representation, the mobile energy of its lived experience survives in the other.

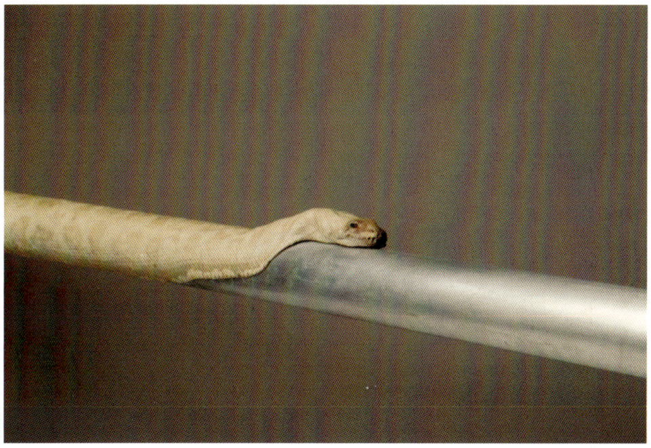

Albino Python, 1997, detail installed in Irish Museum of Modern Art
Photo: John Kellett

The video of the black snake in motion remains disturbingly ambiguous: the vague shape one sees at first, something like a strange rolling eye, only becomes recognizable in the final seconds of the film loop.[32] As a result of this prolonged visual uncertainty, the viewer experiences a shock of surprise when he or she is suddenly face to face with the returning gaze of the beast. We encounter the return of that repressed and forbidden other—our own animal nature. William Blake imagines such an encounter in "The Sick Rose," where "the invisible worm that flies in the night/ In the howling storm" brings both a "dark secret love" and the destruction of life into the flower's "bed/Of crimson joy"(42). In both the Turkish legend and the Christian myth of the Fall, the desire and death that the father tries to banish and the Church tries to transcend always reappear in the intimate heart of things.

In these four temporary site-specific works, Cross takes the viewer into the architectural unconscious, into the most hidden spaces of a repressed past—personal and collective. In the pieces discussed in the next chapter, however, she brings desire and death out into the open, offering an even more direct encounter with those manifestations of the uncanny that haunt us all.

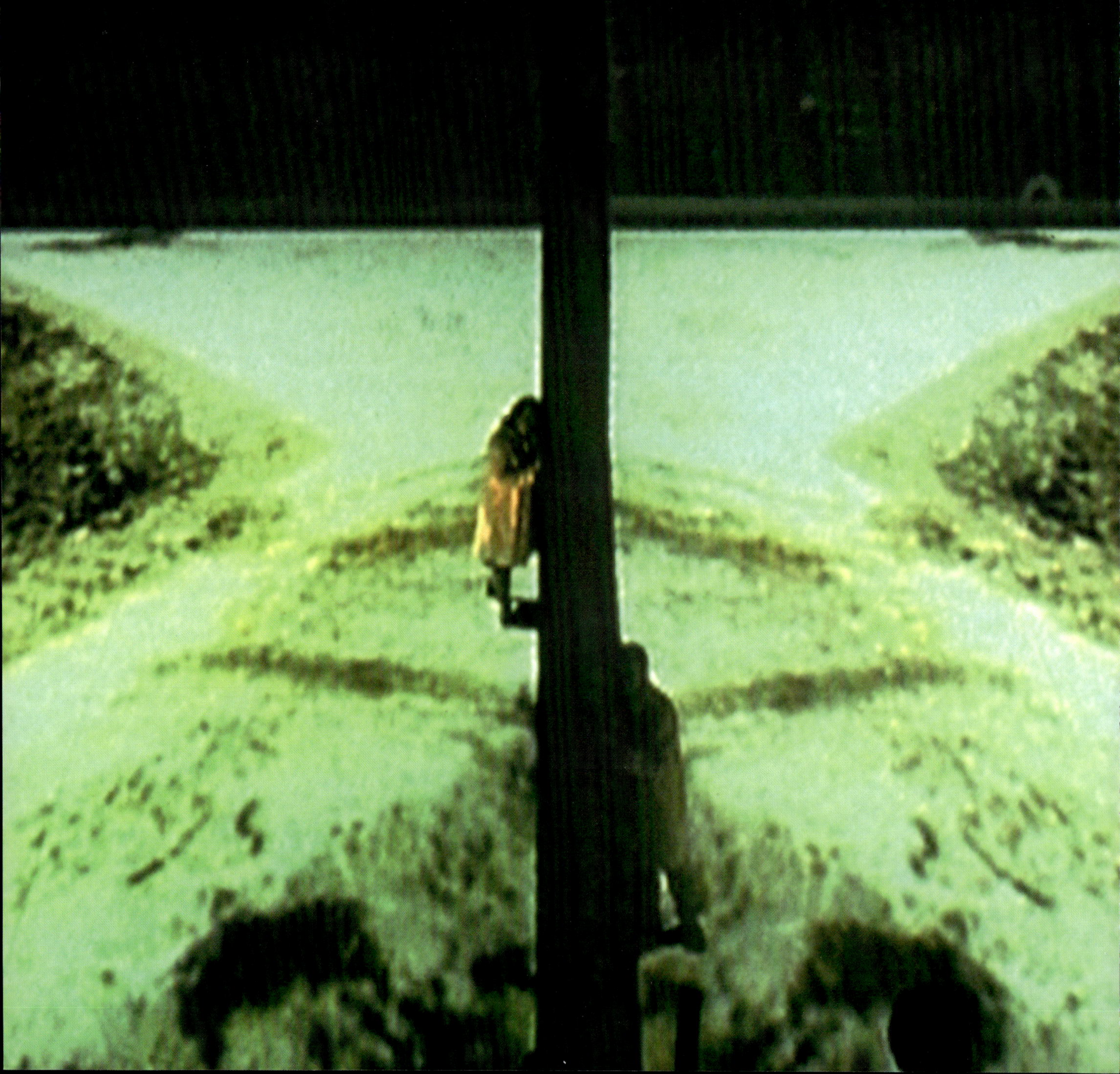

CHAPTER THREE

The Impossibility of Desire

In Cross's site-specific projects, the repressed inevitably returns in the form of historical traces, but also in the form of impossible desires. In the three site-specific works discussed in this chapter—*Slippery Slope, Chiasm,* and *Strangers on a Train*—desire emerges as an imminent but elusive encounter with the other, with representation, and with limit. *Slippery Slope* stages the futile yearning to return to the origin or arrive at the end of desire; *Chiasm* dramatizes the obstacles that invariably separate self and other, the desiring subject and its goal; and *Strangers on a Train* revolves around the haunting remains of an anonymous embrace. In addition to representing the impossibility of desire, these pieces also enact it through their incorporation of the desires and frustrations of the audience. Viewers' engagement with these works remains tentative and open, their understanding partial. Whereas *Slippery Slope* offers a chance

FACING PAGE:
Chiasm, 1999

encounter to the passerby who might easily overlook the installation, the more formally staged performance of *Chiasm* eludes its audience by giving every seat a partially obstructed view. The most direct level of audience participation and frustration is achieved in *Strangers on a Train,* where viewers enter the installation and come face to face with each other at the empty center of a performance in which they are the only actors.

Although Cross conceived of these projects independently of the vast theoretical literature on desire,[33] they often embody and animate the most urgent issues raised by literary, psychoanalytic, and philosophical approaches to the topic. The ambiguity and witty self-reflexivity characteristic of her style distinguish her work from more explicitly didactic and cumbersomely theory-based art. Nevertheless, a brief mention of some modern theories of desire will provide a useful backdrop against which the complexities at work and at play in Cross's aesthetic of desire may stand out most clearly.

Norman O. Brown, an early and influential theorist of desire, argues that man's essential characteristic "consists not, as Descartes maintained, in thinking, but in desiring"(7). As Freud's account of the sexual instinct suggests, however, the "true essence" of desire may be its inherent impossibility, stemming from infantile demands that are "altogether insatiable," "immoderate," and "cannot for the most part be satisfied" (1933, 122-23). Theorists like Leo Bersani and Julia Kristeva make of this insatiability a triumph rather than a failure. As Eugene Goodheart observes, they celebrate desire's refusal to be "constrained by the satisfaction that would extinguish it" (Goodheart 3).

Some have argued that desire is threatened not only by satisfaction, but also by our inclination to codify, inscribe, and symbolize it. Although the containment of desire in systems, words, and images may weaken its primordial energy, desire is continually fuelled by such representations in the unconscious. In sexual life, another critic proposes, one is "captivated by libidinally invested images ... trapped like an animal [in] the 'mechanical throwing into gear of the sexual instinct'" (Staten 175).[34] "Captivated" by insubstantial images, "trapped" in the machinery of the drives, the subject is fated never to possess the object of his or her desire. So desire revolves around an empty space that is at once a potentiality and a negation. As Jacqueline Rose puts it, "Desire functions much as the zero unit in the numerical chain—its place is both constitutive *and* empty" (1982, 32).

Some psychoanalytic theorists, following the lead of Jacques Lacan, propose that this constitutive lack-in-being animates the subject from the most primal animal stirrings of the drives to the complex interactions of human desire in the symbolic. The subject's entry into the symbolic order—into language, reason, law, intersubjectivity, differentiation—never fills that lack, but does enable us to name it (Belsey 55). The symbolic order gives us a structure in which objects of desire may be substituted for a primary (but imaginary) lost object. Desire becomes "human" when the subject turns from those objects towards another desiring subject; but since the other subject is also marked by a privation that leaves him or her lacking, the sexual relation will always be the intersection of two impossible desires (Muller and Richardson 20-21). "In other words," as Lacan proposes, "what it is all about is the fact that love is impossible, and that the sexual relation founders in non-sense" (1982, 158). The only way to move beyond this impasse of frustration may be to acknowledge and represent the limits of desire and the lack that constitutes each individual subject.

Many theorists of desire recognize that the coming together of vision and touch, self and world, self and other is an encounter that remains "always imminent and never realized in fact" (Merleau-Ponty 1968, 147). However, for those more optimistic about desire, such as

Merleau-Ponty, the gap between desiring subjects and their others is not an indication of failure, but a clearing that acts as a "hinge" or "pivot," a "negativity that is not nothing." This hollow, he suggests, is where the idea forms the "lining and … depth" of the sensible/visible world, where thought and feeling converge (1968, 148-49). At once intensely sensual and deeply intellectual, Dorothy Cross's aesthetic of desire brings together the world of ideas and the world of sight, sound, and touch. The three pieces discussed in this chapter represent desire as absolutely impossible and absolutely necessary.

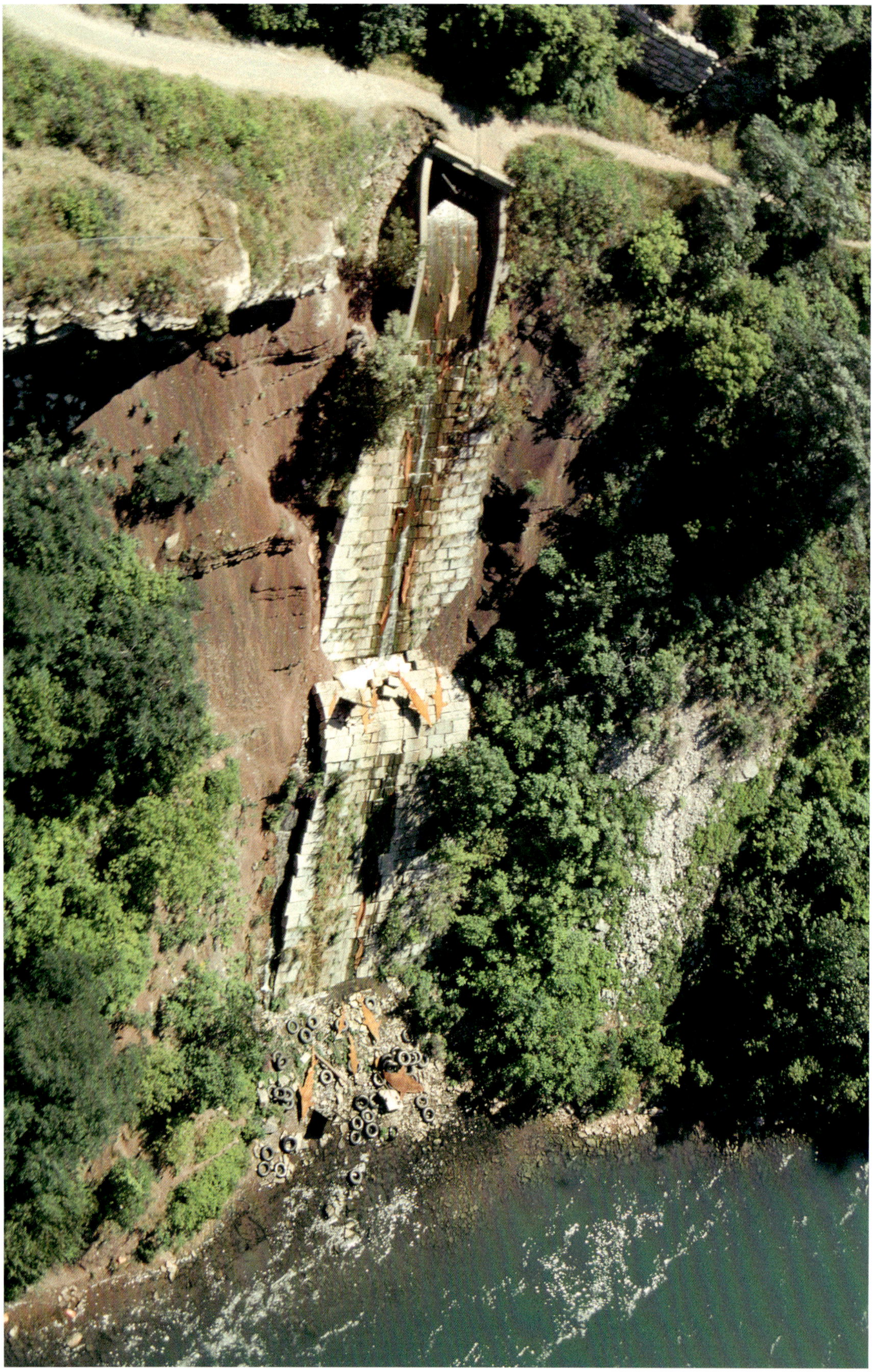

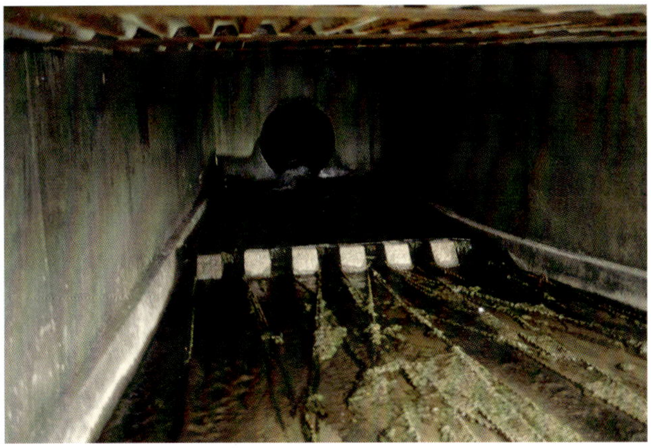

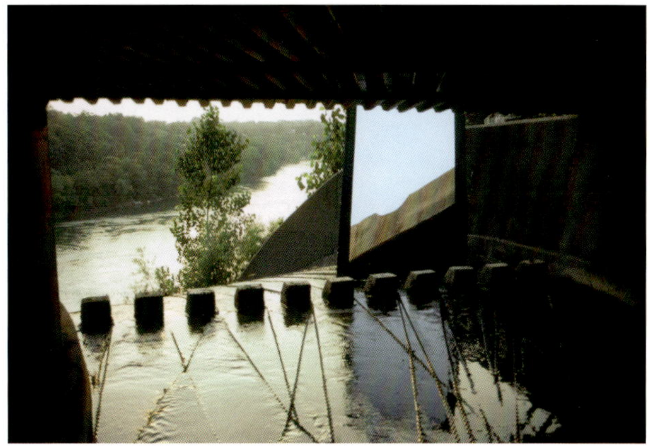

Slippery Slope, interior of sewage outlet

Desire and the Drives: *Slippery Slope (1990)*

Of the three site-specific works considered here, *Slippery Slope* comes closest to a representation of the dynamics of desire at the primary level of the drives. For two months during the summer of 1990, at the Lewiston, New York ArtPark, a visitor walking along a path beside the Niagara River would have come upon Cross's installation. Looking over the edge of a two hundred-foot gorge, the viewer could see, suspended down its side, thirty flat steel cut–out silhouettes representing thirty shark species known to have attacked man without provocation. The sharks' descent is arrested by chains connecting them to a sewage outlet, four feet in diameter, and a spillway emerging from beneath the path. The stages of the sharks' journey are reversed, reflected back up to the viewer in a series of four-by-ten foot, black-framed mirrors installed at intervals down the slope. At ground level, thirty inner tubes await the sharks, as if to float them safely into the river and perhaps ultimately out to sea.

This piece, like those discussed in the previous section, reverberates with the sedimentary history of its location. Once a Native American burial ground, the natural setting of *Slippery Slope* evokes the mysterious atmosphere of a site once animated by spirits. The subsequent use of this part of the Niagara River as a chemical dump inadvertently added a patina of toxic beauty to the scene. A new cultural use has been added to this already richly layered terrain by its present incarnation as part of the two-hundred-acre Lewiston ArtPark.

A similar palimpsest of nature, industry, and culture can be found just up river at Niagara Falls. In the nineteenth century, the Falls inspired artists, writers, and tourists with its natural beauty and power; early appreciations of the spot often describe its impact on the viewer in highly eroticized language.[35] In the first decades of the twentieth century, the thrilling but disturbing energy of the Falls became domesticated and commodified in its marketing as a honeymoon destination. Niagara Falls was transformed into a popular cultural site where the dark side of desire is sanctioned and contained, "given a shady but cheerful tinge"

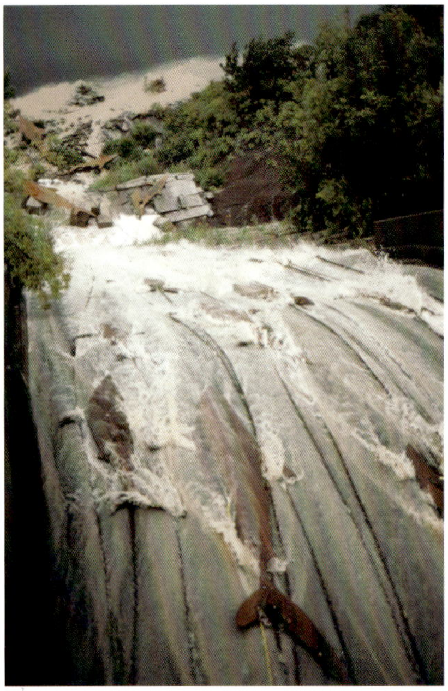 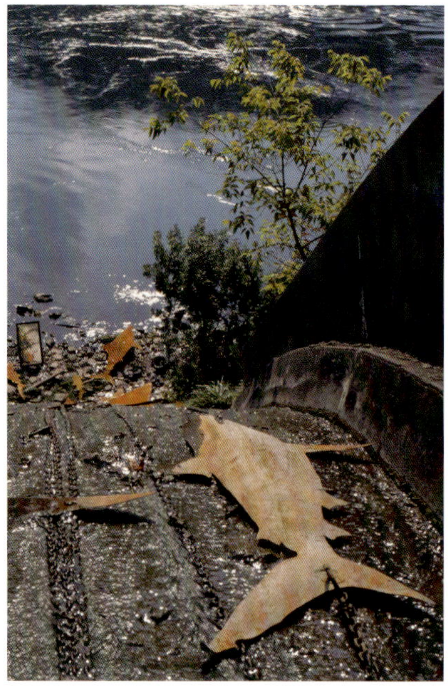 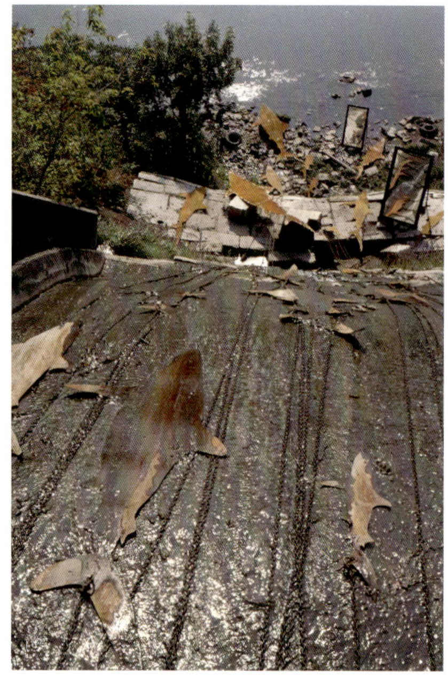

Slippery Slope, sharks descending the spillway. Photo at right: Loring McAlpin

(Dubinsky 211). Reversing the effects of this cultural containment of nature's intensity, *Slippery Slope* returns desire's uncontrollable force to the surface. Cross's piece resonates with the buried history of a natural setting and an indigenous way of life threatened by industrial progress, and with a repressed prehistory of unsocialized desire. The ArtPark's proximity to the infamously contaminated (and ironically named) "Love Canal" reinforces this intimation of dangerous or toxic desire just out of view of the "official" narrative of American romance and industrial progress.

Cross envisions this piece as a "theatre of the river," in which the river's history of reverence and abuse is enacted. The dramatic clash of traditional and modern cultural values, finds its sad outcome in our betrayal of and alienation from nature. Alongside this ecological drama, however, Cross stages a "theatre of desire," in which the river and its waters function as signifiers of what Freud recognized as the "Instincts and their Vicissitudes."

In his analysis of desire, Freud often elaborates on the metaphor of libidinal energy as a flowing stream subject to obstructions—diverted, drying up, going underground, overflowing.[36] *Slippery Slope* gives this metaphor concrete form, drawing our attention to the convergence of the natural water of the river and the sewage and run-off being emptied into it by the artificial slipway. This tainted flow is the poisonous underside of modernity, containing everything expelled by nearby domestic and industrial activities. The sharks strain to escape from this abject source, yet are held captive by it, chained in the very path of its contaminated outflow. During the two months the installation was in place, the sharks' steel bodies began to rust and erode, and the tires below exploded and rotted in the heat. The sharks remain suspended between an excremental point of origin and an equally abject destination. Despite their stalled itinerary, the sharks' immobilized bodies churn and animate the waters that run over them, the pull of gravity generating an image of the inescapable dynamics of the drive.

The implied narrative of *Slippery Slope* resonates with Carl Jung's allegory of desire in which the mythic hero escapes from stifling "maternal" waters by way of immersion in and movement through them, to achieve at last a liberating separation from the mother and a

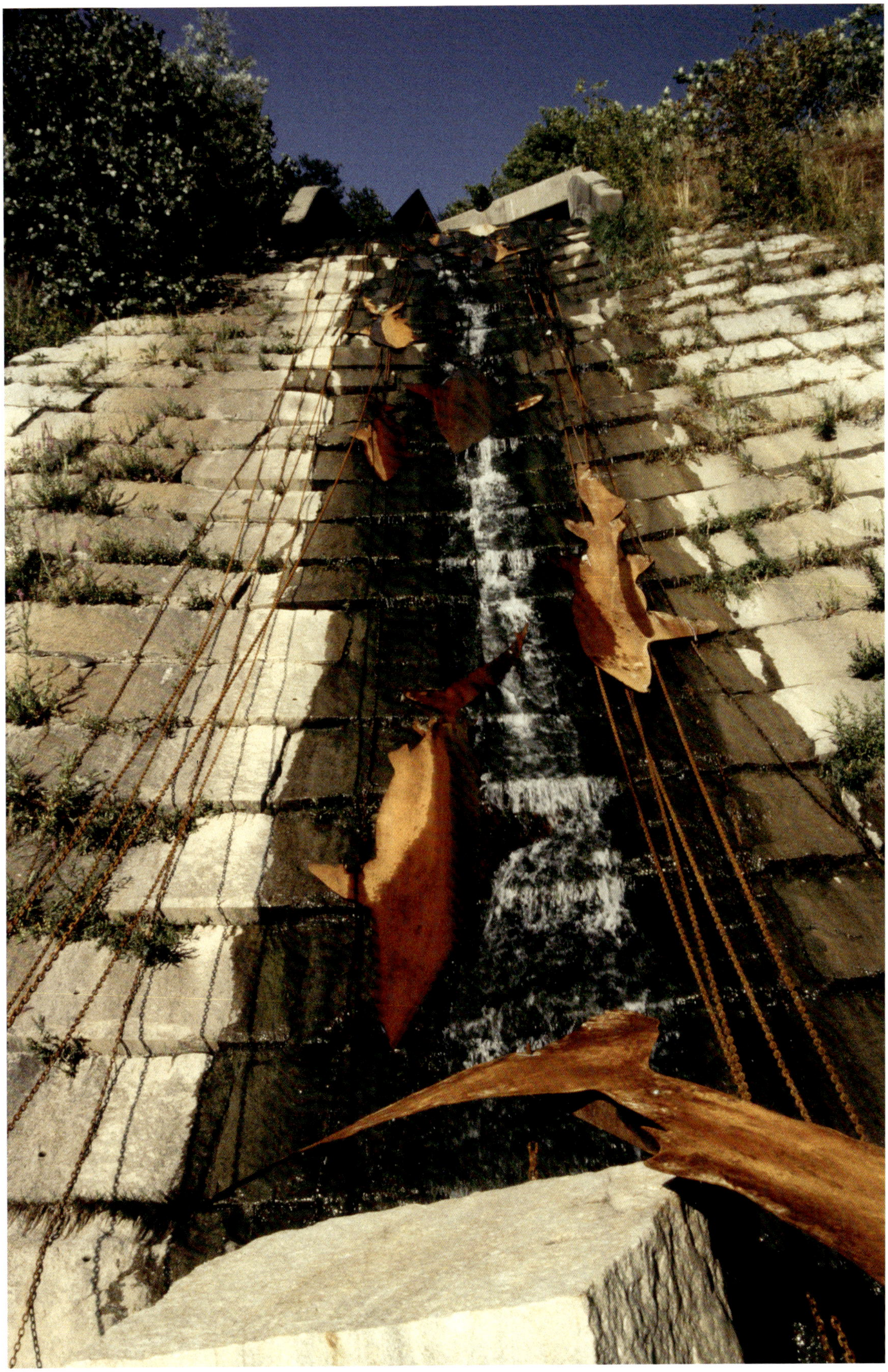

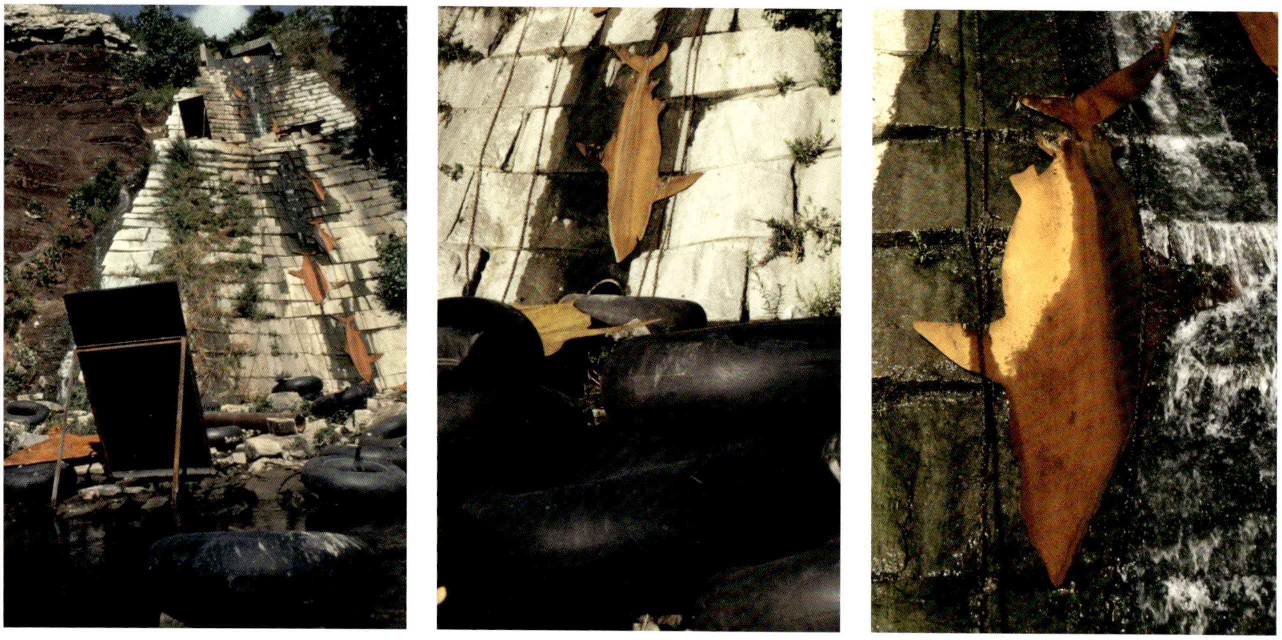

Slippery Slope, bottom of the spillway

rebirth of trapped libido.[37] Influenced earlier in her artistic career by Jung's theories, Cross is familiar with his journey of desire. She short-circuits its promise of rebirth, however, with a more melancholy scene. Withholding allegorical clarity and narrative resolution, Cross stages the precarious uncertainty of what Peter Brooks (in his theory of narrative) calls the "doomed energies" of the middle, where one is suspended between a lost origin and an inaccessible destination (110). The sharks are set on a course down a "slippery slope," with no way to arrest their perpetual fall.

In other works, Cross uses the figure of the shark to evoke the violence and unpredictability at the core of human subjectivity, revealing the entanglements of desire, aggression, and death. In some of her sculptural constructions, the shark's body is only partially visible, as a protruding fin or a collection of fossilized teeth; in others, the shark is reduced to a silhouette etched on glass or burned into wood. Cross invariably acknowledges that the full presence of the shark's power leaves behind only its traces, mediated by the artificial conventions of iconic representation. Even in this diminished incarnation, however, the sharks unveil the repressed violence hidden within the most protected human sanctuaries, from the domestic spaces of kitchen or bathroom, to the more intimate spaces of private lockers and beds of passion.[38] The sharks' intimate presence threatens to shatter the individuality of the subject and his or her status as "human." As the "cannibalistic" aggression of the drive is released in the sexual instinct, the individual subject loses his bearings and is absorbed into the collective identity of the species (Rose 1982, 35). Doubled and divided in the mirrors positioned down the side of the gorge in *Slippery Slope*, each of these dangerous and unpredictable beasts in chains reflects, though in a glass and darkly, our own paradoxical being.

Cross ventures into this grim terrain not to explain it, but to make its darkness visible. In a 1989 gallery installation at P.S. 1 in New York, conceived during the same period as *Slippery Slope*, Cross used the image (and title) *Eclipse* to make darkness and illumination reverberate. This piece includes an upward sloping metal ramp perforated by the cut out shapes of the same species of sharks featured in the Lewiston installation. For the gallery exhibition, however, their

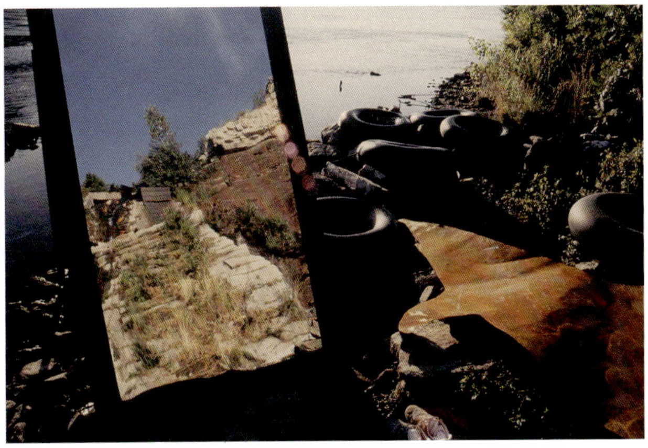

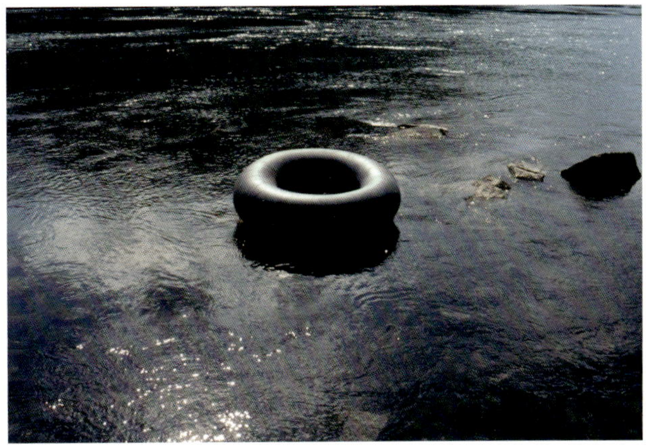

forms are not realized in metal but in light shining through the cut-outs onto the floor below. The curving ramp leads up to a large photograph of an eclipse of the sun mounted in a light box on the gallery wall. The light obstructed by the eclipse streams out from behind the box, a seductive lure for sharks and viewers alike. But the object of desire remains out of reach, and the ascent up the ramp leads only to reversal and fall. Viewers of this installation may recognize their own human dilemma in the cluster of metal shark silhouettes suspended by chains from below the lightbox.

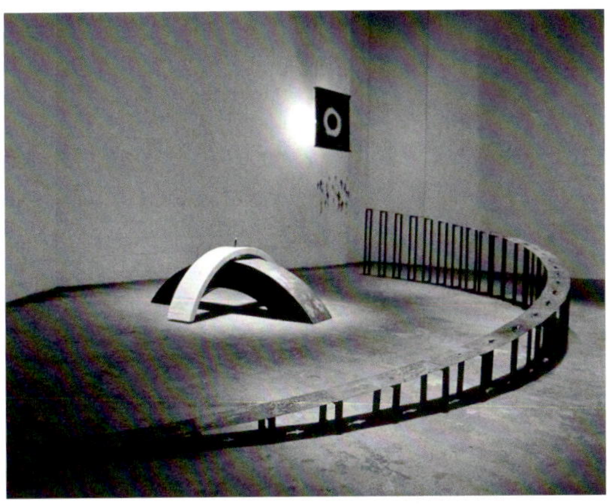

Eclipse, 1989
P.S. 1, New York

In *Slippery Slope*, Cross locates the same conflicted territory of desire outside the gallery, in a natural site that restores the material and bodily foundations of the drives. The lure at the Lewiston installation is not the "light" of Enlightenment, but desire for some uncontaminated watery home just out of reach, where the sharks, present and whole, might regain their fleshly three-dimensionality. The sharks in *Eclipse* are chained to a two-dimensional image of a black circle superimposed over a circle of light; the outdoor beasts, in contrast, are chained to an actual three-dimensional hole, its slimy sewage buildup suggestive of bodily orifices, simultaneously anal and genital.

The sharks in *Slippery Slope* are suspended in abjection—in a "desire for separation, for becoming autonomous and also the feeling of an impossibility of doing so" (Kristeva 1988, 136). Here, Cross reveals the complications of desire, as the tilted mirrors interrupt the drive downward and away from the origin with reflections that throw the gaze back up toward that source. Ascent and fall are sequential in *Eclipse*; in *Slippery Slope* they are simultaneous, capturing the full ambivalence of the drives and desire. The rush forward is at the same time a repetition and a return, and that return of the repressed, as dictated by the death drive, brings the subject to the edge of annihilation. It is always already too late for the cautionary warning, "Slippery Slope!"

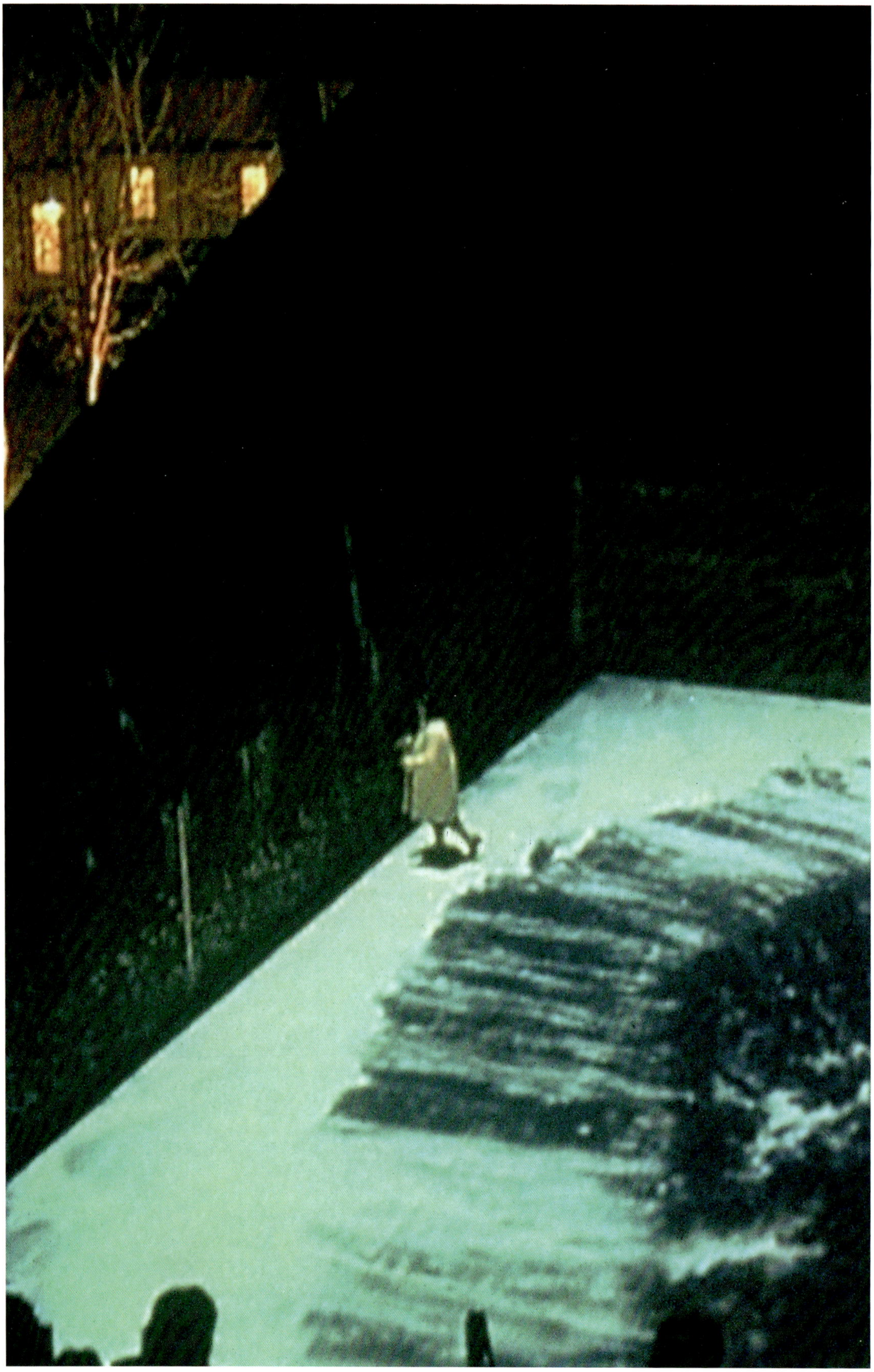

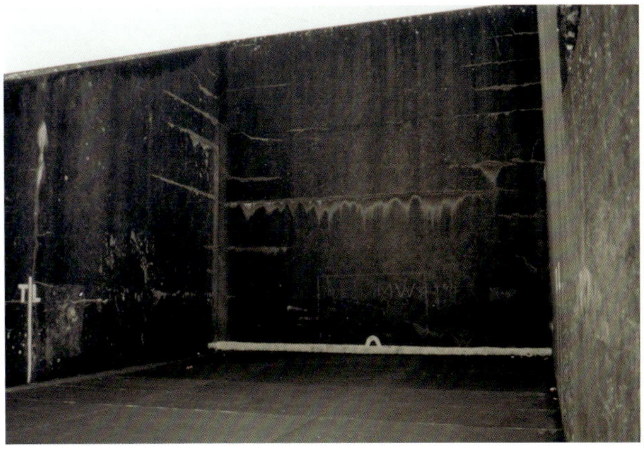
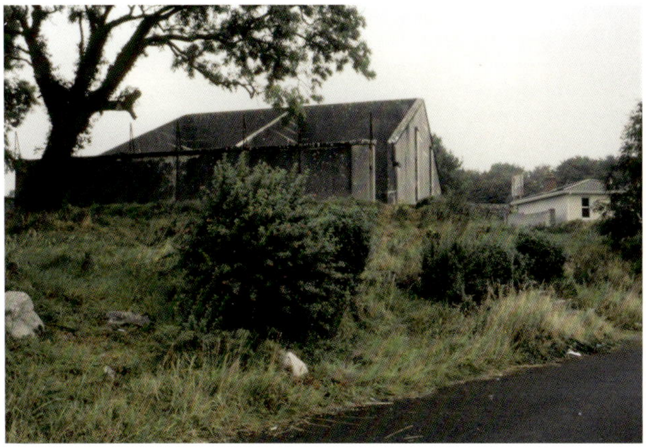

Chiasm, open-air handball alleys, Galway, Ireland

Desire in the Symbolic: *Chiasm (1999)*

Although the outdoor setting of *Slippery Slope* puts the sharks in intimate connection with matter and its transformations, their flat, blank silhouettes keep them trapped in the realm of representation. As Cross puts it, the sharks merely "refer" to something, and their physical descent down the side of the gorge is also a fall into the symbolic. Taking up where *Slippery Slope* leaves off, *Chiasm* is situated firmly within the symbolic order that mediates all signification, intersubjectivity, and love. This piece delivers viewers from the vitality and abject materiality of the body to a realm in which the drives are constrained and organized within the symbolic even as they transgress its limits.[39]

Chiasm has three distinct but intricately interwoven layers. Its foundation is a pair of abandoned, open-air handball alleys in Galway, Ireland. Onto their cement floors Cross projects video images of a limestone tidal pool filmed on the Aran Islands. These adjoining courts, transformed by the projection of the pool and divided by a cement wall, provide the stage on which a tenor and a soprano sing fragments from ten romantic operas, including such classic love tragedies as Gounod's *Romeo and Juliet*, Puccini's *Manon Lescaut*, and Tchaikovsky's *Eugene Onegin*.[40] The three repeated cycles that make up each full performance of *Chiasm* were staged for only two nights in May 1999.

After the design for this piece had been completed, Cross was introduced to a philosophical concept from the writings of Merleau-Ponty that would become its title. Along with its variants—chiasma and chiasmus—the term chiasm denotes structures of intersection or inversion. In physiology, for example, it describes the intersection of two anatomical structures; in rhetoric, it is a figure of speech in which the order of terms in the first of two parallel clauses is reversed in the second ("Beauty is Truth, Truth Beauty"). In philosophy, and specifically in the late work of Merleau-Ponty, chiasm represents a complex mode of relationality, an intimate encounter of the visible and the invisible, subject and world. Although Cross was not initially

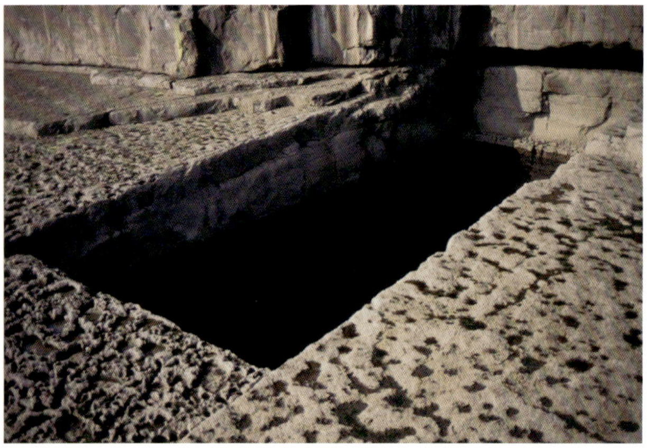

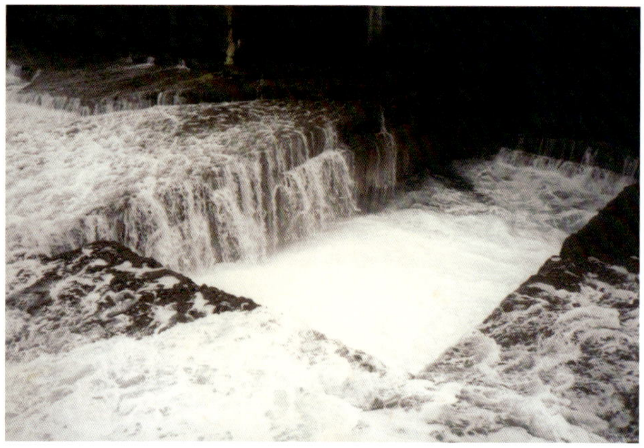

Chiasm, Worm's Hole sea pool, Aran Islands

inspired by Merleau-Ponty's philosophical elaboration of being in chiasm, the striking affinities between their ways of thinking provide a fruitful starting point for an analysis of this piece.

Deviating from the structures of hierarchy, binary opposition, and synthesis that organize traditional Western metaphysics, Merleau-Ponty turns to chiasm as an effect of intertwining, intersection, and inversion in which each element nevertheless retains its alterity. He envisions the relationship between the perceiving subject and the sensible/visible world, between seeing and touching, and between the subject and the other as an exchange in which "each borrows from the other … encroaches upon the other, intersects with the other, is in chiasm with the other" (1968, 261) without losing itself. Although each element resists appropriation into an undifferentiated synthesis, there is no autonomous identity in chiasm, but a mode of being that is hinged rather than stable, characterized by doubling and inversion. As nature and culture, myth and history, seer and seen are brought into intimate encounter, Merleau-Ponty argues, all binary oppositions are thrown off balance, every defining barrier breached. Between body and world "there is a relation that is one of embrace…. And between these two … there is not a frontier, but a contact surface" (1968, 271). From that contact surface everything radiates outward in a kind of Derridean dissemination. The temporary aspect of Cross's site-specific art, and particularly of a performance piece like *Chiasm*, enacts most poignantly the artist's willingness to be dispossessed—of permanence, of identity, of mastery, and of the satisfaction of desire.

For Cross, as for Merleau-Ponty, what shows itself in chiasm is the unconscious, where being trembles as "a being of depths … a being in latency," and where representation constitutes "a presentation of a certain absence" (1968, 136). Merleau-Ponty makes these unconscious effects visible in his description of chiasm as a complex landscape, a "topological space as a model of being" (1968, 210). In his philosophical system, each subject constitutes a "landscape" that participates with "other landscapes," caressing and interpenetrating each other: "[these] landscapes interweave, their actions and their passions fit together exactly" with "an intimacy as close as between the sea and the strand" (1968, 140-41, 142, 130-31). In her version of chiasm, Cross enhances this sensual and erotic aspect of Merleau-Ponty's geographical metaphor.

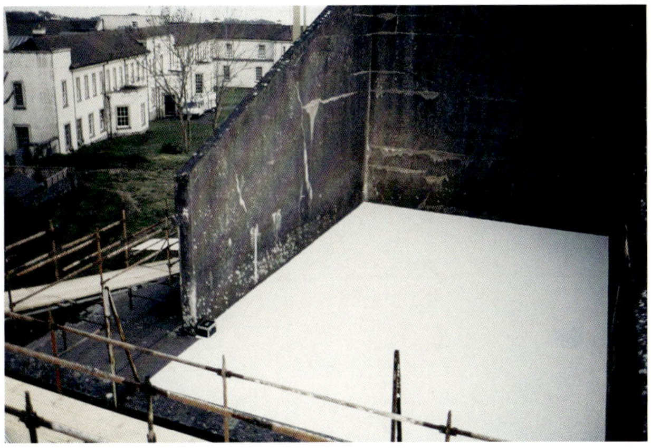

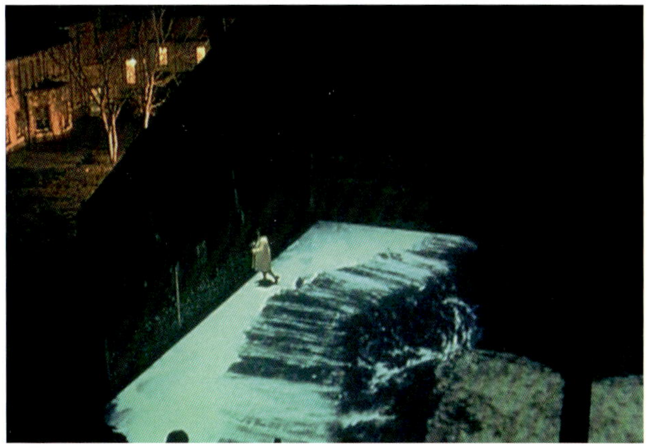

Chiasm, painted court floor with Worm's Hole projection

In "Eye and Mind," Merleau-Ponty elaborates on chiasm in a description that bears an uncanny resemblance to Cross's performance piece:

> When through the water's thickness I see the tiling at the bottom of a pool, I do not see it *despite* the water and the reflections there; I see it through them and because of them. If there were no distortions ... then I would cease to see it as it is and where it is. I cannot say that the water itself ... is *in* space ... but it is not in the pool. It inhabits it, it materializes itself there, yet it is not contained there; and if I raise my eyes toward the screen of cypresses where the web of reflections is playing, I cannot gainsay the fact that the water visits it, too, or at least sends into it, upon it, its active and living essence (182).

In this scene, the natural and the artificial simultaneously converge and radiate out. Tiled floor, water, and surrounding trees are interdependent elements: each brings the others into being without losing its own specificity, and each "materializes" itself without being "contained." Merleau-Ponty describes a scene not unlike Cross's *Chiasm*, in which reflection and distortion are the constitutive lenses through which seeing, being, and desire are animated.

Chiasmic encounters occur in Cross's piece in several different ways. The *site* of the installation weaves together handball courts, tidal pool, and operatic stage; at the level of *discourse*, the artist's arrangement of libretto fragments dramatizes the fertility of unexpected juxtapositions; and in the live *performance* of *Chiasm*, the audience provides the final element of this intricate construction, as viewers are brought into an intimate encounter with site, image, and text.

Any analysis that seeks to disentangle things, Merleau-Ponty warns, only renders them unintelligible (1968, 268). A full reading of the complexities of Dorothy Cross's *Chiasm*, however, requires just such an initial isolation of its elements. Ultimately, however, the chiasmic effects of desire will be revealed in their interweaving.

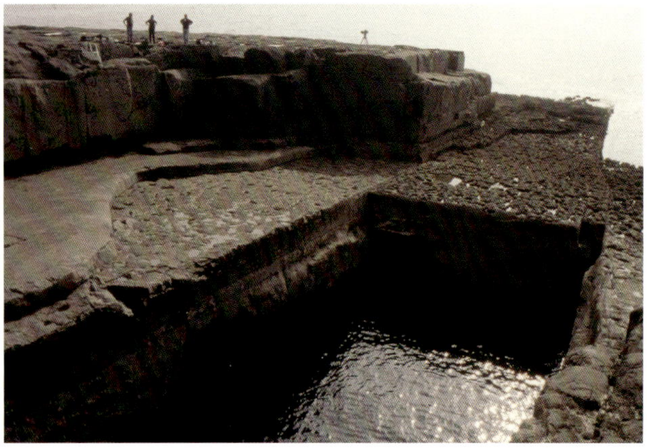

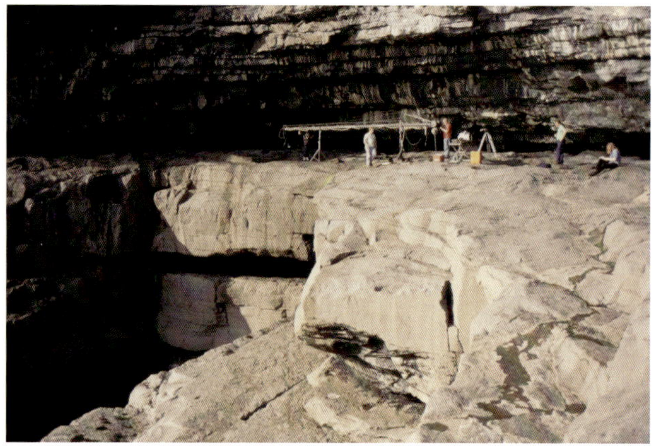

Chiasm, the crew on-site at Worm's Hole

THE MAKING OF *CHIASM* - BY DOROTHY CROSS

There is a sea pool on the Aran Islands off the west coast of Ireland that is a perfect rectangle. Located on the terraced cliffs at the back of the island, it looks as if it were cut by man. The exquisite pool is fed by the ocean through a subterranean opening; the water in the pool rises and falls with the tides and the weather. The natural structure of the pool was formed geologically, created by the collapse of the water-worn limestone shelf. The pool is called Poll na bPéist, or the Worm's Hole.

There are more than 370 handball alleys in Ireland, scattered around the countryside like modernist sculptures, beautiful empty arenas. Handball is the third official sport in Ireland and was very popular in the 1950s and 1960s. It is a game similar to squash, but the ball is hit with the hand. The alleys of competition size measure 30-by-60 feet, and stand 30 feet tall. The proportions of these cast concrete alleys are similar to those of the Worm's Hole.

In 1998 Fiach MacConghail visited my studio and asked if I was working on any new ideas. The Project Art Centre was closing for renovations and the budget was to be used for off-site works. I told him about the handball alleys and the Worm's Hole. I had seen a single alley with a viewing arena beside the road in Tulsk, in County Roscommon, but I later learned that it had been knocked down to build a new sports centre. Shortly afterward, I was driving on the Spiddal road in County Galway and saw an exquisite architectural "quartet" of alleys, two built against two, in St. Enda's school. I drove in and met a man, who turned out to be the principal, painting a corridor. I asked if I could do an opera in his alleys, and he agreed.

The next step in the project was to go with a crew to Inismor, the largest of the Aran islands off the coast of Galway. The Worm's Hole is located about a half mile from the road over very difficult rocky terrain. We carried the crane, camera, weights, and equipment from the road to the pool, where we hid it overnight in a cave to avoid the arduous journey back twice. We filmed the Worm's Hole from every angle; I was interested in how the geometry of the pool mirrored that of the alley floor. We would later project the images from high towers down into the alleys, as if attempting to fit the sea pool into the rectangle of the floor space. We painted the

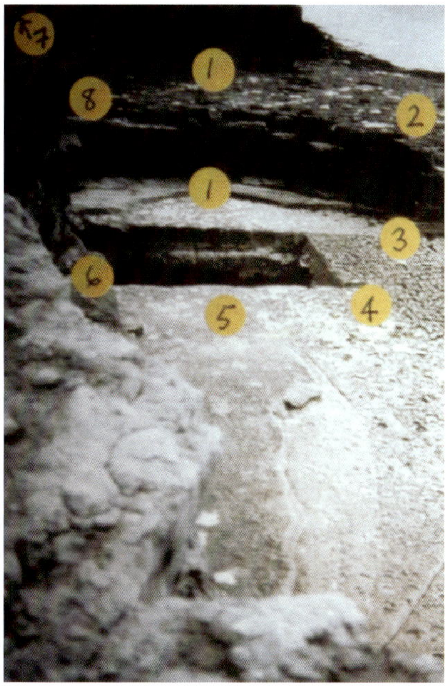

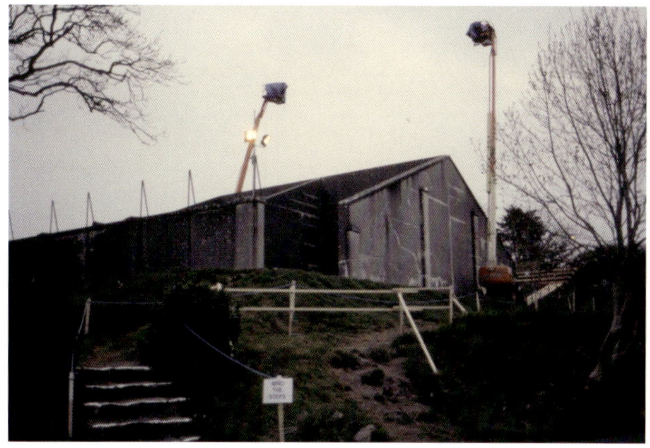

Chiasm, camera position plan and projection towers at handball alleys

floors of the alleys white, and strapped projectors onto cherry pickers 80 feet above the alleys. This required a "flyer" rigger to set up the exact projection each evening; he then had to "fly" to the ground on a rope before the audience came in. Wind would have created havoc on the projections. Luckily, we had no wind, just a full moon, a few bats flying, and a local dog barking at intervals.

During a residency in Roche's Point Lighthouse in County Cork, I studied more than twenty recordings of romantic operas. I wanted to locate small fragments of song depicting extreme love and extreme loss. I listened and read and extracted words sung in German, French, English, Russian, and Italian. I then re-constructed the fragments into a single libretto in which the singers moved from language to language.

The singers began with disconnected phrases, and although they occasionally fell into a duet, they always returned to forgetting and repetition with another fragment from another opera. They sang without orchestration, their voices divorced from the support of instruments. Carol Smith, soprano, and tenor Eugene Ginty moved across the floors of two alleys separated by a 30-foot wall. They walked on projected images of the Worm's Hole swirling and surging below their feet. Midway through the performance they both sang, "Adieu, adieu, de cet adieu si douce est la tristesse," from *Romeo and Juliet*. At this point the libretto seemed to reach a conclusion, only to return to the same, but more fragmented, phrases again. The two singers eventually concluded where they began.

The video images of the Worm's Hole under their feet showed fluctuating strengths of waves of water. As with the waves in the pool, the fragments of music never repeated the exact same pattern, and the singers never stood on the same image singing the same words. Each night the sequence was performed three times. Because the performers' movements were not choreographed, there was a possibility they could arrive at a point on the middle wall exactly in line with each other, but they never did. Standing on a scaffold platform looking down into the alleys, members of the audience could never see both alleys at the same time, and so their point of view was always limited.

THE SITE: NEITHER HERE NOR THERE

Catherine Belsey argues that one cannot "tell the truth of desire.... Desire can neither be seen nor shown [nor] put on display." Unless, she adds, it finds a form at once "non-systematic, untheorized, elliptical, incomplete, uncertain ... and in all kinds of ways *neither here nor there*" (71). The complexly layered site of *Chiasm* provides just such an uncertain ground. Within the genre of site-specific art, this piece creates what James Meyer calls a "functional site," "a process, an operation occurring between sites ... a palimpsest of text, photographs and video ... a temporary thing, a movement"(25). In Cross's piece, handball courts, tidal pool projection, and the various settings evoked by the operatic fragments leave viewers neither here nor there, or simultaneously here and there. These destabilizing spatial effects provide uncertain but fertile ground for an exploration of desire.

The individual layers of *Chiasm* are caught up in multiple networks of unconscious associations, ideological overlays, and the sedimentations of lived history. The Irish landscape has long been recognized for its archaeological richness, from ancient standing stones to more modern ruins—from deserted famine cottages to abandoned handball courts. These courts and hundreds like them were built by the Gaelic Athletic Association around the countryside in the early decades of the twentieth century. In the program of cultural revival, handball was promoted as one of three national Gaelic sports. The surviving alleys are viewed by some with nostalgia, as "desolate and deserted ... relics of a different age" (Healy 63). These abandoned courts provide an occasion for lamenting the advent of modernity in general: "Handball, like so much else in life, has moved on, taking a step indoors into warmth, comfort and sophistication" (63). Other accounts, however, read in the courts' emptiness a testimony to the impact of political violence, famine, and economic disasters that led to massive migration to cities and abroad. While they once stood "at or beyond the edge of settlements," "serving the casual needs of marginalised or disaffected youths," the growing silence of these alleys "connote[s] young men on the move with their cardboard suitcases" (O'Connor 26). Cross herself never loses sight of the historicity of the courts—and that historicity includes their association with past conflicts (which were simultaneously athletic and political), their present condition as beautifully weathered surface and form, and even their potential for future transformations.

Unlike the Stone Age or early Christian ruins that mark the Irish landscape, the handball alleys are not likely to be preserved by the heritage industry. They are too mundane to be narrated or reenacted as legendary history (like the megalithic New Grange tomb), and too austere to be commodified as picturesque kitsch (like the thatched cottage). This uncertain status of the modern "outmoded"[41] drew Cross to the handball alleys, just as the Surrealists were drawn to the Paris arcades—as "spatial allegories of temporal crossing or historical change" (Hansen 194). Having outlived its original function, the handball site becomes open to reincarnation.

Cross describes the courts as "modernist sculptures, beautiful empty arenas" one might happen upon unexpectedly in rural areas, on the margins of towns and villages. Viewed as aesthetic objects, the courts have the same beauty found in early sculptures by Richard Serra, Donald Judd, or Sol LeWitt. Art critics compare the imposing minimalist sculptures by these artists to ancient monuments like Stonehenge or, bringing us almost full circle, to ancient Toltec ritual ballcourts (Krauss 1985, 279). Cross's handball alleys retain, in latency, all of these associations: the history of Irish handball courts of the early twentieth century, of American sculpture of the 1960s and 1970s, and of ancient stone monoliths from around the world.

The courts are not only a site of temporal chiasm—as Merleau-Ponty puts it, "Past and Present *Ineinander*" (1968, 268)—but also of the spatial interpenetration of nature and culture.

In the "expanded field" of modernist sculpture, Rosalind Krauss recognizes a breakdown of traditional categories; defying the conventional definition of sculpture as that which is neither landscape nor architecture, these minimalist sited works are "*both* landscape and architecture"(1985, 284). Although Cross perceives the courts' minimalist beauty through a modernist lens, she also departs from that tradition. Whereas Serra or Robert Smithson erected man-made structures in the natural landscape, Cross finds an artificial structure already situated in the landscape and projects onto its surface the displaced image of a stunning natural phenomenon—the Aran Island tidal pool.

Handball courts and tidal pool come together not just as sites but as citations, the courts referring to a particular period in Irish history, the pool calling up the mythologized geography of the Aran Islands. Although it is metonymically connected to that larger landscape and its myths, this particular tidal pool, named Poll na bPéist, or the Worm's Hole, is unique in its *resistance* to being incorporated into any legend.[42] Remote and relatively inaccessible, such tidal pools rarely appear in the popular representations of Western Ireland that have coalesced into a set of ideological stereotypes.[43]

The peculiar structure of the Worm's Hole makes it too disorienting and ambiguous to be circulated as an icon or commodity. The history of its geological formation constitutes a chiasmic inversion, a crossing over of the relationship of land and sea. Over time, the collision of the surrounding sea against the rocks carved out a subterranean vault beneath the cliffs. When its roof eventually collapsed, a vast limestone pool was created above, and within its perfect rectangle the restless tides are now contained, calm or turbulent at the whim of the weather.

Structurally, *Chiasm* is an incarnation of what Merleau-Ponty describes as a "relation with being [that] is *simultaneously* a taking and a being taken, the hold is held" (1968, 266). Water surrounds or holds the island; the island, in turn, captures and contains the tides. Projected onto the floor of the handball courts, the image of the pool is contained within cement walls, and yet it seems to be "continually moving,... surge and calm" ("*Chiasm*: AP")[44] In *Chiasm* the holding is never final, for the constant motion of the tidal waters seems to dissolve the solidity of the courts. Cross mirrors the video so that a doubled image of the limestone pool (one projected onto each court) rotates from the axis of the dividing wall—as if the tidal waters have set the surrounding stone and cement in motion. The accelerated speed of modernization that produces outmoded ruins like the handball alleys in just a few decades is written over in this cinematic palimpsest by the slower, cyclical time of archaic nature. The resulting chiasmic encounter of these two sites produces what Merleau-Ponty calls a kind of "*Urhistorie*" that is at once historical and pre-historical, an effect of simultaneous "sedimentation and reactivation" (1968, 259).

Cross uses the handball alleys in *Chiasm* as an embodiment of the poignant stillness of the abandoned and outmoded; with the Aran tidal pool she introduces the power of nature as elemental spectacle. Responding similarly to that landscape, Tim Robinson imagines himself as an artist striving to capture the "essence" of the Aran Islands' unique geology:

> If as an artist I wanted to find a sculptural form for my intuition of the Aran landscape I would not think in terms of circles.... A block... would best embody the essence of Aran's landforms—or, since I am dealing with abstractions and have undergone the metamorphoses of contemporary art, the absence of a block, a rectangular void to stand for all blocks.... [L]et this void be filled by water, reversing the relationship of sea and island. Site it on one of the great stages of rock below the cliffs; do it on a prodigious scale, a spectacle rather

than a gallery-piece; let the ocean dance in it, and the cliffs above step back in wide balconies to accommodate the thousands who will come to marvel at this ... sublime and absurd show of the Atlantic's extraction of Aran's square root (61-62).

Confronted with the Worm's Hole, Robinson bows to the superior artistry of nature itself, acknowledging the sea as both "decisive sculptor" and "morose civil engineer"(62).

Whereas Robinson discovers in the Worm's Hole the eternal struggle of "primaeval chaos pitted against fundamental geometry"(63), others have found something less abstract—a place charged with unconscious erotic energies. In her *Chiasm* proposal, Cross's describes the symmetrical patterns created by her mirrored and rotating video of the tidal pool as a "kaleidoscopic Rorschach," alerting us to this peculiar structure's relationship to something hidden below the surface, to something revealing the collective unconscious and desire. Irish painter Gwen O'Dowd also finds an erotic charge in the pool, using it as one image (*Poll na bPéist*, 1992) in a series of paintings of similar geological formations that evoke the body and sexuality in their destabilizing ambiguity and violence.[45]

Cross's kaleidoscopic film, particularly in those parts of the cycle where the singers are not present on "stage," creates a similar disorientation, occasionally suggesting giant granite bones parting to expose the blue pool within, then closing up again in silent slow pulsations. Cross herself observes that the tidal pools superimposed onto the courts resemble two watery graves, the dividing wall a skeletal armature. In her incorporation of the Worm's Hole into *Chiasm* she preserves both its geometrical austerity—its containment of the sea's power—and its haunting evocation of the hidden workings of desire and the death drive.

Seamus Heaney's poem "Lovers on Aran," also draws a connection between Aran geography and the ambiguities of desire:

The timeless waves, bright sifting, broken glass,
Came dazzling around, into the rocks,
Came glinting, sifting from the Americas

To possess Aran. Or did Aran rush
To throw wide arms of rock around a tide
That yielded with an ebb, with a soft crash?

Heaney concludes, as does Merleau-Ponty, that our identities are made from such uncertain boundaries and intertwinings:

Did sea define the land or land the sea?
Each drew meaning from the waves' collision.
Sea broke on land to full identity.

There can be no "full identity" without this collision of self and other, without fantasy and desire. The Aran tidal pool has a double function in *Chiasm*: it introduces what Robinson calls the "natural theatre" of rock and sea, as well as what O'Dowd and Heaney recognize as an unconscious geography of desire. In this site where rock and sea embrace, where pool and court are intertwined, Cross creates her own version of a theatre of desire.

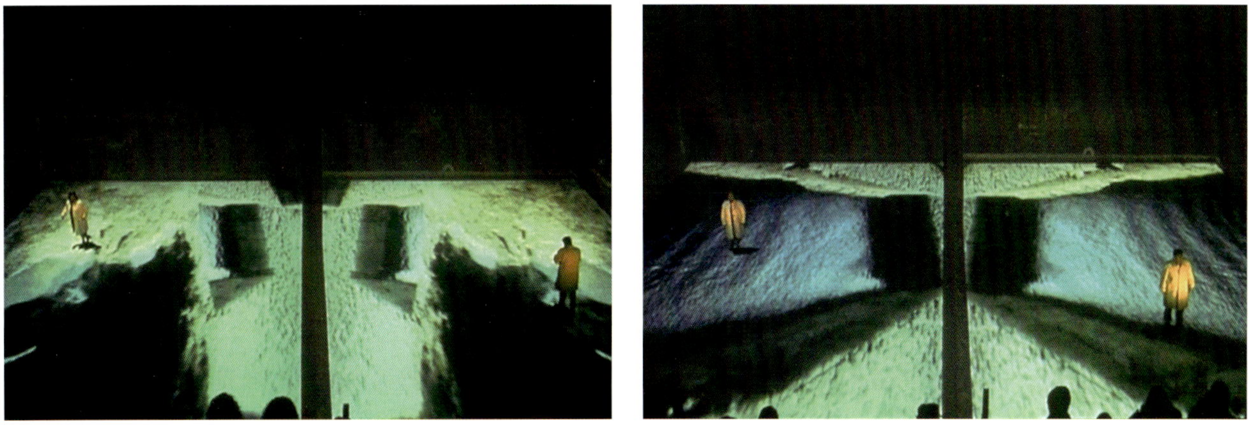

Chiasm, stills from performance video

THE SOUND: GIVING VOICE TO DESIRE

By adding music and words to this piece Cross expands the theatre of desire first enacted in *Slippery Slope*, making *Chiasm* a discursive as well as a visual site. To the palimpsest of handball alley and tidal pool projection Cross adds the final element of operatic performance. The operatic libretto, where extremes of passion are given narrative form and harmonious order, provides Cross with the perfect discourse for her theatre of desire. Literary theorist Catherine Belsey observes that although "desire is more voluble than ever before" in the twentieth century (76), our postmodern culture lacks the codes and conventions to represent the dilemma of the lover.[46] Some contemporary artists and writers look back, as does Cross, to the operatic tradition for an amatory discourse that gives expression to the paradoxical nature of desire as wounded lack and extravagant excess.[47] Opera, Cross observes, arises from the human need to represent love, passion, and loss; her collage of fragments from operas spanning three centuries reveals the constancy and universality of that need. The libretto and staging of *Chiasm* approach what Kristeva calls the "revolutionary" or "ethical" text that "pluralizes, pulverizes, 'musicates'" fixed truths about the subject and about desire (1984, 233).

Cross had already worked in opera before mounting *Chiasm*, most notably in designing sets and costumes for a production of Handel's *Tamerlano* in 1997. For that opera, Cross clothed the singers in animal skins and created a steel wall on the stage, the costumes concretizing the primal vitality of the drives and the set embodying the impossibility of any direct encounter in the symbolic. Even as she embraces the operatic, however, Cross undermines and complicates its effects. Everything that constitutes romantic opera as conventionalized spectacle—its reassuringly familiar images and codes—is unsettled in her theatre of desire.[48] The confusion of space and fracturing of narrative in *Chiasm* put such shattering on display, producing not a spectacle that hides loss, but the spectacle of loss itself. Whereas opera's narratives shape and contain passion, Cross's libretto-collage fractures continuity; stories interrupt each other, events blur into memory, memories dissolve into amnesia and pure sound. Just as courts and tidal pool never quite come to rest in perfect alignment, the efforts of the characters,

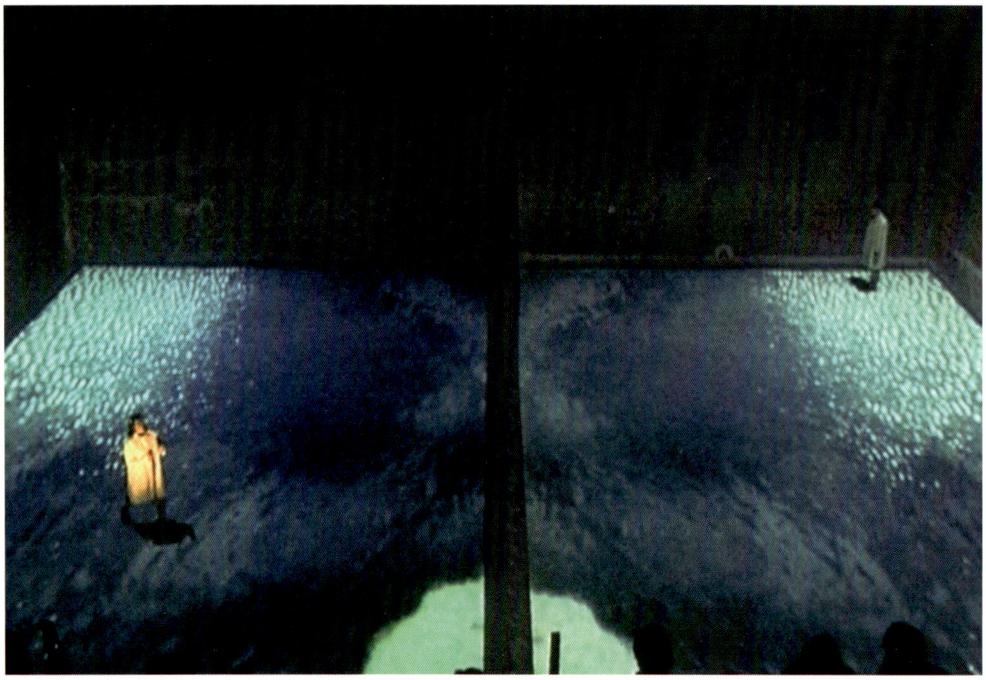

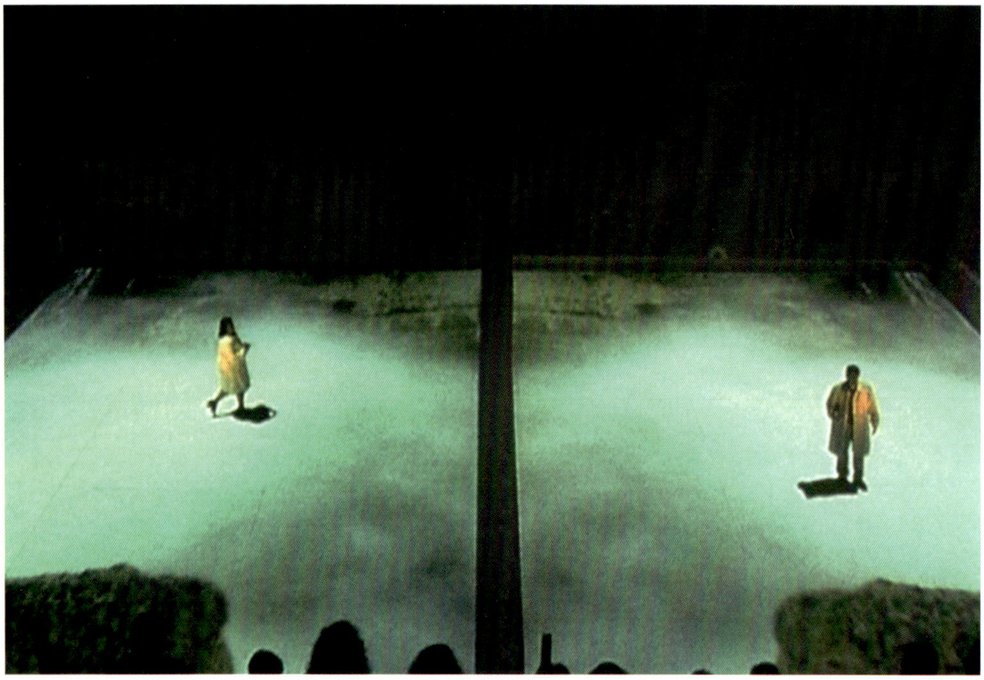

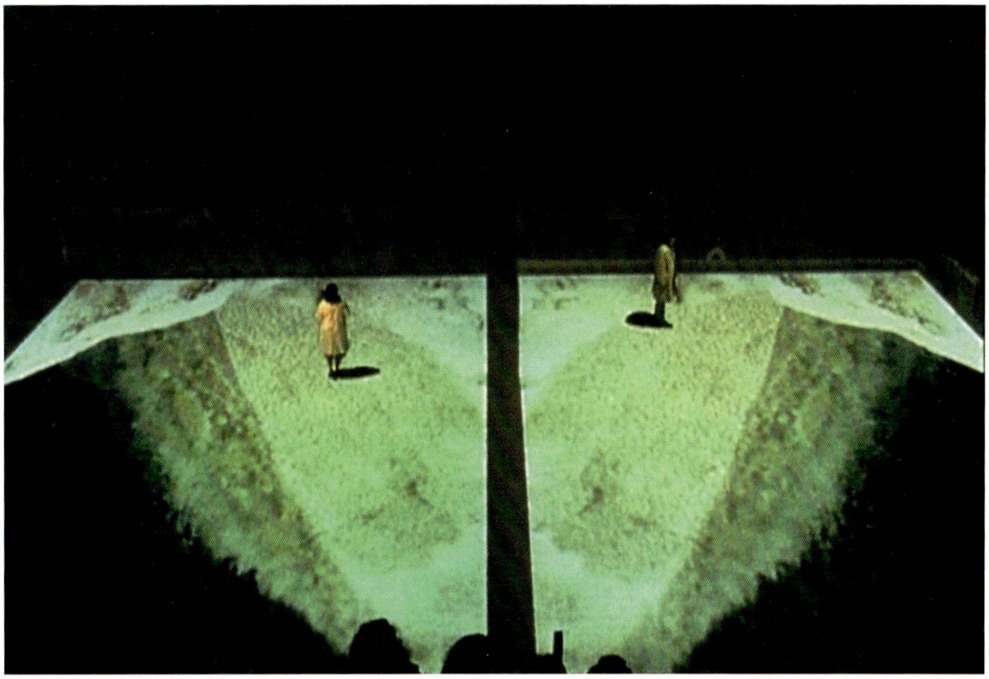

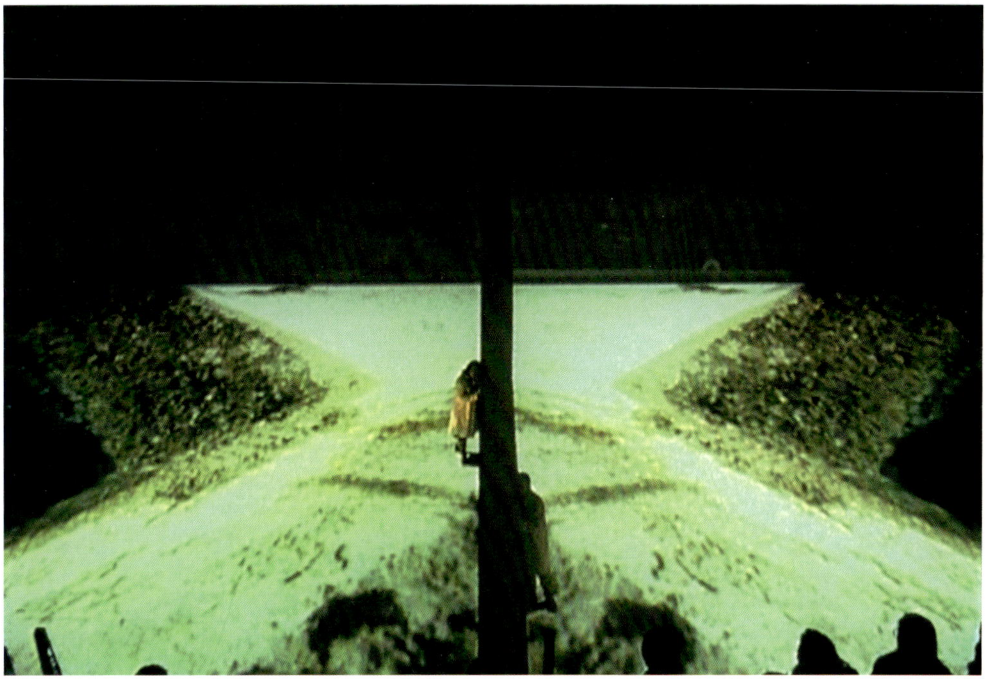

performers, and audience to hold on to any narrative clarity about the present or the past are repeatedly undone.

In traditional opera, the orchestral accompaniment surrounds, soothes, and aestheticizes even the starkest expression of loneliness and despair. As Wayne Koestenbaum points out, when Tatyana describes how desolate she would be without Eugene Onegin, the orchestra accompanies, embraces her with sound: "Tatyana declares her solitude but the orchestra proves her wrong (when she sings 'I am alone' *she is not alone,* an orchestra surrounds her with corroboration and blossoming" (230). By contrast, in *Chiasm* the fractured libretto is "divorced from the orchestral music" (PN), the voices "raw and vulnerable," "shattered" ("*Chiasm*: AP").

Chiasm makes visible and audible what some feminist theorists call the semiotic chora, where energies are transformed into rhythm, gesture, and movement, into "[m]usic ... preliminary to meaning"(Irigaray 1993, 168). The rhythmic music of the drives that emerges in the "raw corporeality" of language (Oliver 1993, 105) can be heard in the operatic voices in *Chiasm*, vibrating with bodily materiality and mediated meaning. As Catherine Clément points out, "language ... always keeps to the shadows" in opera, either distorted by the style of musical delivery or estranged in some foreign language (12, 9). Cross multiplies that estrangement by producing a Babel of five different languages, a breakdown in the conventions of communication that suggests the impossibility of desire and its satisfaction.

Chiasm's textual collage dramatizes how love propels us toward language, how desire demands expression: "To whisper to her 'I love you' would stir deep feelings within me" (ML). Yet language seems barely adequate to the task. Lovers' speech dissolves into sweet but empty "murmur[ing] together"(Oth) or inarticulate sighs, "Ahh, Ahh" (R/J). At the extremes of love's suffering, language escapes into madness and nonsense, as in Desdemona's haunting refrain, "Willow, Willow" (Oth). In opera, Clément observes, "words are strung together for the pleasure of an ear that is finally released from meaning" (17). Cross similarly describes the operatic fragments in *Chiasm* as joined together "like a string of pearls"(PN), their impact as much sculptural as referential or expressive.

When language in its referential function is coupled with musical form, the result becomes simultaneously symbolic and semiotic. Roland Barthes distinguishes between two aspects of the singing voice: the symbolic "phenosong" that functions "at the service of communication, of representation, of expression," and the semiotic "genosong" that reveals the "'truth' of language" in its materiality, "not its functionality" (1985b, 270). Barthes discovers an erotic intensity in the "grain of the voice," where one hears the friction between language and the materiality of "the muscles, the membranes, the cartilage" of the singer's body. This effect is rarely heard in opera because that genre's familiar "image-repertoire" mutes the otherwise threatening transgressive ecstasy of love and loss (1985b, 270, 268). Barthes concedes, however, that one might hear the grain of the voice in opera if it could be randomly viewed, if the constraints of its narrative continuity and unifying spectacle could be disrupted: "I would like to see an opera as free and as popular as a movie theatre or a wrestling arena: you could go in and out according to your mood, you'd spend part of your evening taking a 'hit' of opera"(1985a, 186). The fractured libretto and hybrid staging of *Chiasm* offer just such a randomly viewed transgressive spectacle.

The visual chiasm of real and virtual space in Cross's piece reappears at the level of sound in the intertwining of words and music, song and singer's body. Koestenbaum finds this merging typical of all operatic performance, where words and music come together like the lovers in Aristophanes' myth, seeking in their union the recovery of a lost original wholeness (178-9). Although in opera "language seeks its shadow-bride in music, and music crosses Lethe to find its echo in language"(178), neither quest succeeds. Operas are "works of mourning" (178), and the reunion of lovers is most often exposed as an impossible dream.[49]

In opera, as Clément observes, the characters are "no more than little symbolic figures ... tiny actors." The encounters we witness on stage do not occur at the level of these insignificant figures, but at a more primary level, where "nature and culture seek, thwart, and marry one another—part and tear one another apart"(20). In the singers' operatic performance in *Chiasm*, music and words similarly approximate a potentially annihilating embrace that is never consummated. The fractured form of *Chiasm*'s libretto was inspired, in part, by the haunting quality Cross heard in the voices of opera singers practicing random phrases alone in their dressing rooms before a performance. In *Chiasm*, she places each singer in a solitary court, framing each voice in space, isolated from all meaning, narrative, relation.

The shifting juxtapositions of the collage text, the random blocking of the singers' movements within their courts, the open seating that encourages viewers to watch the repeated cycles of the performance from several different points of view—all of these effects foreground the workings of chance, misunderstanding, and accident. In its association of chance and desire, the operatic spectacle of *Chiasm* resembles the random accidents of desire that Kristeva finds in the Biblical *Song of Songs*, or in the style of the early troubadours—songs of love determined by chance, unfolding in aleatory patterns, in a singing style that is full of "meanderings, pleasureful incantations ... spasmodic windings ... amorous transports," "intertwining, entangling words" (1987, 281-82). As another theorist puts it, the look of lovers is a "look forever organized, or disorganized, around an impossibility of seeing," and only "an unlikely stroke of luck or chance? Or of grace?" might allow two lovers to "catch sight of each other, find each other"(Irigaray 1993, 153, 182).

Chiasm enacts this theatre of chance on a physical level, as the singers wander in fluid space, approaching and receding from the dividing wall like the tide itself. At times, miraculously, they come together there, each tentatively extending a hand to touch the cement surface, each blind to how close or far the other might be. The operas from which *Chiasm*'s libretto is derived are full of lamentations over missed chances and bad timing, painful reminders of the impossibility of desire. Thus, the lovers in *Eugene Onegin* sing in despair, "Too late, too late."

Cross's work reminds us, however, that despite love's vulnerability to the effects of chance, there is also choice, making decisions, taking sides. Like the involuntary fall down the slippery slope of the drives, the fate of desire in *Chiasm* is inescapable. The sad tales of these operas are well known, their course toward disaster irreversible. But there is also the choice to engage repeatedly with that fate; again and again, lovers choose to hurl themselves down the slippery slope. Hearing the reckless courage in the arias of tragic heroines ready to die for love, Clément declares with admiration, "the act of falling, the final gesture, is theirs"(22). As others have argued, love involves choosing to open oneself to others, and it demands the repeated performance and reaffirmation of that choice (Oliver 2001, 74).

Determined by both chance and choice, desire shows itself in *Chiasm* in the encounter of handball alleys and tidal pool, in the repeated cycles of each performance, and above all in the weaving together of textual fragments. Unmoored from the specifics of plot, character, and setting, the libretto is disrupted by sudden shifts that enact the unpredictable nature of desire, consistent only in its inconsistency. The extremes of desire are expressed in metaphors evoking the fire of newly discovered passion ("What's the matter with me! I'm all on fire" [EO]), and the icy despair of betrayal ("There is ... an iciness that numbs me" [ML]). Cross's selections are often provocatively paired, the "cradle of this fatal love" with the "grave ... my wedding bed" [R/J]);"I

"I love you" and "All is over between us" sung almost in the same breath (EO, C). The libretto's confusion echoes the confusions of love itself: lovers falling from the heaven of an "intoxicating dream" (R/J), an "enchanting dream" (EO), to the torments of an "empty dream, the self-deception of an inexperienced soul" (EO). In the grips of desire's confusion, one lover frantically seeks his bearings: "What shall lost Aeneas do?" (D/A), while another luxuriously gives in to that confusion, declaring, "[love's] intensity disturbs my very being" (R/J). For Cross, as for Heaney and Merleau-Ponty, the disturbance of being is perhaps being's fullest realization.

The viewers of *Chiasm* experience a similar confusion as the fractured text transports them without warning from language to language and from place to place. The literal or metaphorical places in which the lovers are situated are often sites of displacement, foreign lands to which they have been abandoned or exiled: an unidentified "desolate plain" or "arid waste" (ML), "wasteland," "tomb," (R/J), or "prison"(C). Ariadne's plight is exemplary: she finds herself on an isolated island with her homeland in view, but always out of reach. The theme of exile, which has particular resonance for Irish cultural identity, is universalized in *Chiasm* as the pain of all insatiable longings. As Freud argues, all love is a form of "home-sickness," a longing for the lost perfect union of maternal love that never existed except in fantasy (1919, 245). The place of desire, then, is uncannily familiar and strange, like the palimpsest of cement court and spinning tidal pool.

On that uncertain ground, the lovers deliver their solos in separate courts, occasionally transcending their isolation in unexpected and glorious duets. The classical poetic figure for such perfect union is chiasmus—a rhetorical form that reflects the perfect mirroring of the lovers' hearts. In John Donne's "The Good Morrow," for example, the speaker celebrates such perfect mutuality in the lover's assertion to his beloved that "Your face in mine eye, mine in thine appears." This trope, in which two become one in love, finds expression in the opening lines of *Chiasm*, in which Ariadne describes the ideal of two lovers merged into one identity: "There was a thing of beauty called Theseus/Ariadne that walked in light and rejoiced in life" (A/N).

In *Chiasm*, the lovers often realize their mutuality in self-sacrifice and self-annihilation: Romeo and Juliet, for example, are each eager to take on the burden of sin for the other; Des Grieux and Manon share their willing enslavement in "chains of love," simultaneously demanding: "Yield to me" and declaring "I am yours" (ML). Ironically, these lovers are joined together most intimately when they commiserate on the "sweet sorrow" of parting (R/J). When the frustrated lovers from *Eugene Onegin* sing in duet from opposite sides of the wall, "So close, So close," their situation is given a stark architectural literalness. In this fragmented libretto such dramatic moments are never resolved in the completion of a plot; *Chiasm*'s score offers only repetition, ending with the same two solos with which it began. This final fragment is the only place in the libretto where Cross manipulates the original music, creating a new duet from solos from two different operas.

In the opening sequence of *Chiasm*, the abandoned Ariadne mourns the loss of a perfect union now no more than a memory; this solo is followed by Des Grieux expressing his amazement at the first sight of his beloved: "A maiden like this I have never beheld" (ML). The loss of love and its first blossoming are thus strangely reversed in order; love is lost even before it begins. The final duet of *Chiasm* reprises this opening sequence, but with a difference: the death and birth of love are now expressed simultaneously and in a harmonious duet, as if to say that love never dies, it is always just beginning again. The duet seems the very triumph of love; the voices of man and woman are joined not just across the cement wall, but across different plots and languages.

Or is this triumph a mere delusion? The singers, after all, remain in their solitary courts, on opposite sides of that undeniable wall. In her original proposal for the *Chiasm* project, Cross cites the myth of Pyramus and Thisbe, finding there the precedent of a "cruel wall" that prevents intimacy of embrace, but allows the lovers the "privilege of transmitting love words" through a tiny opening between its stones. The wall in *Chiasm* lacks such a tantalizing aperture, but as Pyramus and Thisbe's experience proves, the obstruction or repression of desire only intensifies its fire: "the fire burned more intensely for being covered up" (Bullfinch 25). In acknowledging and incorporating the limits of desire, *Chiasm* also heightens its impact; the wall stands in for the structure of the symbolic order, for words that mediate but never satisfy desire. One might apply to Cross's libretto-collage Catherine Belsey's description of the postmodern text as one that "foregrounds the citationality of desire ... speaks desire and defers it, draws attention to the loquacity, the excess of textuality" that is generated by the impossibility of desire (82).

With the wall Cross materializes the limits that constrain all desire, particularly the limits of our knowledge of the other. Des Grieux pleads across the cement wall, "See me, See me" (ML), but the lovers in *Chiasm* remain blind to each other in spite of their movements within the same projected landscape. Although these characters' voices temporarily come together in glorious duets within the audience's hearing, they meet only as disembodied voices, dissolving into thin air. For desire and love to be present without domination or assimilation each lover must realize the impossibility of full recognition and knowledge of the other (Oliver 2001, 64-72). Lovers must work their way toward such a "limitless love" by reaching beyond that "limit-point of the particularity of the subject" (Staten 183), and of the symbolic order. Dorothy Cross's *Chiasm* takes the audience to the edge of that abyss.

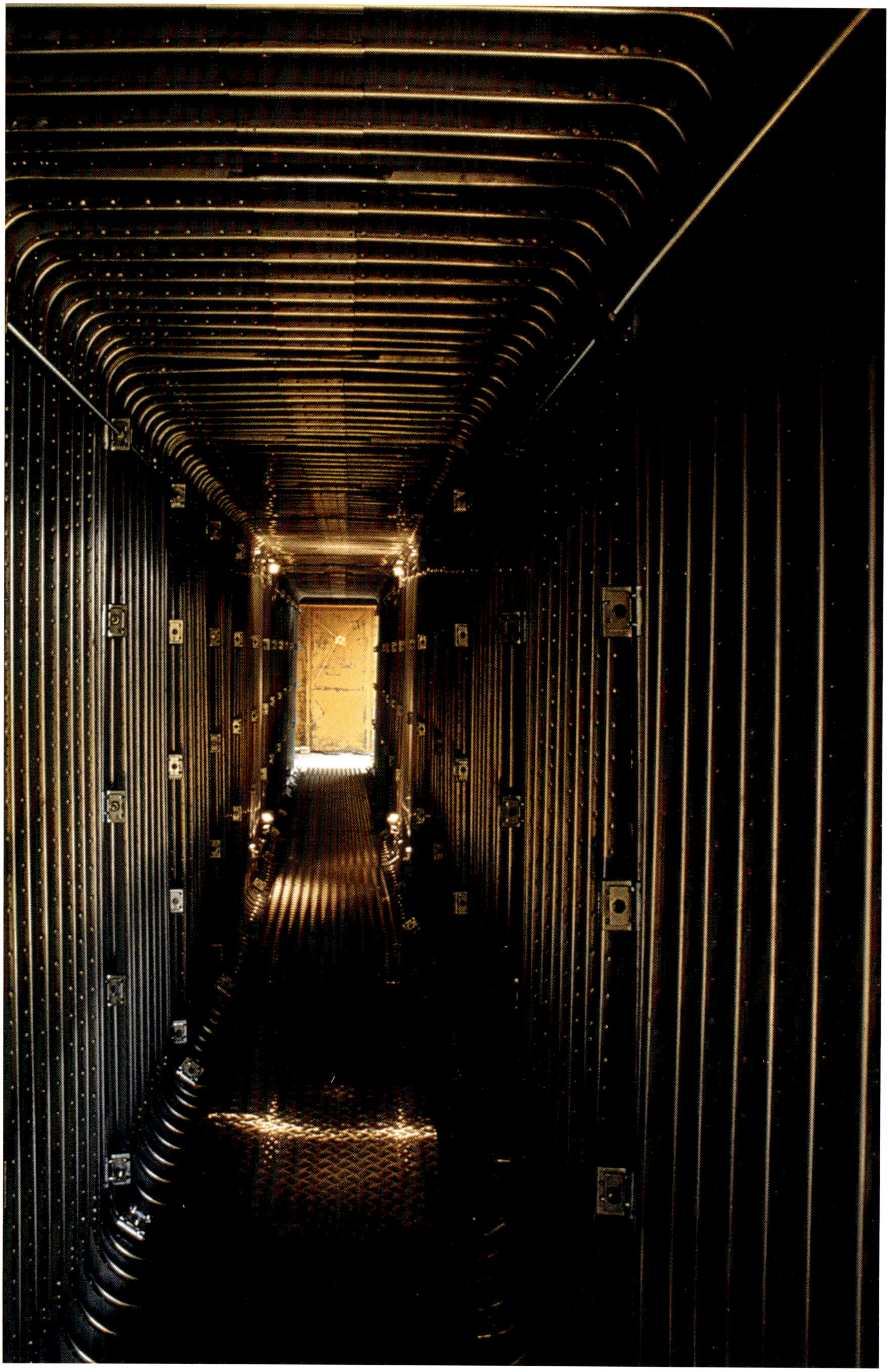

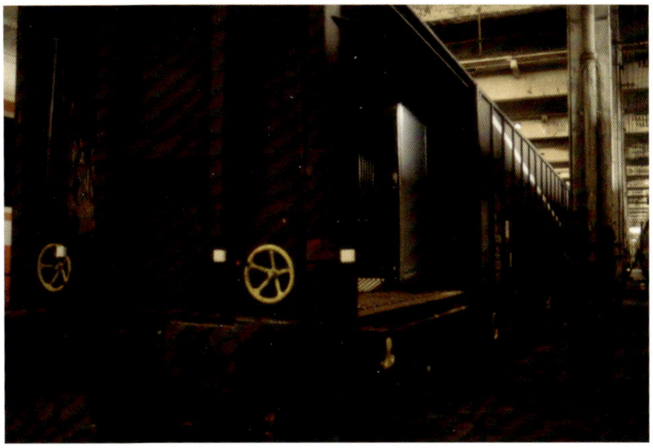

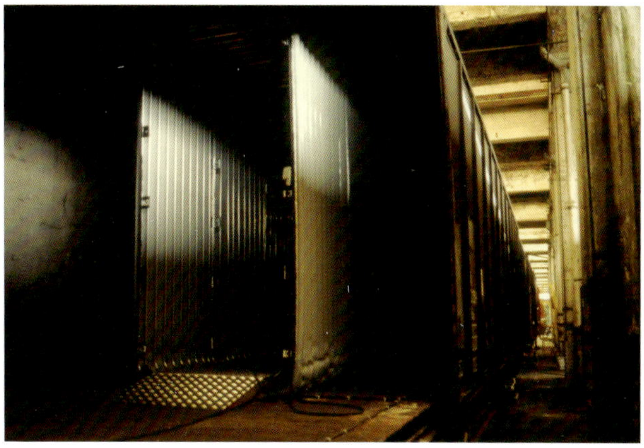

Strangers on a Train, exterior of baggage car

The Limits of Desire:
Strangers on a Train (1996)

Chiasm demonstrates that an encounter with the other is always an encounter with limits—limits of time, space, subjectivity, and representation. *Strangers on a Train* stages an intimate encounter with the limits of desire, not just *for* an audience but *with* an audience as one of its active components. This piece was created as part of a group show entitled *Sidetracking*, for which fourteen artists were each invited to make a work using one train carriage from a railroad yard of decommissioned vehicles. The original plan was for all the cars to be coupled together for a journey from Brussels to Maastricht as a nomadic site-specific event. These obsolete trains stirred up Cross's memories of those equally dated romantic black and white films in which anonymous lovers meet, kiss, and part forever in the course of a brief journey.[50] The artist initially conceived of *Strangers* as a work about love, but it evolved into a work about memory and loss.

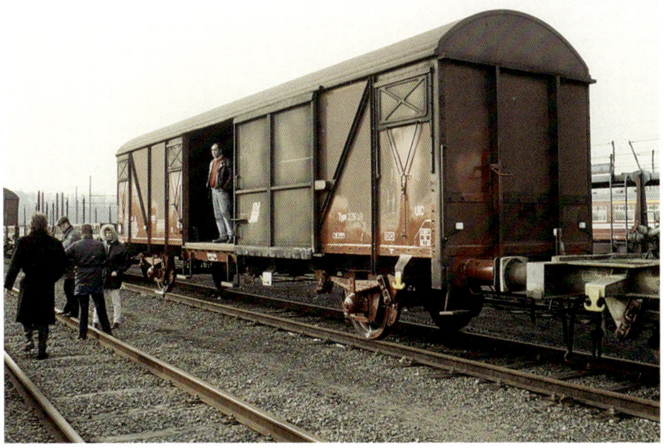

Strangers on a Train, on location at the railroad yard, Brussels

For *Strangers on a Train*, Cross uses an old baggage car inside of which she constructs a sixteen-meter tunnel. The inner walls are made of several bolted-together, concertina-style doors like those used as buffers between railway cars, and its floor is covered with a diamond-patterned chrome. The space is lit within by delicate spotlights that lend it the atmosphere of a mysterious space-age conveyance. In this used and worn baggage car incongruously lined with a pristine futuristic conduit, old fashioned romance meets sci-fi austerity. Removed from the abject natural materiality of *Slippery Slope* and the complex spectacle of *Chiasm*, and emptied of any personal or historical particularity, *Strangers on a Train* depicts the universal effects of desire and its limits stripped down to their barest essentials.

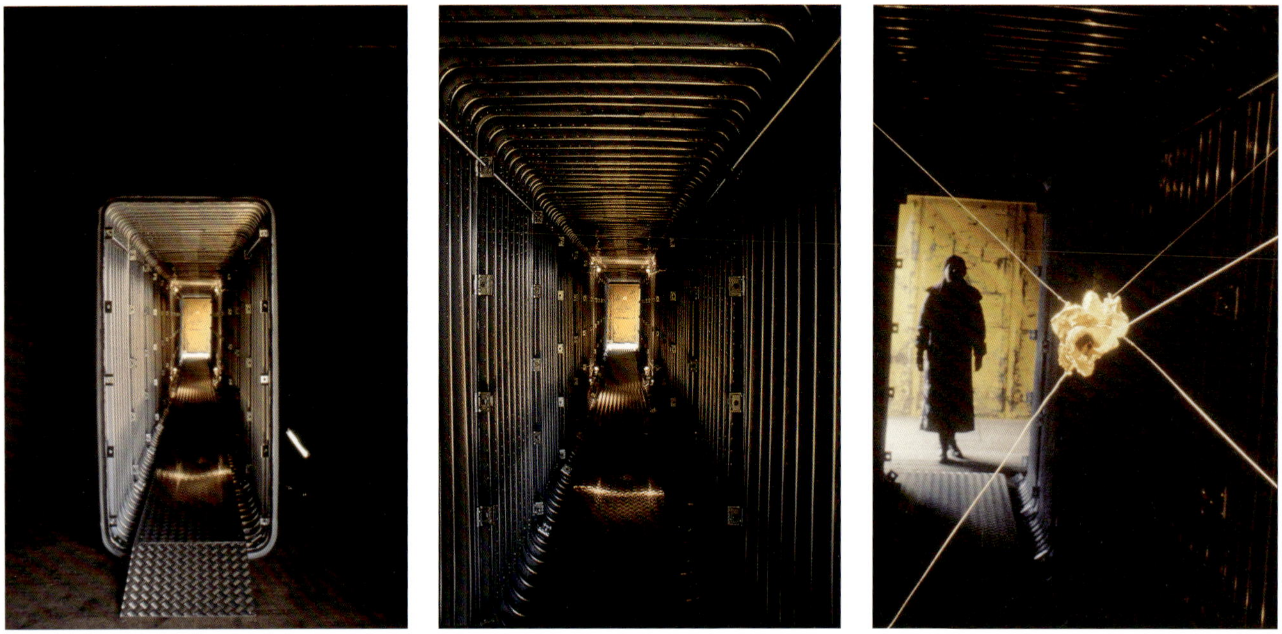

Strangers on a Train, viewer's perspective

The baggage car can be entered from either end, but its enclosed space is doubly insulated from the outside world by its windowless outer shell and its even narrower internal tunnel. Viewers proceed to the center of the car where they meet face to face as strangers on opposite sides of a mysterious small sculpture entitled *Kiss*, suspended from a delicate web of wires. This gilded form was produced from a dental plaster mold cast from the insides of the mouths of two people kissing. The tunnel directs viewers to this sculptural form that marks the limit they cannot cross; they must turn back at *Kiss* to exit by the same route they entered. *Strangers on a Train* thus enacts an approach to the unknown other and the limits of such an encounter.

All the ambivalence of desire is embodied here: at once intimate and impersonal, human and mechanical. The scientific precision suggested by the inner tunnel is disrupted by the more human imperfection of the crude, off-center stringing up of *Kiss*. The metallic enclosure that depersonalizes the space is contaminated by the representation of one of the body's innermost cavities suspended at its center.

The inevitable path of the drives is made literal by the tunnel and the traffic flow it controls; the gilded sculpture, on the other hand, reflects our need to symbolize desire, to fix and preserve an idealized notion of love. The original conception of *Sidetracking* as a multiple, mobile, site-specific installation would have further emphasized this ambivalent and uncertain ground of the drives and desire. Responding to train travel on both a literal and a symbolic level, as Freud and Lacan have done, Cross shows how we are all "caught in the rails" of desire (Lacan 1977, 167).[51] The human need to re-stabilize self and world through representation and narrative is always re-asserted against the threat of that unmooring.

Such narrative re-orientation is called up in *Strangers* by the linearity of the train itself—by the rails on which it is designed to run its predetermined course—and by the controlled and controlling passageway running through the baggage car. Although the title recalls a familiar genre of narrative films from the 1950s, Cross's *Strangers*, like Cindy Sherman's *Film Stills*, makes vague allusion to stories never told. The placement of *Kiss* at the center of the car imposes return and repetition, obstructing any continuous narrative progress to resolution or

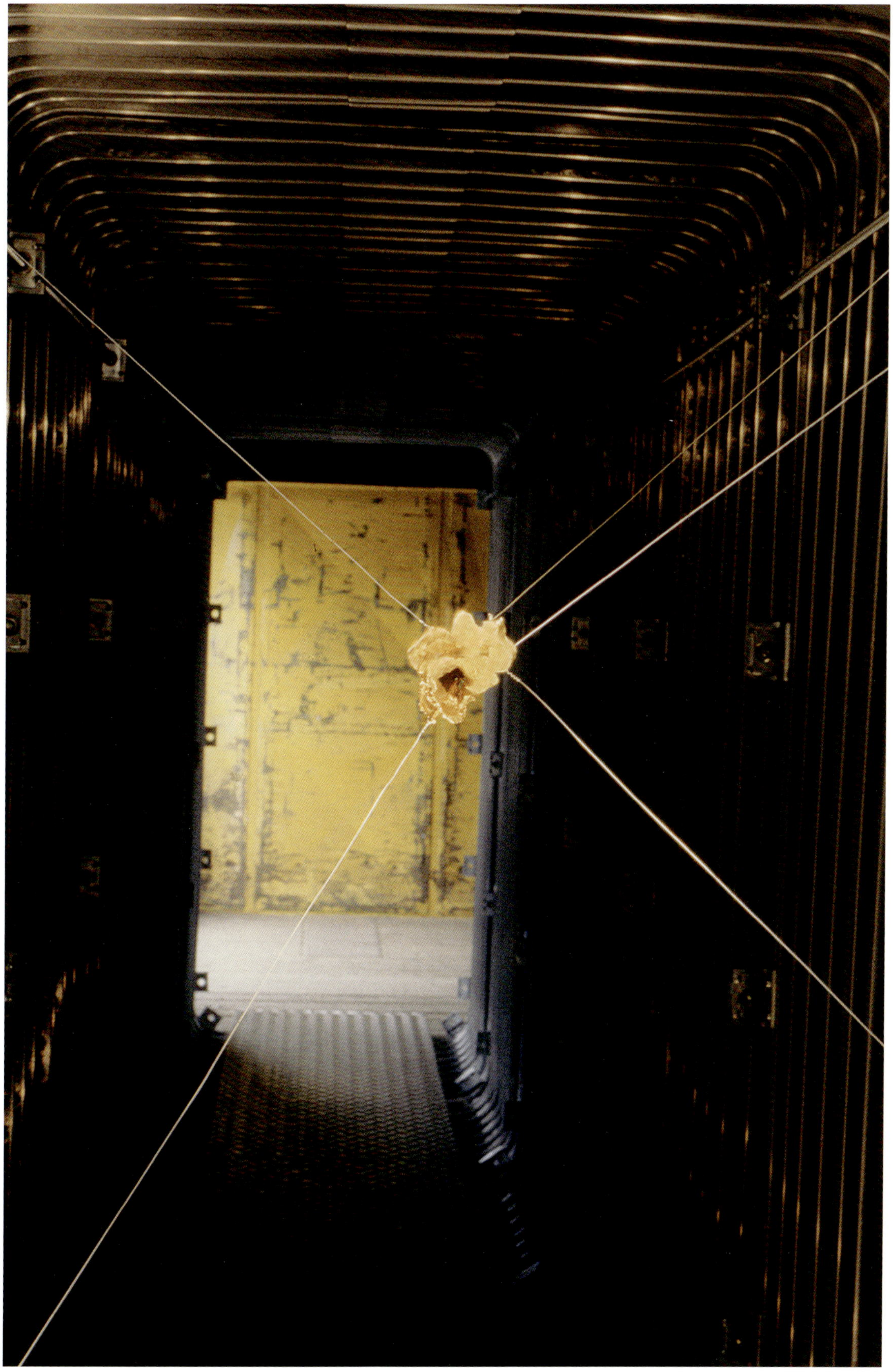

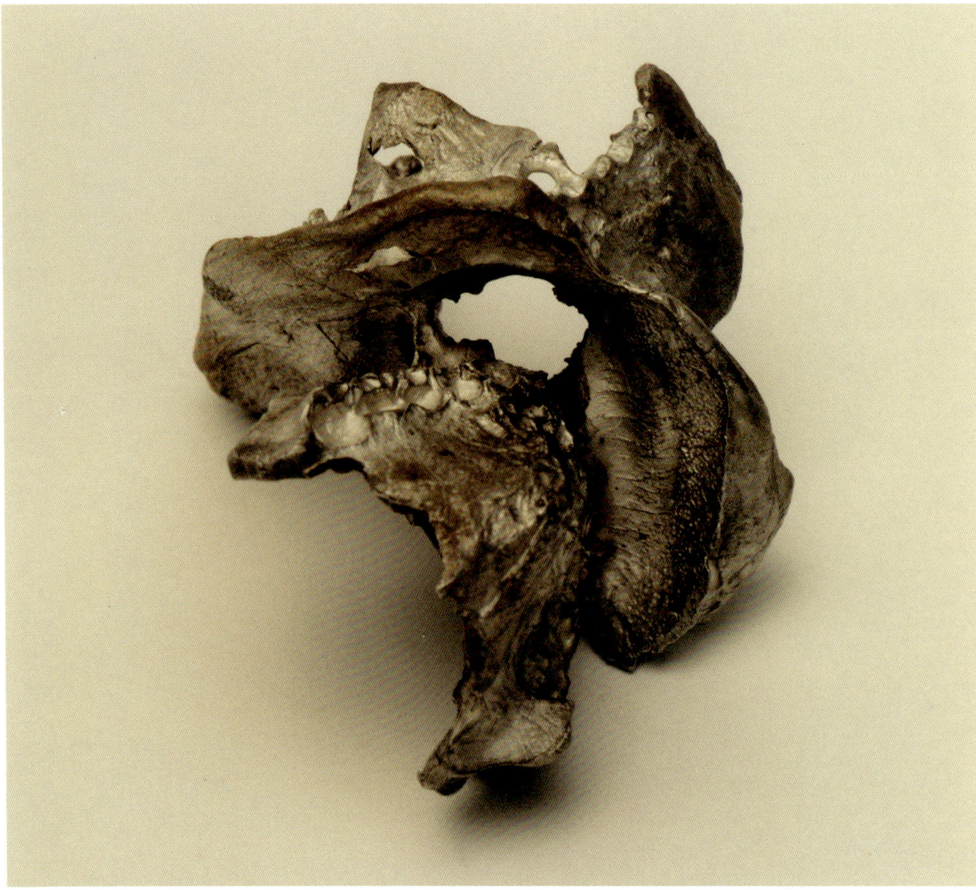

Kiss, 1996
Photo: John Kellet

climax. In undermining the very cinematic conventions its title evokes, *Strangers on a Train* resists and disrupts the narrative domestication of desire.

The nature of that narrative undoing, however, is paradoxical, even uncanny. Unlike the more definite wall in *Chiasm* or the chains immobilizing the sharks in *Slippery Slope*, desire's obstruction in *Strangers* remains open, permeable. Through the hole at the center of *Kiss*, a hole formed where the lovers broke through the dental plaster to make most intimate contact, an intertwining of viewers' gazes is made possible. Something of the chiasmic nature of desire is captured in this gilded reliquary, delicately elevated for reverent contemplation. Like Marcel Duchamp's *The Bride Stripped Bare by her Bachelors, Even* (1915-1923), a work that represents the impossibility of desire in an inscrutable mechanism encased in glass, Cross's piece offers simultaneously a transparency one can see through and an opacity that defies comprehension. Our tendency to idealize the union of lovers is reflected in the precious material and elevated display of *Kiss*; yet the impossibility of such a perfect union is suggested by the way in which the entire installation pivots around the hole or void at its center. This "skeleton of a kiss," as Cross describes it, is the remnant of a random passionate encounter, an ephemeral moment of intimacy represented by this delicate void. Although desire will always elude or exceed its representations, one can at least preserve and treasure the traces of its passage.

It is in the nature of the symbolic order that all signifiers are signifiers of an absent referent, and *Kiss* accordingly makes symbolically present a desire that remains offstage. Yet this signifier is more than an arbitrary placeholder—for unlike word or image, this sculpture is also the more direct and concrete indexical trace of bodies and events, like a footprint or shadow.

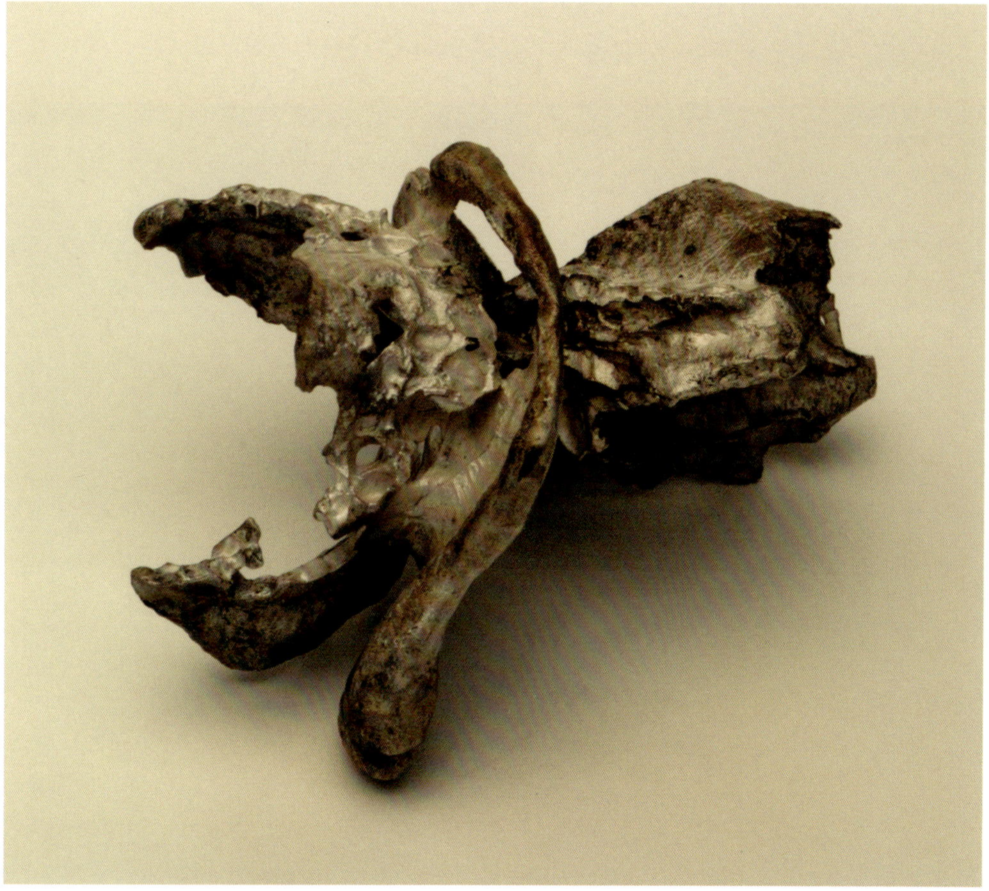

Kiss, 1996
Photo: John Kellet

Formed directly by the body, the indexical sign bears witness to the body's absence from the scene. The skeletal form of *Kiss* constitutes the remnant of a desire that lingers. Refined to an abstract form resembling saintly bone, *Kiss* appears as something delicate and precarious at the center of the machinery of the sexual drive. It marks the site of an encounter with loss and with the limits of desire and subjectivity. Perhaps no different from the participants in any amorous relationship, the anonymous viewers who come face to face in Cross's baggage car meet and part as strangers. Such fleeting encounters suggest not so much a failure of relation as an abdication of the desire to possess or appropriate the other. In *Strangers to Ourselves*, Julia Kristeva argues that we must learn how to deal with the stranger (the one inside as well as those outside ourselves) with respect and tenderness, to resist fixing or incorporating the other into our own likeness (169-92). Such requisite tender generosity might occur in the fleeting encounters made possible in Cross's baggage car.

In *Strangers on a Train* the audience is set in motion, displaced and alienated from the familiarity of home, family, and self, and made vulnerable to the inevitable return of repressed desires. As they move inward from baggage car, to interior tunnel, to internal orifice, viewers approach an almost primal uterine space where desire first forms around an object that is always already absent. *Chiasm* and *Strangers on a Train* demonstrate the gift and curse of the symbolic order that reduces the body to abstract sign and dematerialized form. The Midas touch of language confers value, but distances us from the human immediacy and warmth of bodies coming together in the flesh. *Strangers on a Train* makes explicit the uncanniness and transitoriness of all encounters, offering viewers the full experience of limit and loss rather than their denial.

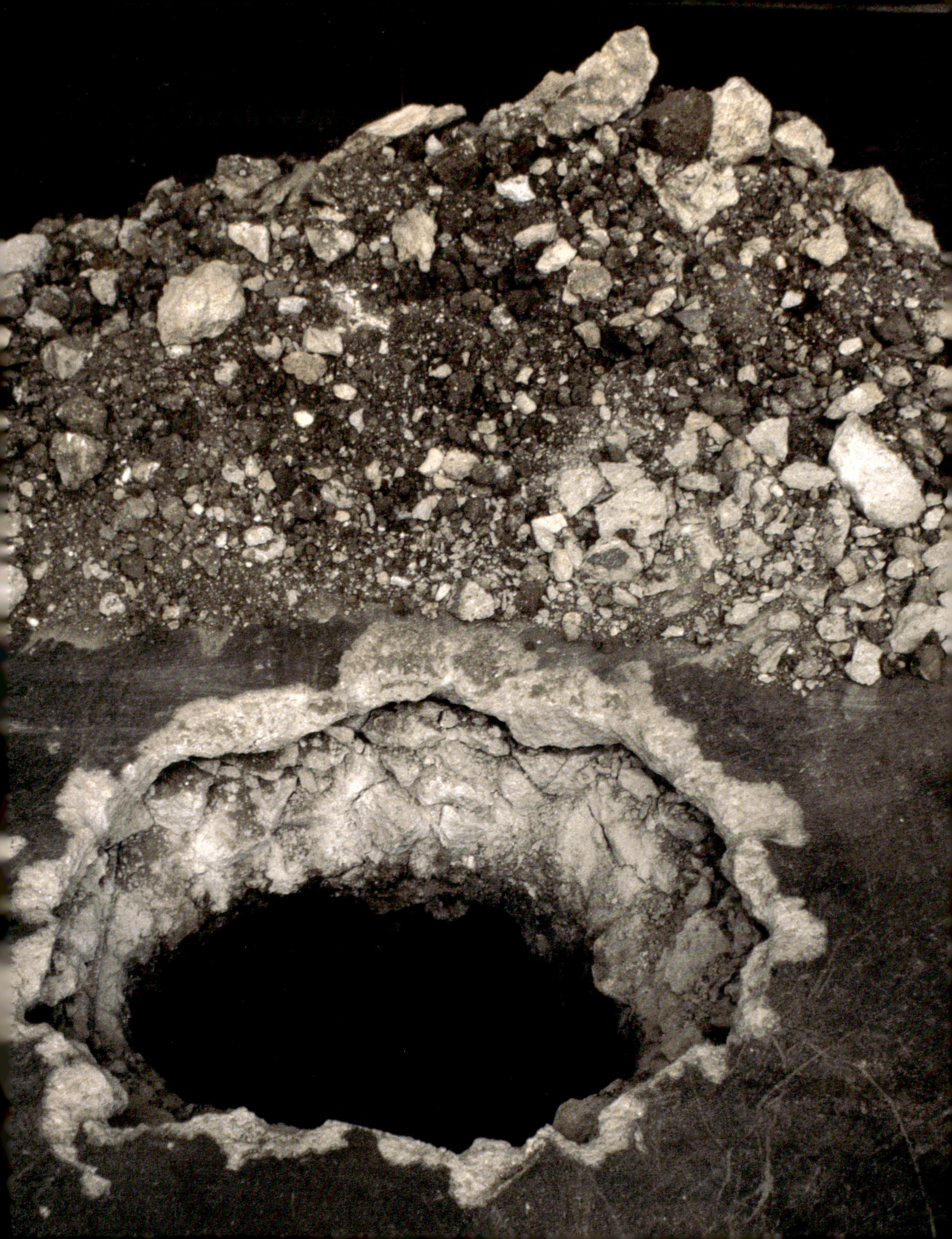

CHAPTER FOUR

The Inevitability of Loss

The works discussed in the previous chapter demonstrate Cross's understanding that desire and loss, like Freud's life and death instincts, function interdependently. Theorists of desire and death often remark on this paradoxical relationship: "Death, the seeming opposite of life, emerges as its ground, its vanishing point, *and* its sustaining force" (Bronfen and Goodwin 11). Cross's art reveals the complex ways in which loss obstructs and animates desire, history, religion, and language. In many of her sculptures, videos, and site-specific projects, Cross succeeds in making loss palpable, productive, even playful; as she transforms death and absence into art, she conjures up the poignant beauty not of any specific lost object, but of ephemerality itself. This chapter represents two of Cross's site-specific works that deal explicitly with mortality and memory: an installation entitled *CRY*, conceived and

FACING PAGE:
CRY (detail), 1996

produced at ArtPace in San Antonio, Texas in 1996, and a performance piece called *Ghost Ship*, staged in Dublin Bay in 1999. To understand how loss, absence, and death function in these works, one must consider Cross's artistic meditations on death over the past twenty years.

Death appears in Cross's work not in its strangeness, but in its uncanny familiarity. For one of her earliest projects as an art student, Cross produced a series of etchings inspired by the omnipresence of the void in Beckett's writing. She was struck by his unflinching view of death as a shadow present even in life's first stirrings. As Pozzo declares lugubriously in *Waiting for Godot*, "They give birth astride a grave, the light gleams an instant, then it's night once more" (Beckett 58). In a work included in her 1995 solo exhibition *Inheritance*,[52] Cross produces a visual counterpart to this tragi-comic observation. Struck by the formal similarity between the shape of the brain pan and the position of the fetus curled up in the womb, she creates a computer-generated composite image in which an X-ray of an adult human skull is overlaid with an X-ray of a fetus nestled within the brain cavity.[53] The entire life narrative of the species, from birth to death, is collapsed into this image of our phylogenic fate. "The first thing you inherit," Cross remarks, "is your own death." This composite image plants the seeds of that fate in the brain, suggesting that our mortal inheritance is as much cognitive as genetic.[54]

Death is lodged not only in our brains, but in our most intimate daily habits, and Cross's work often reveals mortality in all of its merciless banality. Her model, once again, is Beckett, who "is the penultimate in terms of equating the most mundane things with death: picking your nose and death, or making a cup of tea and death" (Cross qtd. in Colpitt). The banality of death shows itself in several of Cross's sculptural works where the familiar and familial enclosure of the domestic sphere is disturbed by some uncanny presence. Cross uses the term "domestic" to refer to a common inheritance of quotidian monotony, of "lifestyles, repetition, and time" that ultimately "collapses in on itself" (qtd. in Colpitt).

For an early piece entitled *Bath* (1988), for example, Cross refits a small cast iron bathtub with a wooden lid supporting a high tower at one end; the lid is cut through by a metal shark fin ominously approaching the tower's base. Death lurks, as Cross puts it, in each of our "little ocean[s]," in our most mundane rituals (qtd. in Colpitt). In *Teacup* (1999), she juxtaposes refined social ritual and imminent disaster in a two-minute video loop set into a fine china teacup, repeating there a miniature scene of shipwreck. These sculptural and video works dramatize death as a pre-existing presence (*Inheritance*), as a threatening approach (*Bath*), and as a return of repressed danger (*Teacup*).

Dealing with death in her site-specific works, Cross extends this focus on the individual psyche and the domestic sphere to include the broader cultural and discursive means by which we try to deal with mortality.[55] Some of these responses arise from what the artist sees as a Jungian collective unconscious, but they are subsequently shaped by forces that are more culturally specific. In the introduction to their collection of essays on death and representation, Elisabeth Bronfen and Sarah Webster Goodwin argue that "much of what we call culture comes together around the collective response to death.... Death is thus necessarily constructed by a culture; it grounds the many ways a culture stabilizes and represents itself"(3-4). Cultures ancient and modern attempt to transform and obscure the brute fact of death by producing spiritual narratives of the soul's immortality, epistemological narratives of scientific progress, and generational narratives of familial or national continuity. Cross puts these cultural frames on display in *CRY*, where she reveals their failure to contain the "very extraordinary ordinariness, the uncanny everydayness" of death (Critchley 179-80). In *Ghost Ship*, she offers viewers fragmentary and discontinuous glimpses of that uncanny remainder.

In these temporary works, death and loss are contextualized in relation to the history of each site, to images derived from local memory and collective imagination. The conscious and unconscious attitudes of viewers toward loss are not rendered abstractly, but engaged physically in real time and space. Cross emphasizes the performative aspect of these two pieces, explaining that they are "completed by the audience." As performance/installation works, *CRY* and *Ghost Ship* function as theatrical events that "respond to a psychic need to rehearse for loss, and especially for death" (Phelan 3). Both works make productive use of the spatial exigencies of site-specific art and the temporal exigencies of performance. In her sculpture, video, site-specific installations, and opera stagings, Cross's work has dealt with the inevitability of loss and the broad range of cultural responses to it. In each medium she discovers that representations of death can only be approximations, gestures toward something ultimately unrepresentable. *CRY* and *Ghost Ship* are as much concerned with the limits of representation as with the limits of mortality.

Much of the theoretical discourse on death situates it in relation to the impossibility of desire and to the limits of representation. Death often functions in these meditations as the undeniable evidence of the inadequacy of all sign systems: "Just in case you thought there was no distinction between representation and reality, there is death" (Barreca 174). Representations of death become "metatropes for the process of representation itself," in which each attempt to communicate loss is forced to rely on a "signifier with an incessantly receding, ungraspable signified" (Bronfen and Goodwin 4). This limit of representation is not so much a failure as a defensive strategy. We don't really want accurate representations of death, even if we could produce them, but rather representations that are "idealized fantasies of wholeness we invent or create" to screen out the brute reality of death (Ragland 82). *CRY*, in particular, elaborates on the conflicted duality of these representations that simultaneously acknowledge and deny loss.

Simon Critchley argues that all "[r]epresentations of death are misrepresentations … representations of an absence" (26). Cross is one of several contemporary artists attempting to work through this impasse of representation by exploring rather than covering up the absence that constitutes its foundation. She expects both less and more from representation. Even as she accepts its inevitable failure to replace, preserve, or reconstitute a living presence, she marshals the power of representation to illuminate loss and transform reality. Absence, made present by whatever representational means, will always have that liminal quality of the trace—or the ghost: "representation functions like a revenant … [that] always has death as one of its signifieds" (Bronfen and Goodwin 12).[56] Cross makes a similar connection in relation to *Ghost Ship* when she muses that "ghosts are very much like art—people are afraid of them"(qtd. in "Ghostly goings on" 61). In many of her works, Cross makes productive use of such discomfort, uncertainty, and disorientation by taking viewers to the edge of an abyss that ultimately cannot be bridged, where conventional representation arrives at its limit. *CRY* and *Ghost Ship*, in particular, achieve an alternative mode of representation that acknowledges and makes productive use of those limits.[57]

Cross's representational strategy in *Ghost Ship* exemplifies what Kristeva calls the "nonrepresentative spacing of representation." The only method by which one can approximate death or loss, Kristeva argues, is by an indirection that would be "not the *sign* but the *index* of [the] death drive.… The ultimate imprint of the death drive, the *dissociation of form* itself"(1989, 27). *Ghost Ship* realizes this indexical representation by way of the "trace" with stunning simplicity. Both *CRY* and *Ghost Ship* take viewers beyond traditional forms of representation that tend to deny, mask, or sublimate the horror of death. They offer instead an alternative mode of representation that accepts limit, remains open to the return of the repressed, and holds on to the materiality of the indexical trace of the object.

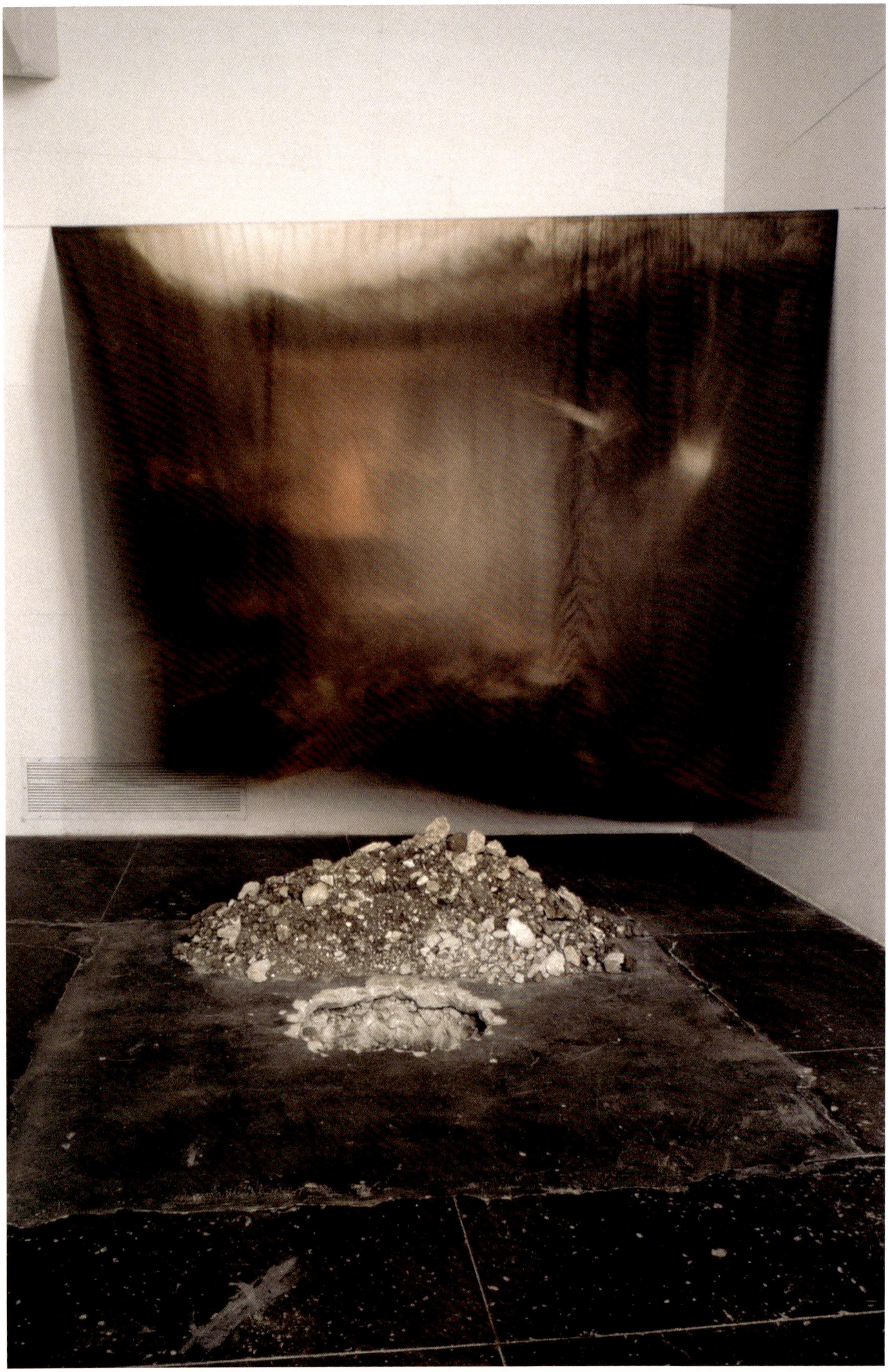

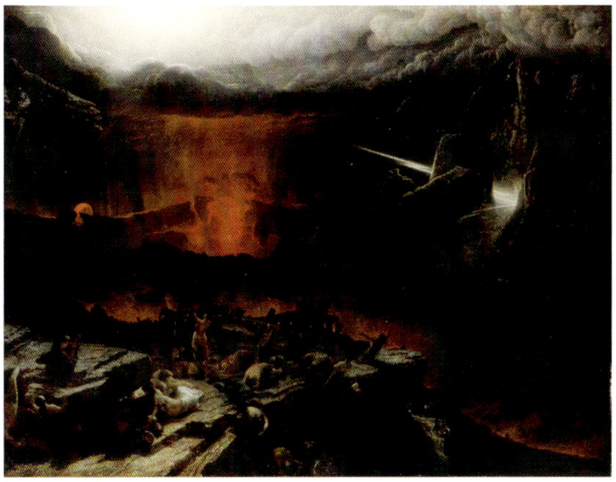

Francis Danby, *The Opening of the Sixth Seal,* 1828, oil on canvas

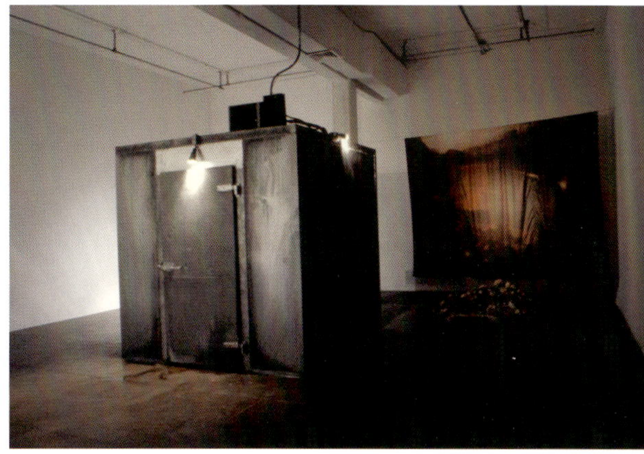

CRY, view of the installation

Responding to Death:
CRY (1996)

CRY was developed during a three-month residency at ArtPace Center for Contemporary Art in San Antonio, Texas. Although technically a gallery rather than a non-art site, ArtPace has inspired several of its artists-in-residence to respond to the history of the gallery's converted space and to the context of the surrounding culture and geography. Cross conceived of and created *CRY* partly in response to elements she encountered by chance at the Texas site: fifteen pages of churches listed in the local phone directory, the frequency of fires in the dry landscape and the fire-fighting techniques developed to control them, and the snake breeder's farm she discovered just down the road.

The ArtPace gallery was used previously as a car repair shop, and its cement floor still bears the marks of heavy machinery and labor. In *CRY*, Cross responds to a certain ghostly presence of machinery in the space. In the center of the gallery she installs a small walk-in freezer, which she describes as, "a warn, galvanized-steel refrigerator that stands alone like a mausoleum …[while on] its roof a small engine throbs" ("Heat and Cold" 49). Viewers enter the narrow space of the freezer two at a time to discover inside a variety of frozen dead snakes arranged on frost-coated shelves, looking as if they might at any moment uncoil and slither off. To one side and behind this structure, a fireman's protective silver gloves and helmet with gilded visor are theatrically lit on the floor of the gallery.

By incorporating snakes and fire into her work, Cross collaborates with the cultural specificity of the Texas site. In two other elements of *CRY* she acknowledges her presence there as a foreigner bringing her own cultural baggage, the movable "site" that constitutes her Irish heritage. Working as a nomadic *bricoleur*, Cross combines the local characteristics of San Antonio with two items she brought with her from Ireland: a postcard of Francis Danby's nineteenth-century apocalyptic painting, *The Opening of the Sixth Seal*, and one of three existing casts of *Kiss*. This small sculpture finds its place to one side of the freezer, next to the fireman's

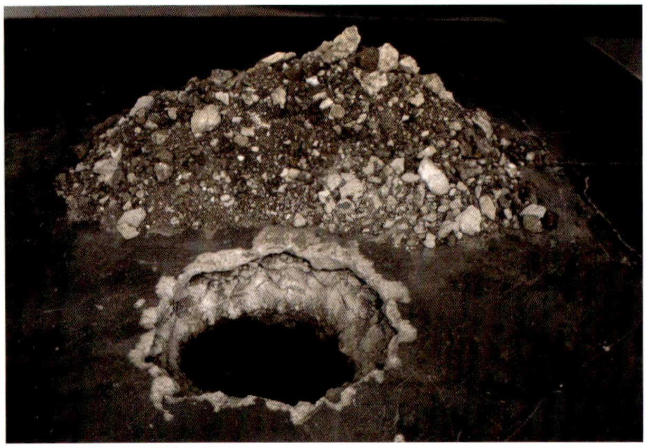

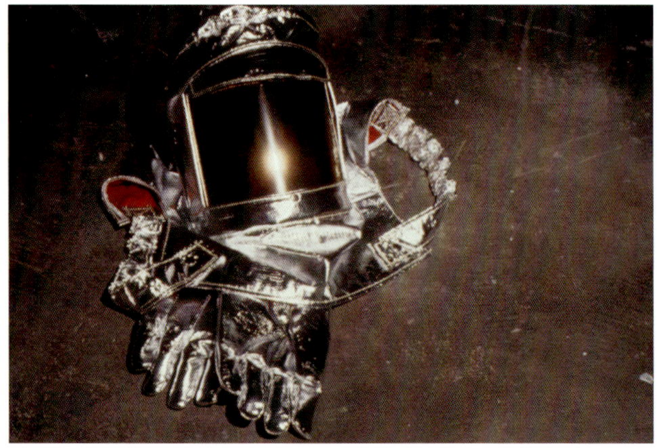

CRY, details of hole and fireman's gear

gear, where it is similarly displayed and illuminated. Danby's image of final judgment and annihilation, hung on the opposite side of the freezer, is reproduced on sheer fabric kept in motion by a set of oscillating fans. In front of this drapery the artist dug a crude six-foot vertical hole into the gallery floor, leaving the unearthed dirt and stones piled nearby. The constellation of these various cultural elements makes the site of *CRY* a hybrid site—part nineteenth-century Ireland, part twentieth-century Texas. Viewers entering the ArtPace gallery find themselves on uncertain ground.

In *CRY,* Cross contrasts what she sees as an American tendency to deny or overcome death through science and technology with an Irish, perhaps particularly an Irish Catholic, submersion in it:

> I am interested in how death used to be integrated into society and ritual,
> and no longer is, especially in America, where death is totally denied....
> In Catholicism, you're told life is preparation for death; death is the ultimate,
> whereas [in America] it is the opposite (qtd. in Colpitt).

The title of the installation plays with those conflicting attitudes. It refers to the science of *CRY*onics, a process by which dead bodies are frozen in liquid nitrogen until they can be revived or cloned at some later date; at the same time, it echoes the *CRY* of mourning, a lamentation that persists in spite of the promises of science *or* religion.

In this installation Cross brings together America and Ireland, as well as technology and religion, in a structure she compares to the interior architecture of a cathedral—two "naves" flanking the central "tabernacle or mausoleum." Cross's "cathedral," however, is dominated by the freezer in which frozen snakes evoke the American dream of defying death through the wonders of modern science. The apocalyptic painting and the vertical tomb dug into the gallery floor suggest an Irish immersion in both the spiritual salvation narratives of the church and the simple "rot and reality" of physical death (Cross qtd. in Colpitt).

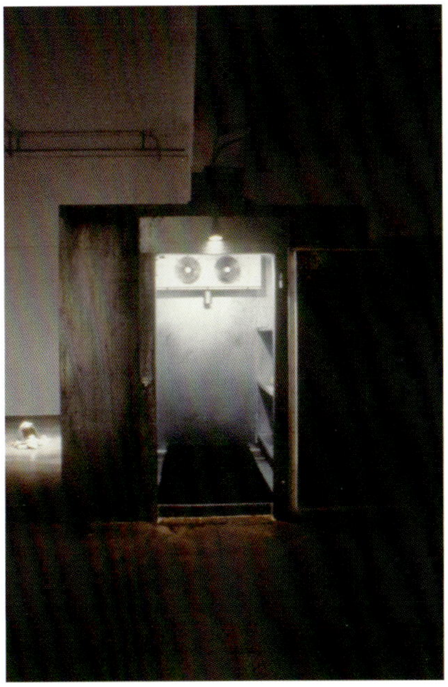
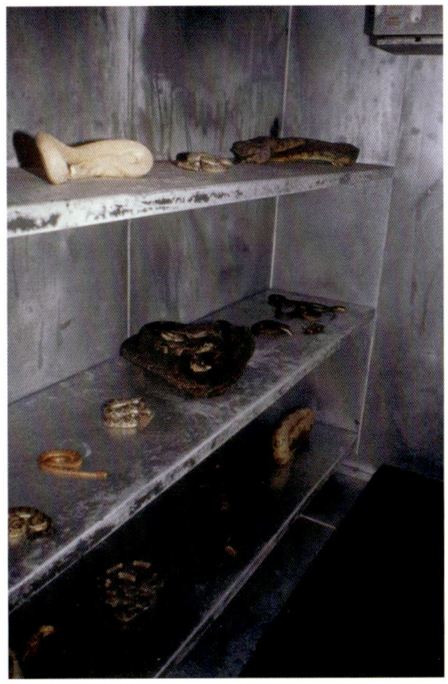
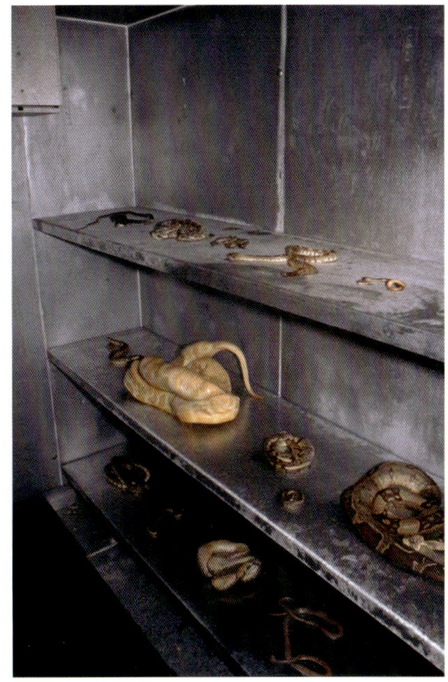

CRY, exterior and interior of freezer

In its complex totality, *CRY* brings together these two different cultural attitudes toward death. Ultimately, the piece reveals that efforts to evade annihilation (whether through science, religion, or love) are played out on the uncertain ground of annihilation itself—the gaping hole in the gallery floor, the billowing apocalypse on the gallery wall, the freezer doors opening into the Texas heat, the formless remnant of a kiss. A closer examination of the individual elements of *CRY* will show how in our uncanny encounter with mortality, all the structures and assumptions by which we orient ourselves in the world dissolve into thin air.

SCIENCE AND TECHNOLOGY VS. DEATH

The uncanny is, among other things, an epistemological disturbance in which life and death, familiar and unfamiliar, animate and inanimate are confused. One common response to this cognitive disorientation is an intellectual effort to arrive at certain knowledge and mastery. Scientific discourses from anatomy to genetics, and scientific methods of preserving, classifying, and displaying specimens for study all attempt to defuse the mystery of life and death by fixing them in language and in matter. The problem of epistemological mastery, however, is that to preserve life for study one must impose on it a deadly immobility; in anatomizing death, one renders its finality inescapable. In *CRY* Cross slyly disrupts the absolute authority and certainty of scientific ways of knowing in general, and of cryonics in particular.[58]

The model of Western science, based on empirical and positivist methods, derives in part from the way the pursuit of truth is defined in traditional Western metaphysics. In a philosophical novella by one of Cross's favorite authors, Marguerite Duras, this tradition and its limits are dramatized. Duras' *The Malady of Death* relates the story of an anonymous man who hires a woman for several nights, seeking to penetrate through her the unknown and unknowable truth about sexual difference, death, and love. The woman perceives the fatal impossibility of his desire to know: "I don't want to know anything the way you do," she says, "with that death-derived certainty, that hopeless monotony … that deadly routine of lovelessness" (48).[59]

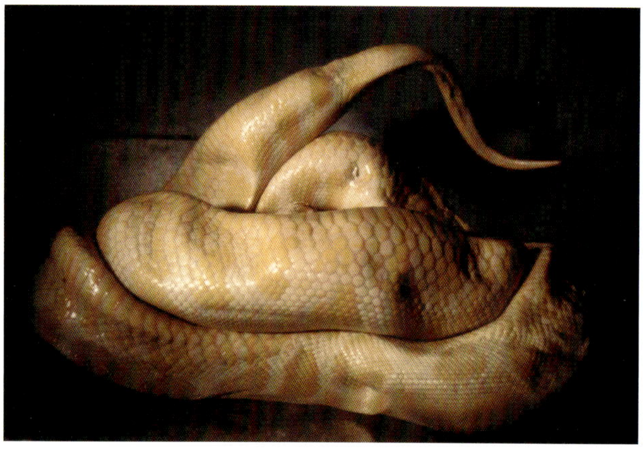

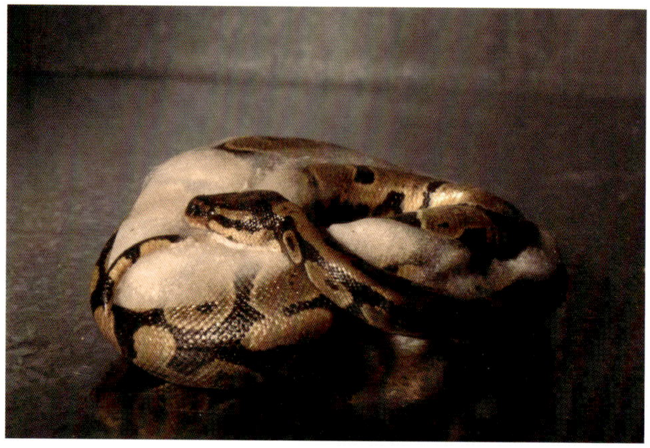

CRY, snake portraits

Duras recognizes a kind of knowing that destroys its object in the process, always missing its living mark. Like the novelist, Cross discovers her philosophical affinity not in the tradition of Western metaphysics that ties knowledge to illumination and possession, but (as *Chiasm* demonstrates) in the counter-philosophy of thinkers like Merleau-Ponty who try to move philosophy away from the desire to "grasp" and preserve the truth, and toward the fertile and fleeting entanglements of the visible and the invisible, of sight and touch, of life and death.

In an article on *CRY* in *Tate: the Art Magazine*, Cross provides a quotation from a manual on cryonics, "The Technical Feasibility of Cryonics," that exemplifies everything she rejects about Western science and metaphysics: "Tissue preserved in liquid nitrogen can survive centuries without deterioration. This simple fact provides an imperfect time machine that can transport us almost unchanged from the present to the future: we need merely freeze ourselves in liquid nitrogen" (qtd. in "Heat and Cold" 50). Cross finds it "ridiculous, negative, tragic to sustain one life only that's never going to progress." Resisting this emphasis of cryonics on preservation, on the desire to move from present to future "unchanged," she chooses instead to embrace the ongoing life processes of decay and loss.

CRY alludes to many different methods of preservation; the frozen snakes evoke cryonics, but also recall the science of taxidermy, or religious methods of preservation such as ancient mummification or Christian reliquaries. Science and religion are united here by their similar practices of preservation and by the similar questions those practices raise: What is the status of the body preserved in laboratory or mausoleum? Is the corpse perceived as life in suspended animation or as death's incarnated double? The frozen snakes in *CRY*, like animal bodies preserved by taxidermy, paradoxically use death as a method of preserving life.[60] Such methods resemble the fabrication of death masks, which "preserve, artificially, [the] bodily appearance … to snatch it from the flow of time, to stow it away neatly, so to speak, in the hold of life" (Bazin 9). *CRY* demonstrates that the "hold of life" inevitably gives way.[61]

Cross is one of several contemporary artists whose works explore the limitations of scientific methods of knowing. Damien Hirst, for example, mimics and mocks the procedures of

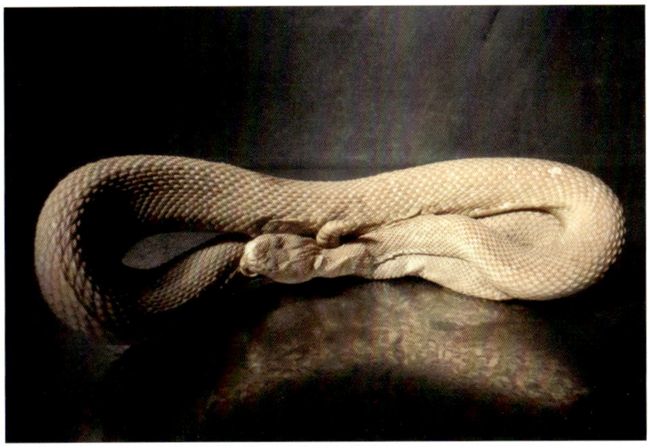

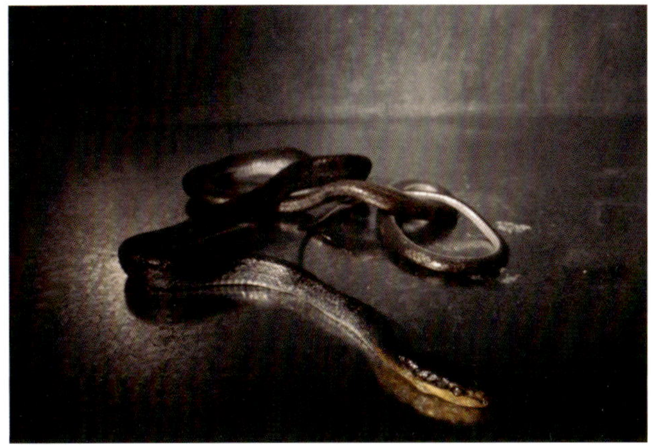

scientific study by suspending sharks or cows in tanks of formaldehyde. In *CRY* the pretensions of science are similarly humbled. The previous use of the ArtPace gallery space as a garage puts science and futuristic technology (not to mention artistic production) on the same ground as the cruder mechanics of car repair. *CRY*'s allusion to the science of cryonics is more comical or poignant than awesome; Cross ironically describes its "grandiose mausoleum" as no more than a worn little freezer, its engine audibly straining against the intense heat in the gallery. Cross turned off the air-conditioning in the exhibition space so that viewers would feel "a shock and a reprieve" as they entered the cool air of the freezer (qtd. in Colpitt). The price of such a reprieve is that the deadly cold, in which the body is protected from decay and available for scientific inspection, keeps out the heat of life and passion.

THE FATE OF THE BODY

When Cross uses bodies and body parts in her sculptural works, her interest is not in their scientific preservation but in the possibility of transformation and reincarnation, putting the body back into circulation in some new form. In the "udder" works she refashions cow hides with udders into a variety of constructions that give the cow new functions, new identities.[62] Other works perform a similar service for the snake, redeeming it from its "abominable reputation" and opening it up to unexpected new meanings (Cross qtd. in Bonaventura 20).

The snakes used in *CRY* call up a broad range of cultural associations. Cross sees the snake as a beast that once held a position of central and positive importance in early matriarchal religions, but was subsequently demonized by the Judeo-Christian tradition, and even further "disempowered in recent times" (qtd. in Colpitt). The freezer display is not only about the death and preservation of the body, but also, as she explains, about "the history of something psychically annihilated," something that has lost its place in the cultural imagination. Looking beyond the scientific relegation of the snake to the status of specimen, and beyond its Christian designation as the archetypal symbol of evil, Cross recognizes the snake's beauty and vulnerability.

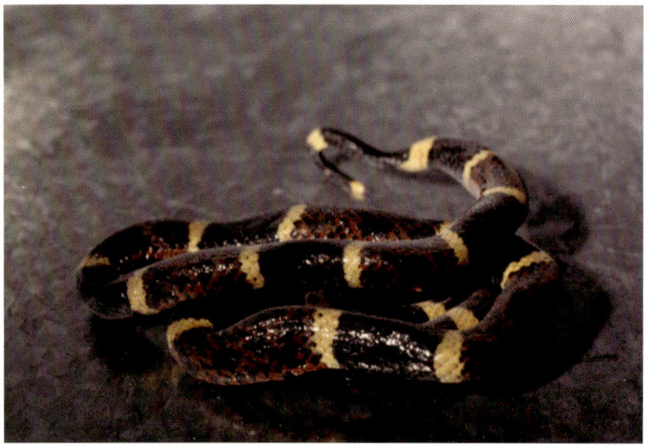 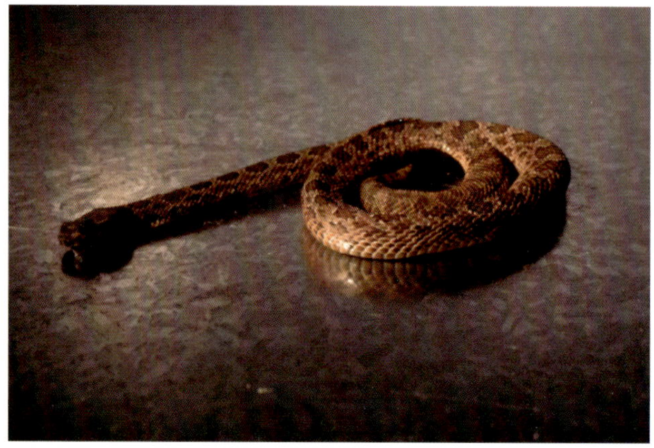

For an earlier work entitled *Bandaged Snake* (1995), Cross dissects a dead snake and removes its heart. The extracted heart is then tenderly displayed in a small metal box with glass lid, set next to its bandaged body.[63] She asks us to think, for the first time perhaps, about a snake's heart, about its inner life and the scars it bears. In a related work, *Gallows* (1995–96), Cross enigmatically stages a mass execution of snakes that seem to slither up the plywood structure, either forced to endure their fate or embracing their annihilation in a gesture of self-sacrifice. Cross's most poignant piece in this series is *Lover Snakes* (1995), a sculpture in which two dead snakes entangled in a sensuous embrace nevertheless keep their hearts at a distance—literally encased in silver reliquaries attached to their bodies by delicate silver wires. All of these snakes, like those in the freezer of *CRY*, suggest both our vulnerability and our modes of defense—against the wounds of love, loss, and death. The snakes "mirror the bafflement and inadequacy we all sometimes experience," just as they mirror our hurt (Bonaventura 20). Noting with satisfaction the difficulty of determining a snake's sex, Cross transcends the gendered interpretations that often oversimplify or misrepresent her work. "More than anything else," she insists, "I am interested in common mortality, common love and common struggle, and the snake provides the perfect metaphor for that commonality" (qtd. in Bonaventura 19).

Like the snakes in these earlier works, those in *CRY* generate multiple associations and meanings. In their ancient mythological resonance they symbolize spring and regeneration, but also danger and death. In their physical presence in the installation, they evoke in viewers the "small uncertainty that [the snakes] may revitalize, if unfrozen" (Cross qtd. in Colpitt). One is simultaneously repulsed by the snakes' bodies and empathetic with their mortality. Cross further provokes viewers' squeamishness and sympathy by describing with enthusiasm her harvesting of the snakes for the installation from the neighboring snake farmer's stock:

> He brought me round the back ... and opened three domestic freezers which bulged with frozen snakes. He allowed me to burrow alone, up to my elbows in reptiles, breaking through the ice and plastic bags to select the most

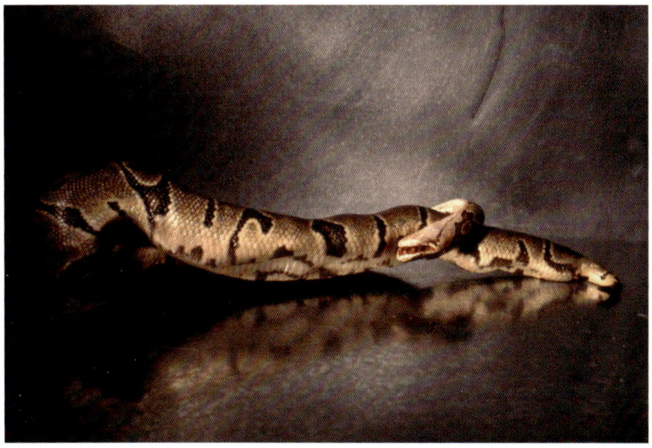

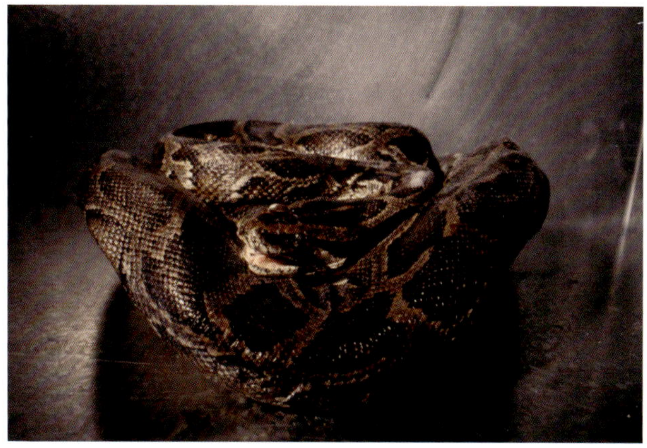

> beautiful snakes.... He told me stories of the snakes. I chose one that had been alive the week before. She had died giving birth. She was a large, beautiful, butter-coloured albino boa ("Heat and Cold" 49).

This image of the artist rooting around in the abject materiality of death, is at once gruesome and hilarious. Despite the indignity of being massed together in their plastic bags, the snakes are individualized and anthropomorphized, each with its own story.

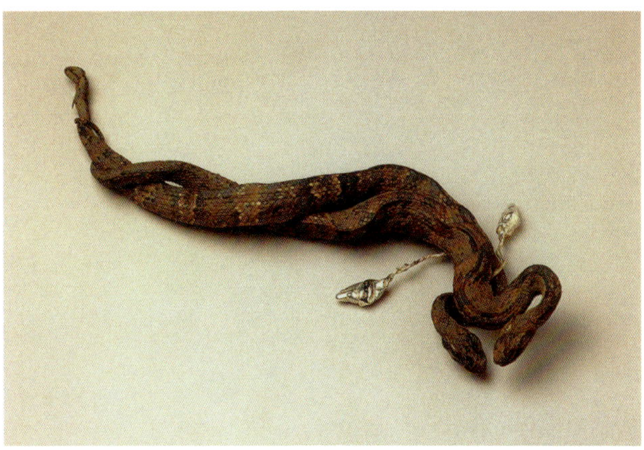

Lover Snakes, 1995
Photo: John Kellett

CRY is not only about the desire to preserve dead bodies, but also about our efforts to protect the still living body. Next to the Danby reproduction, in which fire is not local but apocalyptic, these preparations seem absurdly inadequate, futile accessories for a rendezvous with disaster. With their theatrical gilding and display, helmet and gloves evoke a strange combination of space age technology and religious icon. The base materiality of the body, so insistent in the freezer snakes (as it is in Cross's "udder" pieces), is replaced here by idealized prostheses: body armor that promises mastery over death and destruction—salvation through technology. Although the gear magically "deflects the heat and reflects light" ("Heat and Cold" 49), these objects are merely part objects, fetish objects that try to make up for the mortal body's vulnerability and lack. In the manner of all representational images, helmet and gloves preserve the body only by displacing it; there *is* no body in *CRY*, only its protective shell. The fireman's gear is a monument to our desire to protect ourselves from the flames—flames of eternal damnation, but perhaps also the wounding flames of life and passion. Somewhere between the decorative and the functional, the silver helmet and gloves highlight the absurd artificiality and inadequacy of our technological defenses against mortality and loss.

Whereas science deals with matter, protecting and preserving the living body or its simulacrum, religion holds out the possibility of the soul's disembodied transcendence. In *CRY*, the "nave" opposite the fireman's gear is dominated by Francis Danby's depiction of the moment of Resurrection and Rapture in the *Book of Revelation*, when all of nature is thrown into upheaval, all matter exploded or transfigured.[64]

Danby's painting conveys the complexity of this apocalyptic moment: earth and heavens turned upside down, horizontal time thrown out of joint by vertical space, the dreadful fate of some souls diverging violently from the imminent deliverance of others. The painter acknowledges the difficulty of his task in one version of the painting's title: *An Attempt to Illustrate the Opening of the Sixth Seal* (my emphasis).[65] The Biblical text describing the opening of the sixth seal is only one moment in a larger salvation narrative that clarifies and justifies the cosmic catastrophe. Extracted from that framing narrative, Danby's painting seems even darker than its textual source.

When Danby's painting was first shown in London's Royal Academy exhibition in 1828, it had to be moved to a larger room to accommodate the crowds fascinated by its apocalyptic sublimity (Nolan 1). Viewers were simultaneously attracted to and repelled by these images of the reversal of all known natural and social order. The popular taste for such images in the nineteenth century owes as much to political upheavals of the time as to religious fervor. As a result, the apocalyptic sublime became popularized as an aesthetic fashion and was fraught with ambivalence. The Gothic novelist William Beckford, who purchased *The Opening of the Sixth Seal* for 500 guineas (Nolan 1), commissioned and then rejected several of Danby's apocalyptic designs. The artist himself alternated between dismissing the genre, "the subject is not one after my own heart [but]... most likely to sell," and confessing to its addictive appeal, "I think I am almost cured of painting dark pictures, but I shall ever like them best" (qtd. in Graham-Dixon 38, 40).

The style and subject matter of the apocalyptic sublime provoked in this nineteenth-century artist and his viewers a deep ambivalence that found expression in a compulsion to repeat. After the painting was attacked in 1848 by one viewer who objected to the anti-slavery message that many contemporaries read into Danby's painting, the slashed-out figures of king and slave had to be repainted by the artist.[66] The composition was reproduced several times in mezzotint editions, and one set of imprints was sold off as individual raffle tickets, the winner to be awarded the original painting. *The Opening of the Sixth Seal* was finally acquired and installed in the National Gallery of Ireland in Dublin, where it is now available in postcard reproductions like the one Cross brought to Texas. These various modes of reproduction are culturally controlled repetitions in which the threat of the apocalyptic drama of death and final judgment is mastered, neutralized, and even domesticated as touristic memento.

The power of the apocalyptic sublime is undercut by this proliferation of copies, the effects of "mechanical reproduction" diminishing the original painting's "aura" and impact.[67] For Cross, however, the repetition of an image or object is always an opportunity for transformation. For the *CRY* installation, she reproduces and enlarges Danby's painting on a twelve-by-nine foot sheet of fabric. Two oscillating fans keep the fabric in perpetual motion, introducing into the gallery the natural effect of winds, like those depicted in Danby's turbulent scene. Both the printing process and the movement created by the fans render the moment of apocalypse more imposing and animated, but also more obscure. Just as the freezer and fireman's gear expose the dependency of science on machinery and artifice, the oscillating fans, like the Wizard of Oz behind his curtain, create effects that are purely theatrical. This literal "thinning out" of the image reduces it to a ghostly memory of both the original painting and its Biblical source.

The apocalyptic tradition in which Danby worked may seem distant and dated, but the fascination with annihilation to which it appeals persists in more modern forms. Julia Kristeva has argued that, since World War II, a "new rhetoric of apocalypse" has emerged to represent the "monstrous nothing" threatened not by God's final judgment, but by "gas chambers [and] atomic bombs" of our own making (1989, 223). This new rhetoric of the apocalypse moves, she believes, in two different directions: toward a "wealth of images" and toward a "holding back of words" (1989, 224). *CRY* moves in both of these directions simultaneously. As the X-ray image of skull and fetus in Cross's earlier work from *Inheritance* suggests, death is not something outside of us threatening our autonomy and integrity, but something deeply inborn.[68]

DOWN IN THE HOLE

Roland Barthes argues that, in modernity, encounters with death often occur in unexpected places, "outside of religion, outside of ritual." He perceives death's paradoxical effects, for example, in the frozen moment of the photographic image that, like cryonics and taxidermy, "produces Death while trying to preserve life." In particular, his discovery of a photograph of his dead mother taken when she was a child shocks him like an "abrupt dive into literal Death" (1981, 92). In *CRY*, Cross juxtaposes Danby's bathetic and lurid apocalyptic painting with the hole dug into the gallery floor—her version of Barthes' "abrupt dive into literal death." The diaphanous lightness of the sheet bearing Danby's image is countered by the undeniable materiality of a hole dug patiently by the artist through cement, earth, and stone, by hand, and ultimately from inside the gradually deepening space. Engaged in such work, Cross enters into a relationship with death and loss that is tactile, temporal, and spatial, unmediated by science, religion, or even aesthetics. Cross describes the work of excavating the hole as awkward and slow, digging "down into nature, into the dark territory … down into the unconscious. You couldn't see the bottom." The collective catastrophe of the entire human race figured on a cosmic scale in Danby's painting is contrasted by this narrow hole, large enough for only one body. This solitariness of death, Cross observes, is hardly unfamiliar: "we do live in our own vertical tombs … we are living death every day." Whereas Danby's apocalyptic sublime tempers the horror of death with the religious promise of redemption and with sublimation through aesthetic pleasure, Cross's hole reveals death in its unadorned "rot and reality" (Cross qtd. in Colpitt).

The hole, both as materialized space and as immaterial signifier of absence and loss, has been a fertile source for Cross over the years. She pursues its potential in *Bible* (1995), for which she drills a perfect hole through her family's illustrated Bible. Producing what she describes as "a controlled void" through word and image, Cross introduces that sign of absence on every page. The hole makes palpable and present the body that has been repressed in Christian mythology, and the material void appearing on each page becomes a signifier with multiple meanings. It appears by chance as the hole of grief in Mary's heart, and in the heart of Abraham as he sacrifices his son; it makes literal and visible the alienating gap between father and prodigal son, and it obliterates the face of the Good Samaritan, assuring his anonymity. In several of her works, Cross exposes this hole or gap that defeats our desire to make contact with each other, whether within the family or with those designated as "outside" and "other." The inclusion of *Kiss* (which Cross also used in *Strangers on a Train*) in *CRY* gives evidence that even our most intimate relations are pierced through by alienation and loss.

In contrast to the technological approach represented by the fireman's gear and the freezer, *Kiss* introduces into the installation a very different response to death and loss. Displayed and illuminated on a small table, this sculpture made from the inside of two lovers' mouths kissing does not fix or simulate the body, but signals its absence. Whereas the fireman's helmet and gloves offer *outside* coverings for the body, *Kiss* shows us the hidden *inside*. This strange form evokes precisely the intimacy of touch denied to the frozen snakes and obstructed by the protective gear. Yet this intimacy can only be represented indirectly by the index or trace it leaves behind. Cross's ironic presentation of the promise of romance or idealized love as a way to transcend suffering is more gentle than her critique of the promises of science or religion; ultimately, however, love is exposed as an equally inadequate defense against loss.

Although we turn to love in defense against life's wounds, as Freud observes, that suffering "re-emerges from within love itself as love's very condition" (Dollimore 183-4). *Kiss* embodies life's wounds in the central hole formed by the most intimate point of contact between the lovers' mouths, that point where protective barriers are laid aside and the fire of passion breaks through. With this pierced shape, the mere skeletal trace of passion, Cross reminds us that the intimacy of desire, like the strangeness and familiarity of death, is precisely what can never be possessed or represented, except perhaps by a tender void. Our modern apocalypse of desire is fundamentally, in Lacan's punning formulation, "*troumatique*"—*trou* is the French word for hole.[69] The hole of absence carved out by the rough pit in the gallery floor is repeated in *Kiss* in a more precious and delicate form.

When asked in an interview if the *CRY* installation was her "way of coming to terms with death," Cross responds with uncertainty. Could such a coming to terms be possible given that "obliteration is so close all the time?" She speculates further that *CRY* is perhaps "more about beauty than anything else" (qtd. in Colpitt). If *Strangers on a Train* "was meant to be a piece about love but ended up being about holes and loss," it could be argued that *CRY* began as a piece about death and loss, but became a piece about beauty. Viewers entering the freezer are invited to look past their fears to see the beauty that survives or perhaps even derives from death. *CRY* does not produce the classical beauty of eternal harmony and wholeness, but rather something closer to the Surrealists' celebrated "convulsive beauty," in which animate and inanimate, the veiled and the erotic, the static and the explosive converge (Breton 19). In contrast to a death mask that attempts to hold on to a recognizable appearance of life, *Kiss* presents a formlessness that remains unrecognizable, alluding obliquely to the death that lies beyond all representation. The beauty evoked in *CRY* does not mask or sublimate our anxieties about loss; it is the austere beauty that stems from an encounter with death "without the rose-tinted spectacles of any narrative of redemption" (Critchley 27). *CRY* confronts viewers with the hole, the wound, the split within each subject.

THE VOICE OF SILENCE

Elaine Scarry meditates on the divided and dividing experience of death in which the "body is emphatically present while that more elusive part represented by the voice is so alarmingly absent that heavens are created to explain its whereabouts" (49). Viewers experience this constitutive division as *CRY* splits their attention between the dead snakes' "emphatically present" bodies and Danby's depiction of a narrative moment of suspension, the world awaiting the voice of God in final judgment. But given our distance from Danby's apocalyptic sublime, contemporary viewers are likely to experience the absence of voice as haunting silence rather than imminent revelation. Cross herself is struck by the stillness of the installation—likening it to an opera set awaiting or abandoned by its singers. "You're wondering," she muses, "'where's the voice?'" Barthes locates the horror of death in this very silence, in the "platitude" of "nothing to say about the death of one whom I love most.... I have no other resource than this *irony*: to speak of the 'nothing to say'" (1981, 92-93).

Cross addresses this inadequacy of language in an earlier piece entitled *Convention* (1995), for which she assembles a group of snake bodies in a circle, a delicate glass bubble emanating from each head. Playing on the double meaning of "convention" as traditional social practice and as an assembly or gathering, this piece simultaneously displays the hollowness of language and social ritual and insists on their efficacy in bringing us together. We come together at language's empty core, perhaps pulled into it as into a vacuum, joined once again in the commonality of our mortal destiny. In her reading of *Convention*, Joanna Isaak recognizes the tremendous creative energy at work, imagining "fiery tongues and hot dragon breath blast[ing] the sand into glass, blowing it into bubbles. Word without flesh. The birth of air" (Isaak and Cross 42). The empty glass bubbles signal not a lack but a continual becoming, not deadly stasis but the life-sustaining "birth of air."

In his meditation on photography and death, Barthes identifies an effect he calls simply "l'air," some indefinable expression or look in the photograph of a lost loved one, where the reality of death suddenly takes one by surprise, leading one "to that cry, the end of all language: 'There she is!' ... words fail" (1981, 109). That singular "air," that unique manner or presence of the loved one in the image, is as insubstantial and fleeting as its homonym "air."[70] In *CRY*, miraculously and literally, "l'air" speaks. In a sign language communicated directly to the skin, air speaks to us silently through the abrupt change of temperature between gallery and freezer, and through the movement of air generated by the fans. Working with this most ephemeral matter, Cross animates loss as a living process experienced on and through the body. Comprehending death as simultaneously a physical event and a "metaphysical problem" (Bronfen and Goodwin 20), *CRY* sets this duality vibrating in a Morse code that reaches beyond the limitations of language and cultural discourse.

Cross remarks on the affinity between the *CRY* project and a photograph she came across of a sign displayed over the freeway in San Antonio—a sign that simply spelled out the word "Wail" (qtd. in Colpitt). In this silent and depersonalized exclamation, in this primal "yowl of our own mortality," Cross recognizes a language that functions beyond the conventions of grammar, beyond the speaking subject.[71]

Listening for the voice, poised for sound, viewers in the *CRY* exhibit hear only the hum of machines—the "little life force" of the freezer engine straining to preserve life on ice, the oscillating fans reanimating the fixed image of death, and the ghostly mechanical traces that haunt this formerly industrial site. Beyond language and representation, the machinery of the death drive, animating and animated by desire, makes itself heard.

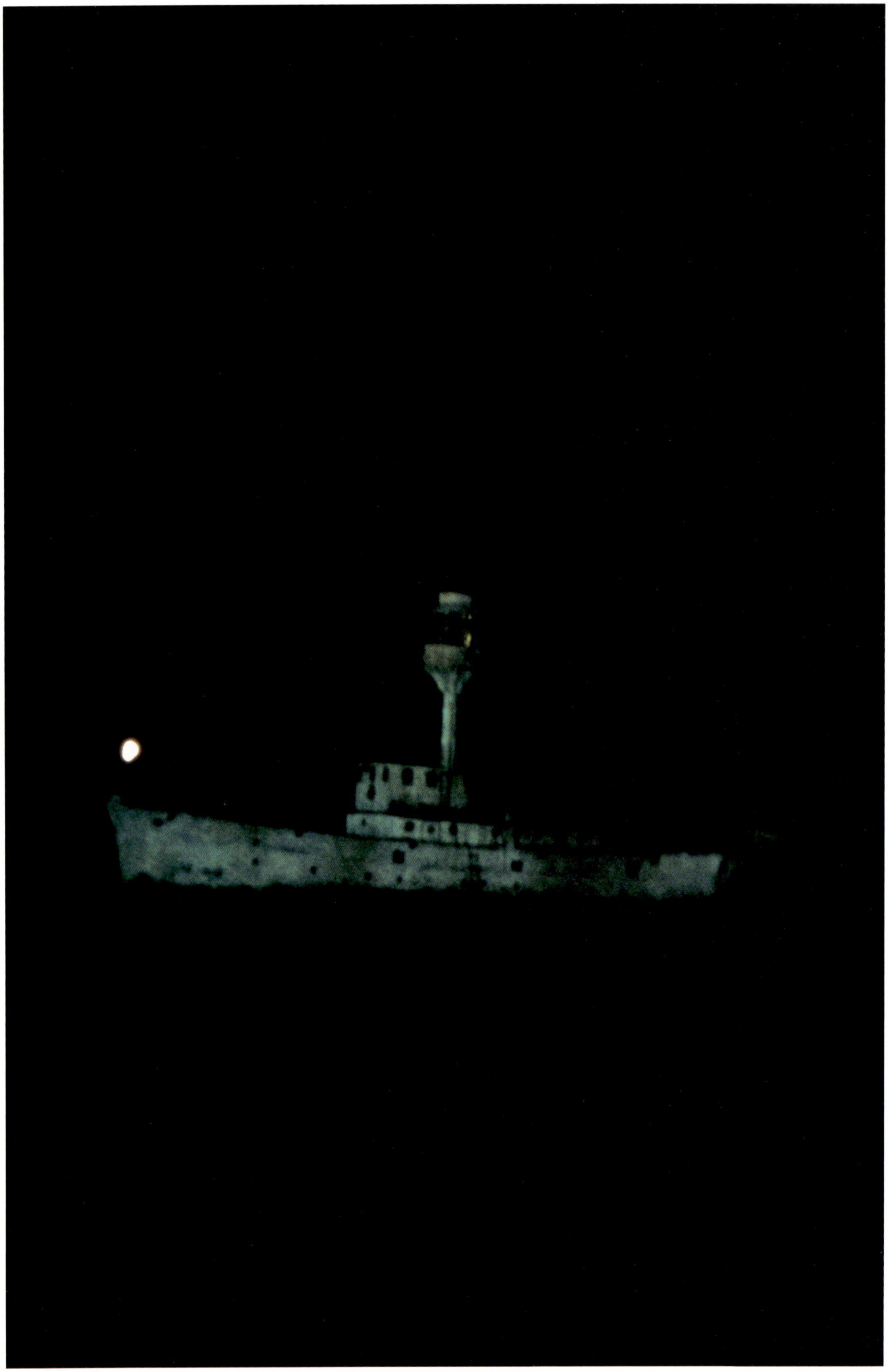

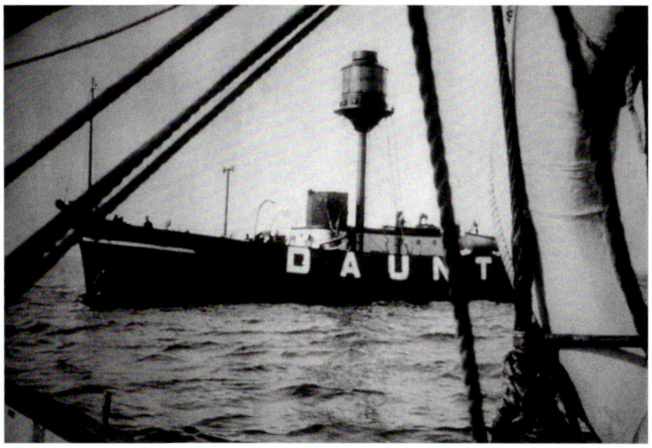

Albatross moored at Daunt Reef, Cork. 1930s. Photo: T. Fergus Cross

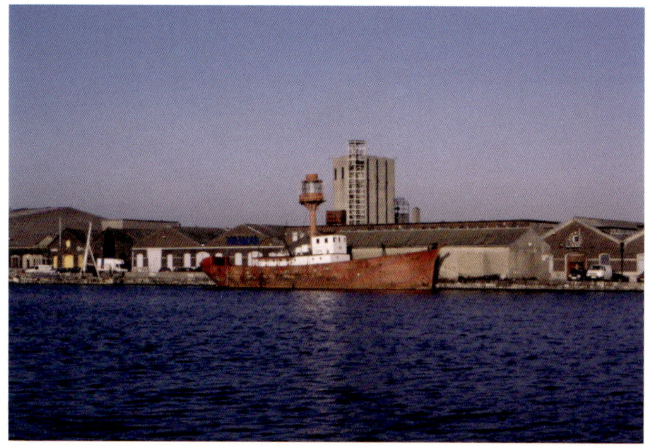

Ghost Ship, Albatross moored in the Dublin docklands

The Illumination of Darkness: *Ghost Ship (1999)*

Cross's site-specific work *Ghost Ship* offers a radically different experience of loss. In *CRY*, the artist invites viewers to enter the space of death literally (the freezer) and imaginatively (the hole). In following the installation's multiple approaches to death and loss, viewers must shift focus continually, adjusting to different contexts and grappling with new challenges to habitual ways of thinking. Whereas the Texas piece assembles a shifting constellation of disparate images, *Ghost Ship* is elegantly comprised of a single object. *CRY* makes us conscious of being in a body and in a specific relationship to space; *Ghost Ship* is more about repetition, about time as duration, about disembodied memory. *CRY* is a sculpture-installation constructed, in part, of absence and air; in *Ghost Ship*, Cross paints with light. *CRY* is an ordeal to be undergone; *Ghost Ship*, in contrast, is a gift—the gift of memory as spectacle.

In 1999 Cross found and borrowed a decommissioned lightship that had been abandoned for several years in a Dublin dockyard. She covered its worn red surface with phosphorescent paint and set it afloat in Dublin Bay. This description makes the transformation sound like an effortless process. In fact, the project was plagued by bureaucratic as well as natural difficulties, and required tremendous patience, money, and the collaboration of many helpers.[72] Each evening for three weeks, over a three-hour period, the ship was exposed to UV light, then left to glow and fade. This obsolete and long-forgotten vessel was made visible again by the poignantly beautiful repetition of its appearance and disappearance. Cross was not interested in the *son et lumière* effect of the ship's UV illumination. Her goal was the far more subtle and mysterious afterglow produced as the absorbed light gradually faded and disappeared. A three-minute video of these final moments of the ship's visibility was subsequently shown in two other site-specific screenings—one in Liverpool and one in Swansea, both ports of embarkation—and in a gallery in Boston, Massachusetts.[73] In 2003 *Ghost Ship* was screened in a group show at Massachusetts College of Art (*Mystic*, Winter 2003), where it was accompanied by two

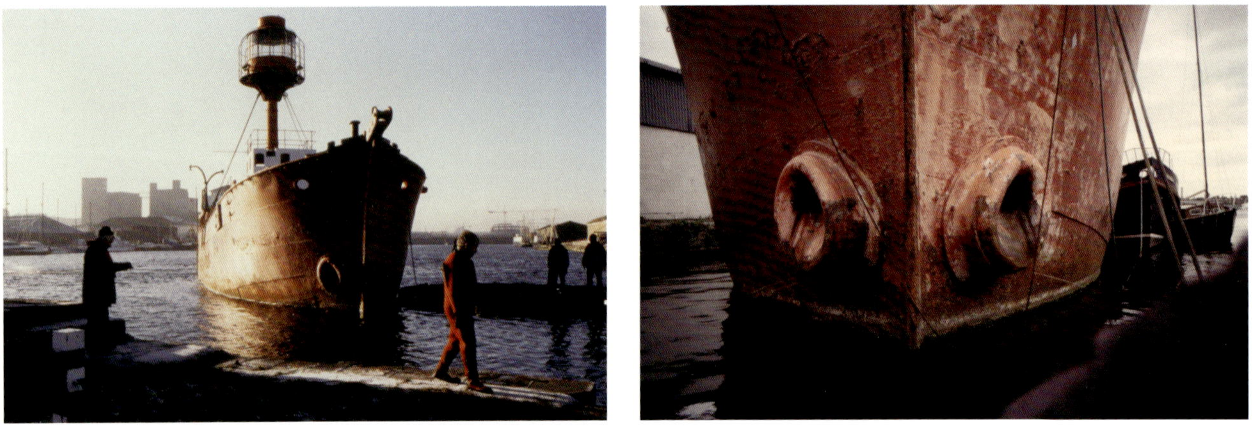

Ghost Ship, Albatross entering the drydock

miniature models of the ship: one painted red, as was the original, and the other covered with phosphorescent paint. In the continuing evolution of this piece from site-specific apparition, to site-specific video projection, to gallery installation, both site and object are continually transformed and displaced. *Ghost Ship* has been a movable and a moving site, in more ways than one.

Of all of Cross's site-specific works to date, *Ghost Ship* is the most public, its reception the most broad-based and enthusiastic. The piece was funded by the Nissan Corporation's yearly award for a non-permanent public art project; impermanence and loss are thus not only the thematic content of the work, but its prescribed form. In contrast to the relatively private experience of each viewer in the *CRY* installation, the public spectacle of *Ghost Ship* brings the human drama of the inevitability of loss out into the open. Because this piece makes the audience such an integral part of its realization, it poses the challenge of alternative modes of representation and new ways of seeing. The history, mechanics, and psychology of sight have long been subjects of intense interest to Cross. *Ghost Ship* stages a particularly complex exploration of seeing in relation to history, time, repetition, and the traces of personal and collective memory.

The Liverpool Biennial, in which the *Ghost Ship* video was first screened, was organized under the title *TRACE*. Participating artists were invited to consider how "materials or objects allow us to reconstruct histories through personal memories and associations" (Bond 11). Cross's work often employs this "mnemonic function of materials and objects," causing viewers to respond viscerally, as well as intellectually, making use of physical, as well as psychic memory (Bond 14). Matter has always mattered to Cross, in her work as a sculptor, as well as in her appreciation of how objects are transformed by time. She is interested in the way in which objects rusted or worn with use carry the bodily memory of the intimacy of touch that has shaped them. Cross celebrates the specificity of matter in its abject materiality (as in the snake bodies or cow udders), and in its participation in a lived human history of physical labor and creative imagination.

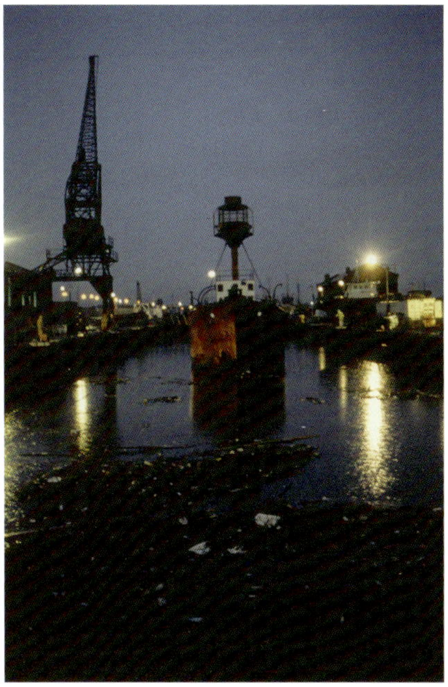

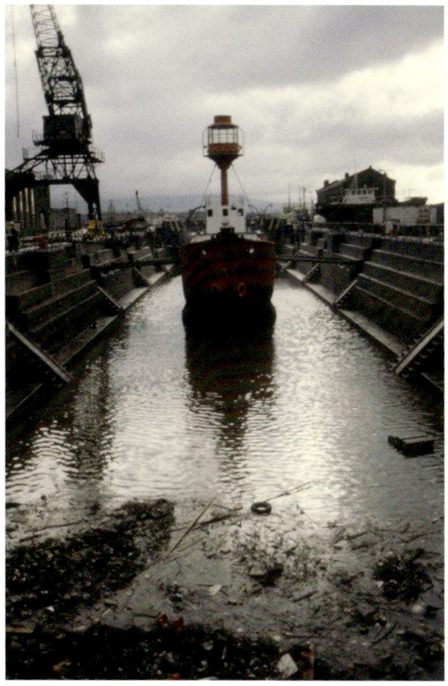

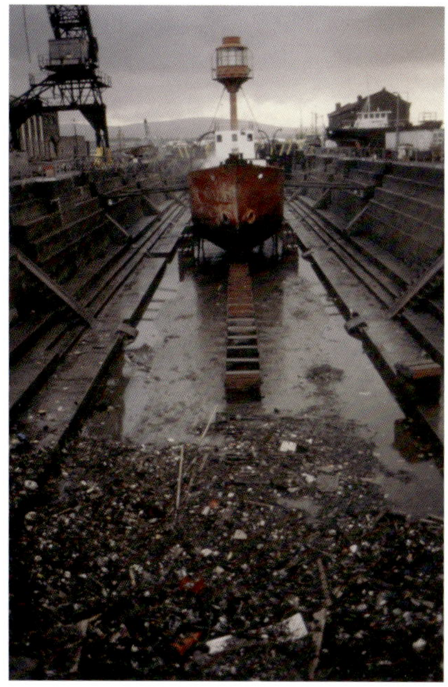

THE MAKING OF *GHOST SHIP* - BY DOROTHY CROSS

As a child, I moved with my family during the summer to a small house by the sea for three months. My father had a boat. As a special treat every year, he brought us out to visit the lightship that was moored two miles offshore.

Lightships were located around the Irish coast on reefs that were too deep to build lighthouses. This 128-foot long ship, *Albatross*, was painted bright red with large white letters spelling the word Daunt, the name of the reef on which it was moored.

The lightships were engineless, moored by great chains, bow and stern, to the bottom of the sea. The lamp was kept alight by lighthouse men who lived three weeks on board and three weeks on shore. On our trip we carried newspapers and cigarettes for the men; we threw these supplies up on deck and then returned to the mainland.

In the 1970s most lightships around Ireland were decommissioned and replaced by satellite buoys, and today only three ships remain in use. In the 1980s, after ten years away from Ireland, I returned to Dublin. Every day, for several years, I cycled past a faded, red lightship on my way to a studio in an old powerhouse in Dublin Bay. The ship was derelict, vandalized, and beautiful. It turned out to be the same ship I had visited as a child with my father. In 1999, the Irish Museum of Modern Art held an open submission competition for the Nissan Art Award, which had been set up to support a non-permanent work to be made in the Dublin area. My very simple idea to turn the lightship into a Ghost Ship was awarded the commission.

I then had to borrow the ship. It had been given to the Sea Scouts of Ireland by the Commissioners of Irish Lights and had been used for several years as a training ship for kids. After a rather surreal series of phone calls, the Sea Scouts faithfully agreed to lend me the ship. The *Albatross* had not been moved for ten years, which created certain problems. We had to employ divers to clear the locks to let the ship exit safely into the river. Because the lightship is engineless, we had to use tugs to move it. For some reason, the Dublin Port Authorities required that the ship be moved rather often. One move located it next to a coal depot; of

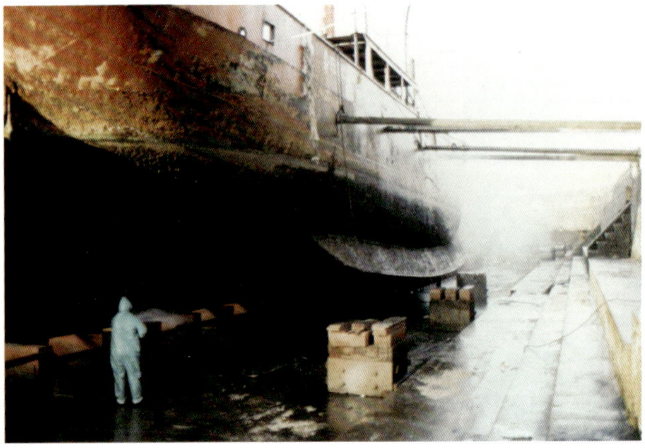

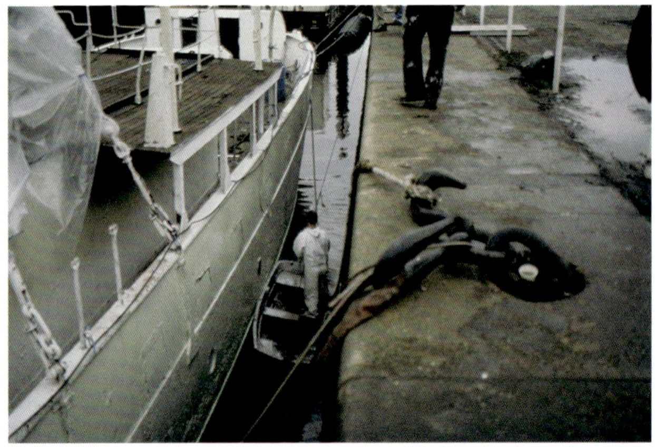

Ghost Ship, cleaning and painting *Albatross*

course, when the wind blew, the ship was covered in black coal dust and had to be hosed down. Insurers insisted on the hull being tested for strength, so at dawn one morning we tugged the ship into a nineteenth-century dry dock that looked like a Roman amphitheatre. The ship was shored-up with great wooden poles, and the water was drained from the dock. The hull was then examined by ultrasound and pressure-hosed to remove mollusks and crustaceans. The hull was strong.

In spite of this good news, a certain hysteria continued to mount among the Dublin bureaucrats: insurance paranoia, suspicion, and resistance. Costs soared, and the project was shelved. Due to the public curiosity and calls to the Museum asking when *Ghost Ship* was happening, it was resurrected; and, in February 1999, it appeared in Scotsman's Bay, Dublin.

To create the glow, we built an out-rig on the hull and superstructure to attach large UV lamps. A generator was put on board, and a timer boosted the lights every ten minutes. The ship was covered with paint of the highest phosphorous content, costing a fortune per litre. Charlie, the painter, applied it like gold dust. The painted ship absorbed the light and glowed. When moving round the ship at night, the surface appeared translucent. If the ship had been towed to the tropics we would not have needed UV lamps as the sun could have boosted the ship in one blast to glow until darkness. Due to the Irish climate, we had to supply extra UV light.

Ghost Ship remained in Dublin Bay for three weeks. Its glow varied according to the weather. It was at its best on dark clear nights. At the end of each night the glow faded to almost nothing and disappeared.

HISTORY MATTERS

The lightship is a material remainder of a period of Irish history during which daily life was dominated by the sea—a source of sustenance, pleasure, and danger. Cross laments the loss of this intimate relation to nature, as modern life shifts the attention of the Irish people away from the seacoast and "inward toward the cities": "The Irish coastline is being neutralized,

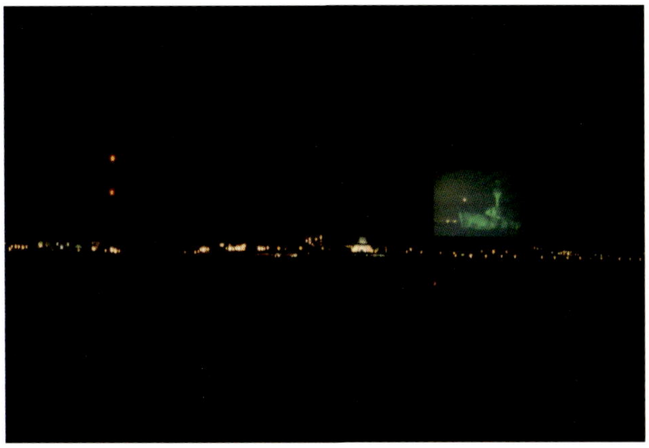 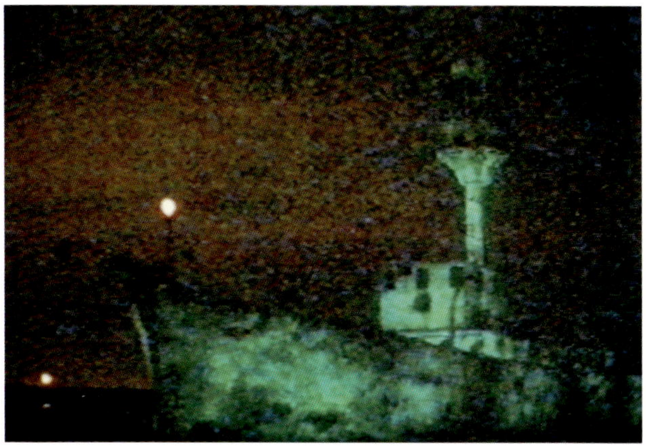

Video screening of *Ghost Ship*, Liverpool Biennial, 1999

automatized, Europeanized" ("*Ghost Ship*: Artist's Statement"). In the original performances of *Ghost Ship*, as well as in subsequent projections of the film in Swansea and Liverpool, Cross creates opportunities for gatherings in which all eyes look once again outward, to the sea. In this piece she reincarnates, along with the ship, the collective memories of a particular way of life being slowly eroded and forgotten.[74]

Where geological conditions made the construction of a lighthouse unfeasible, lightships were permanently moored offshore and equipped with beacons to warn other vessels of unseen dangers below the surface. A small crew of men lived on these ships for three weeks at a time, and their floating habitations became a site of congregation as community members brought supplies to the isolated crew.[75] Existence on these ships was dangerous; moored and engineless, they were highly vulnerable in stormy seas. All but three of Ireland's lightships have now been replaced by unmanned electronic buoys, one more instance of the trajectory of modern life away from human community and toward mechanization. *Ghost Ship* was designed to draw attention to what has been sacrificed in the process of modernization, and to rekindle some of that lost collective spirit and imagination.

On a personal level Cross recalls her childhood in Cork, growing up near the water and under the influence of her father's love of the sea. Among her memories are boat trips with her father out to a lightship moored offshore. *Ghost Ship* resonates with this specific personal and cultural history and with the many legends about phantom vessels familiar in the folklore of Ireland and other maritime cultures (Ryan 24). Cross remembers that as a child she saw them as "beacons of the imagination," and the spectacle she has created decades later re-illuminates the lightship in its imaginative as well as its material aspect.

Cross discovered a way to pay tribute to this fading history when she came across a decommissioned lightship moored in Dublin Bay. By a strange coincidence, the vessel turned out to be the same one that her father had photographed in the 1930s, and that she had visited as a child off the coast of Cork. The ship is identifiable by the name *Daunt* inscribed on its side, referring—as was the custom—to the name of the hidden reef to which it alerted incoming ships. Once a decommissioned ship is displaced from its original site and function, it takes back its own name—in this case, *Albatross*. If one thinks of Baudelaire's poem about that sea bird, the lightship is aptly named; like the poet's albatross, Cross's ship is awkward and ugly out of its proper element, and the artist longs to restore its grace and beauty by setting it afloat once more: "to reestablish it as a ship … to give it another phase in its life."[76] No longer tied literally or by name to a specific site, the vessel is given a more mysterious and mobile identity under the name *Ghost Ship*. In the past lightships were "vessels with a message" (Ryan 24); Cross's renamed phantom ship carries a new message of warning—not against dangerous reefs, but against forgetting.[77]

Like the handball alleys in *Chiasm*, the ship lures the artist with the beauty of the obsolete; its red, rusty hull is rendered more poignant by its disrepair and neglect. Cross immediately recognized its aesthetic potential as a beautiful piece of found sculpture, "a Richard Serra with history and heart." She is drawn to what the lightship retains of a collective memory of life lived more intimately in touch with nature—its beauties and its dangers—and to what it harbors of her own childhood memories of her father. But she is also drawn to the ambiguity of its present condition: no longer fulfilling its original function, the ship is suspended in time, awaiting some unknown future. Cross's goal in this project is not to restore the ship to its original state and function, creating a kind of floating heritage museum simulation. Rather, she wants to "illuminate" its disappearance. She evokes the lightship's history not to fix the past but to repeat its passing, to make visible the process of loss.

SEEING THE LIGHT

In *CRY* Cross approaches an alternative mode of representation, creating effects that combine the crude materiality of snake bodies and excavated earth with matter in its most intangible form—air. In *Ghost Ship* she weds the material remains of the lightship to the ephemerality of light. What does it mean to make representations not in paint or marble, but in light? The most familiar and literal example of this method, of course, is photography. In his theoretical analysis of this medium, Barthes describes the historical moment when "a scientific circumstance (the discovery that silver halogens were sensitive to light) made it possible to recover and print directly the luminous rays emitted by a variously lighted object. The photograph is literally an emanation of the referent"(1981, 80). Cross stresses this same quality in *Ghost Ship*, which absorbs and then emanates its own illumination. Unlike the photograph, however, the sight of Cross's ship is not the trace on light-sensitive paper of a now absent body but the body itself, performing its own appearance and disappearance. *Ghost Ship* constitutes its own indexical trace. Light in this work is not just a method of image-making, but the very heart of the matter.

In its original function the lightship was a defense against the unknown, against disaster, enlightening other ships to the presence of unseen dangers. Those parts of the ship that once cast a warning light—the high tower, the deck, and windows—are now mysteriously dark and abandoned. What was once a ship with an illuminated message has become an empty floating signifier. The ship is present in its materiality, but spectators see only a hollow shell, the ghostly skeleton of a ship.

There is a kind of seeing that illuminates an object in order to fix and master it with certainty in the glaring light of En*light*enment logic and knowledge. The light of *Ghost Ship* has a more uncertain and destabilizing quality. As Cross puts it, the lightship was "painted out and then retrieved by light, discontinuously" ("*Ghost Ship*: Artist's Statement"). As captured in the video, the light first flashes and then fades as the ship metamorphoses from rusty hull, to luminous phantom, to something resembling a strange and barely perceptible underwater beast. In contrast to the focused singularity of Enlightenment thought, the more complex alternations of illumination and endarkenment of the *Ghost Ship* multiply meanings and identities.

In metaphorical language that seems eerily appropriate to Cross's *Ghost Ship*, Barthes describes the effect in certain photographs of "a floating flash" (1981, 53), or what he calls the "*punctum*"—that detail in which an image escapes cultural codes, naming, and analysis, remaining accessible only to memory (1981, 42). Barthes encounters the *punctum* when some unintentional detail "shoots out of [the photograph] like an arrow, and pierces [him]" (1981, 26). He also feels its advent when time blurs and expands to include not only the "*that-has-been*" captured in the photographed image, but the future death that already haunts its subject, and even its spectator: "A sort of umbilical cord links the body of the photographed thing to my gaze: light, though impalpable, is here a carnal medium, a skin I share with anyone who has been photographed" (1981, 96, 81).

As a "carnal medium," the light of *Ghost Ship* offers each viewer a sensuous pleasure enhanced by the slow rhythm of its repeated cycles of light and dark. Cross's project makes use of the magical effect of flickering light that brings a fixed photographic image to life or a sequence of stills to animation. The phantom ship's alternating appearance and disappearance provokes the mesmerizing fascination of that "specific beat of desire" that Rosalind Krauss discovers in the work of "artists of the optical unconscious": "a desire that makes and loses its object in one and the same gesture, a gesture that is continually losing what it has found because it has only found what it has already lost" (1993, 216). The spectacle of *Ghost Ship* drew viewers back night after night to the shore of Dublin Bay, gathering them in communal stillness to witness this spectacle of desire and loss. The repeated cycles of light and dark in the original performance, and the repetition of that performance in subsequent film projections, make viewers conscious of time as duration measured in slow-motion alternations. And this is Cross's gift. The gift of time slowed down for the contemplation of loss, not as a singular catastrophe but as an ongoing process with its own poignant beauty.

In *CRY* death is present as something that has always already occurred; in *Ghost Ship* its advent is continuous. The lightship lingers, refined to the trace of a trace of something that, as Cross says, is "never quite dead." Through its various incarnations and displacements, the lightship lives on as a ghost, and as that other ghost—art.

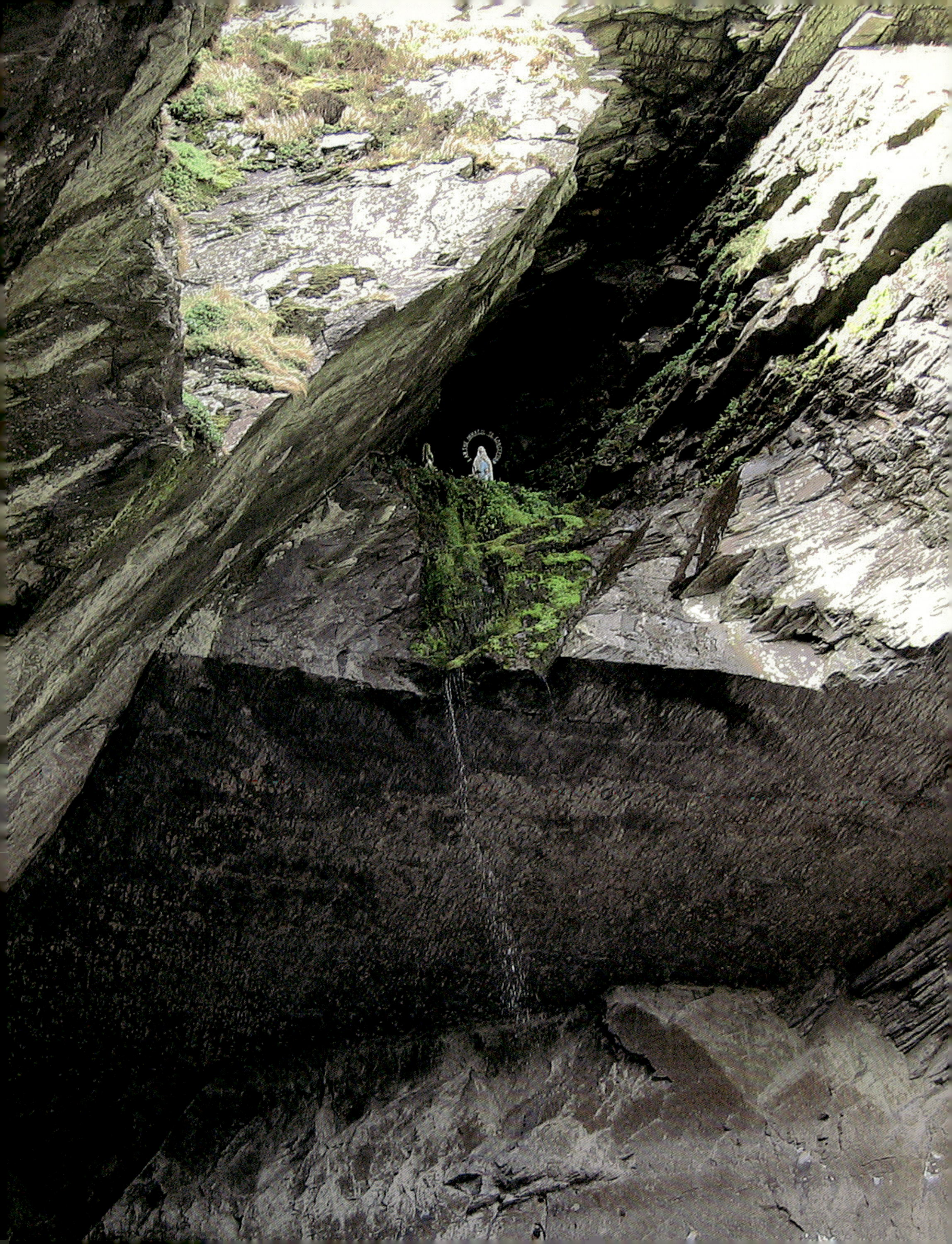

CODA

Beauty: The Admirable Face of Loss

> *Is beauty inseparable from the ephemeral and hence from mourning? Or else is the beautiful object the one that tirelessly returns following destructions and wars in order to bear witness that there is survival after death...? ...* [B]*eauty emerges as the admirable face of loss, transforming it in order to make it live.*
>
> —Julia Kristeva, *Black Sun: Depression and Melancholy* (1989)

Julia Kristeva suggests that we look to art for its healing power, for the "sublimatory hold [it offers] over the lost Thing" (1989, 97). An artist like Dorothy Cross, who is committed to dispossession and transmission, relinquishes that hold when the work is given over to the viewer for completion. Cross continues, with each new work, to "remake nothingness better than it was ... here and now and forever, for the sake of someone else" (99). This mediating aspect of Cross's art is evident in all of the works presented in *GONE*, but it is realized with striking power and beauty in her most recent site-specific project, *Stabat Mater*. Although this multi-media performance piece could not be included in this volume, I offer a brief description of it here because it bears witness to what is *GONE* and keeps faith with what continues.

FACING PAGE: Site of *Stabat Mater*, 2004, Virgin's Grotto at Slate Quarry, Valentia Island, Ireland

Off the western coast of Ireland, on the island of Valentia, there is a huge cave dug out of the side of a mountain, presided over by a statue of the Virgin Mary. Here, in collaboration with Dublin's Opera Theatre Company, for three nights in late August 2004, a small baroque ensemble and two singers performed the eighteenth-century sacred music of Giovanni Battista Pergolesi's *Stabat Mater* for an audience assembled outside the cave, huddled together against the cold and rain. The history embedded in this site recalls the slate mining industry that flourished on Valentia in the nineteenth century, providing slate for London's Houses of Parliament and for the Paris Opera House. A major collapse of the stone vault closed the mine in 1911, and a statue of the Virgin Mary was later installed in a high crevice in honor of the dead and surviving mine workers. The "Grotto" has become an attraction for tourists visiting the region, and serves occasionally as a pilgrimage site where Mass is performed. The slate industry on Valentia was reactivated in 1998, and the cave is once again a working industrial mine.

This site, where historical memorial, religious shrine, and industrial site converge, is further transformed by Cross into a Wagnerian stage set, its arched cathedral-like ceiling suggesting an archetypal and primal space. This mysterious opening into the earth is inhabited, anachronistically, by a modern structure the artist had installed—a large metal scaffolding supporting a video screen that can be moved along tracks running from the front to the back of the cave. The musical performance takes place in front of the screen, which displays a still close-up of a singer's open mouth. After the final "Amen," the performers wander back into the dark recesses of the cave, and the screen moves forward to the outer edge of the cave's mouth.

The lingering echo of the singers' voices is cut short as the video screen and soundtrack suddenly spring to life with the chaos and cacophony of industrial machinery digging, cutting, and polishing stone. The austere intensity of the *Stabat* performance is drowned out by the no less awesome power of machines and men at work. The video details not only the industrial production now brought back into operation, but also the natural surroundings. Rain sweeps over workers, sparse vegetation, and the Virgin Mary alike. Occasionally the video cuts from these scenes back to the singing mouth; straining, one can just hear (or imagine one hears) faint sounds of that pure soprano persisting even in such inhospitable circumstances. The camera travels inward to the cave's hidden depths where the singers sit by an internal pool, evocatively lit from below, a space of quiet contemplation surviving within the industrial clamor. These are the productive encounters Cross loves: of ancient and modern, inside and outside, darkness and illumination, noise and silence, industry and art, performers and viewers.

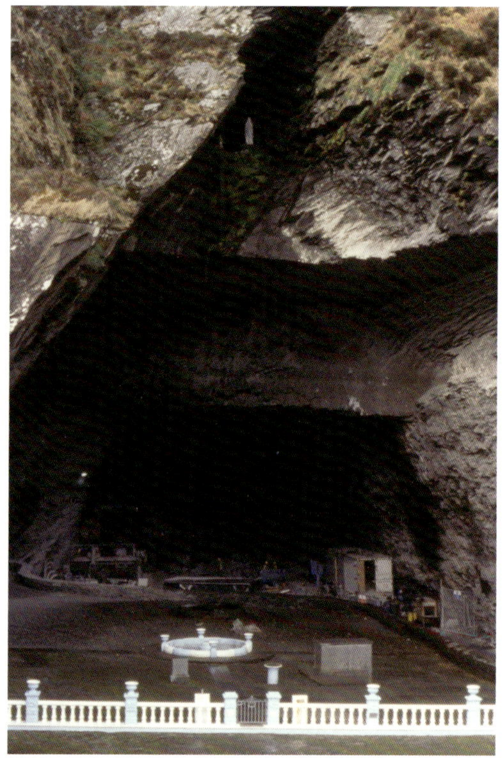

Site of *Stabat Mater,* 2004, Slate quarry, Valentia Island, Ireland

The image of the hole, which appears so often in Cross's work to mark absence and loss, looms large here as the gaping mouth of the cave. Yet that void has been transformed into the frame of a precious spectacle in which loss is not denied but set off like a jewel. Cross originally thought of using the cave as the setting for a performance of *Orfeo*; the poet-singer's descent to the underworld to retrieve his beloved Euridice would emphasize the role of art as mediating between life and death, art coaxing life out of the void. The final decision to stage *Stabat Mater* in the cave offers an experience of mediation that is at once more intimate and more public. The young Pergolesi, dying in monastic isolation, set to music this plea to the Virgin Mary to make one feel, as she feels it, the intensity of the Passion—to join in her mourning. In the language of the libretto, such communal suffering gathers Christ, Mary, and the faithful around the fertile wound that transforms shared suffering into a fountain of love, *dolorosa* into *fons amoris*.

Cross's staging of *Stabat Mater* gathers audience and performers together around a similarly fertile void where mediation is performed not by the Virgin Mary, but by the chiasmic intertwining of nature and industry, of music and visual image. In this complex and uncertain space where viewers find themselves simultaneously exposed and sheltered, Dorothy Cross generates an art of ritual, endurance, risk, and stunning reward.

* * * * * * * * * * * *

Works that belong to the genre of temporary site-specific art are always already haunted by their own ephemerality. Dorothy Cross's sited works are distinctive in that they never give up (or give up on) the ghost; they are sustained within and beyond the limits of their materialization in time and space. Cross's aesthetic practice of transformation and transmission remains enigmatic. How does her work make the return of the repressed productive and transformative? How does it keep faith with desire even in the face of desire's impossibility? How does she make the inevitable wounds of loss bearable and communicable to others? In the concrete immediacy of their realizations and in the aftereffects that linger like the glow of the *Ghost Ship*, Cross's site-specific works offer one response to these questions: Beauty. Her art achieves a singular beauty that is made more intense by its subtle articulation of loss, and more precious by its exposure to chance and risk. Such beauty carries *GONE*ness in front of it, transformed, as a gift to be shared. Cross's goal is not to leave viewers with a product, a final object of beauty, but to enable them to experience what she describes as a "a collision … a bursting into beauty" that reverberates beyond its disappearance. It is my hope that this volume and the exhibition it documents will echo some of those reverberations.

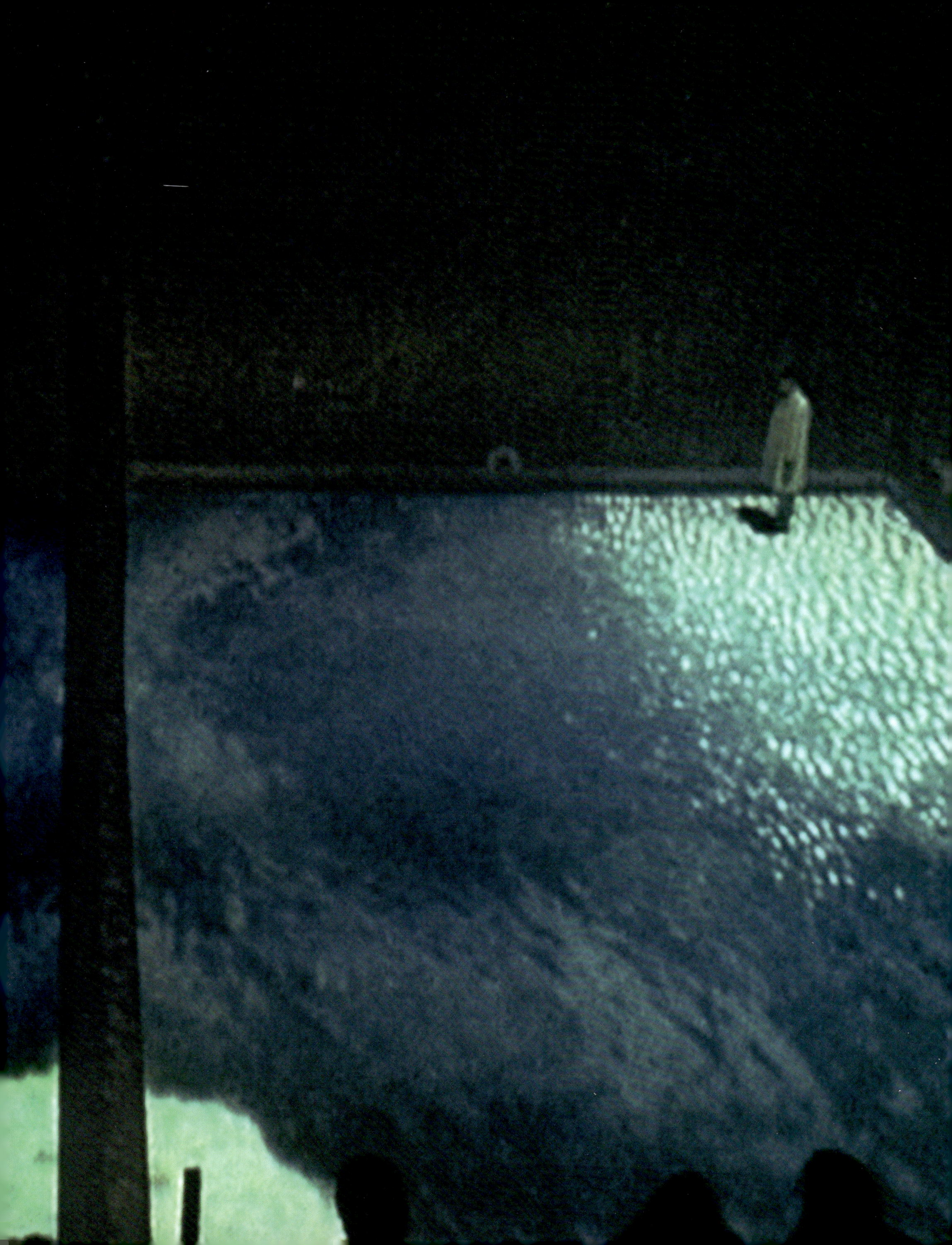

APPENDIX

Chiasm Libretto

The following collage-libretto was compiled by Dorothy Cross from:

Ariadne auf Naxos, by Strauss [AN]
Romeo et Juliet, by Gounod [RJ]
Manon Lescaut, by Puccini [ML]
Eugene Onegin, by Tchaikovsky [EO]
Dido and Aeneas, by Purcell [DA]
Orfeo ed Euridice, by Gluck [OEDE]
Carmen, by Bizet [C]
Les Troyens, by Berlioz [T]
L'Orfeo, by Monteverdi [LO]
Pêcheurs de Perles, by Bizet [PDEP]
Otello, by Verdi [O]

[Bold type indicates duet, conversation, or singing a phrase together.]

[AN] Ariadne: Ein Schönes war: heiss Theseus-Ariadne
und ging im licht und freute sich des Lebens.
There was a thing of beauty called Theseus-Ariadne
That walked in light and rejoiced in life.

FACING PAGE:
Chiasm, 1999

[ML] Des Grieux: Donna non vidi mai simile a questa!
A dirle; "io t'amo" a nuova vita l'alma mia si desta.
A maiden like this I have never beheld! To whisper to
Her 'I love you' would stir deep feelings within me.

[RJ] Juliet: Ahhh! Je veux vivre dans le rêve qui m'enivre.
Ah! I want to live in this intoxicating dream.

Romeo: L'Amour, l'amour! Oui, son ardeur a troublé tout mon être.
Love, love! Yes, its intensity has disturbed my very being!

Juliet: Où suis-je? Où suis-je?
Where am I? Where am I?

[DA] Aeneas: What shall lost Aeneas do?

[C]: Carmen: L'amour est un oiseau rebelle.
Love is a rebellious bird.

[EO] **Tatanya/Onegin: Tak blizko! Tak blizko!**
So close! So close!

[RJ] Romeo: Oh nuit divine! Je t'implore!
Laisse mon coeur à ce rêve enchanté.
O divine night! I implore you, leave my heart
To this enchanted dream!

[ML] Des Grieux: O tentatrice! É questo l'antico fascino che m'accieca!
Oh temptress! Here again the same chains that once bound me!

Manon: É fascino d'amor, cedi, cedi, son tua!
They are chains of love. Yield, I am yours!

[PDEP] Nadir: Je crois entendre encore caché sous les palmiers sa voix
tendre et sonore comme un chant des ramiers.
Hidden beneath the palms I seem to hear her tender, rich voice, like a song of doves.

[O] Desdemona: Oh com'è dolce il mormorare insieme;
Te ne rammenti?
Oh, how sweet it is to murmur together.
Don't you remember?

Otello/Desdemona: E tu m'amavi per le mie aventure ed io t'amavo per la tua pietà.
And you loved me for the dangers I had passed
And I loved you for your pity.

[ML] **Des Grieux/Manon: Dolcissimo soffrir!**
Sweet suffering!

[EO] Tatanya: Akh, shto so mnoi ya vsya goryu.
Ah! What's the matter with me! I am all on fire!

[LO] Orfeo: Tempo è ben d'approdar sù l'altra sponda?
Is the time right to cross to the other shore?

[DA] Dido: Remember me! Remember me!

[ML] In quelle trine morbide…nell'alcova
dorata v'é un silenzio gelido, mortal,
v'é un silenzio, un freddo che m'agghiaccia!
Behind the soft folds of those curtains in that golden alcove,
There is a cold deathly silence, an iciness that numbs me!

[EO] Tatanya: Kto ti? moi angel li khranitel, ili kovarni iskusitel?
Who are you? My guardian angel or a wily tempter?

[RJ] **Juliet: Ah, je n'ai pu m'en défendre! J'ai pris le péché pour moi!**
Ah, I could not help it. I have taken the sin upon myself.

Romeo: Pour apaiser votre émoi, vous plaît-il de me le rendre?
To allay your anxiety will you give it back to me?
Juliet: Non, je l'ai pris! Laissez-le-moi!
No, I have taken it, leave it with me!
Vous l'avez pris! Rendez-le-moi!
You have taken it! Give it back to me!

[EO] Lensky: Ya lyublyu vas, ya lyublyu vas, Olga,
kak odna bezumnaya dusha poeta tolko lyubit.
I love you, I love you Olga with that love known only to a poet's heart.

[C] Carmen: Oui … entre nous c'est fini.
Yes, all is over between us.

[ML] Des Grieux: Vedi, vedi son io che piango, io che imploro.
See, see, it is I who weep, I who implore you.

[ML] **Manon/Des Grieux: Dolcissimo soffrir!**
Sweet suffering!

[O] Desdemona: Al mio signor mi raccomanda…
muoio innocente… addio
I myself commend me to my lord.
I die innocent, farewell.

Otello: Addio.

[RJ] **Romeo/Juliet: Adieu, adieu, adieu, adieu! De cet adieu si douce est la tristesse.**
Goodbye, goodbye, goodbye, goodbye! Parting is such sweet sorrow.

[AN] Ariadne: Ein Schönes war**...**
A thing of beauty...

[RJ] Romeo: Salut! Tombeau! Sombre et silencieux.
Hail, gloomy and silent tomb.

[ML] Des Grieux: E nulla! Nulla! Arida landa...non un filo d'acqua...
O immoto cielo!
There is nothing, nothing! Arid waste, not a sign of water...
O immovable heavens!

[O] Desdemona: Salce! Salce! Salce!
Willow! Willow! Willow!

[PDEP] Nadir: De mon amie fleur endormie, au fond du lac silencieux,
J'ai vu dans l'onde claire et profonde étinceler le front joyeux et les doux yeux et les doux yeux!
At the bottom of the silent lake, in its clear depths
I saw glittering that happy brow, and those sweet eyes of my beloved sleeping flower.

[RJ] Juliet: O Romeo, pourquoi ce nom est-il le tien?
O Romeo, why have you been named thus?
La haine est le berceau de cet amour fatal!
Hatred is the cradle of this fatal love.
Que le cercueil soit mon lit nuptial!
Let the grave be my wedding bed!

[RJ] Romeo: De grâce demeurez!
For pity's sake stay!

[RJ] Juliet: Où suis-je?
Where am I?

[C] Don Juan: La fleur que tu m'avais jetée dans ma prison m'était restée...
The flower that you threw me remained with me in my prison.

[EO] Tatyana: Bit mozhet, eto vsyo pustoye, obman neopitnoi dushi.
Maybe this is all an empty dream, the self-deception of an inexperienced soul!

[ML] Manon: Sola, perduta, abbandonata in landa desolata! Orror!
Intorno a me s'oscura il ciel. Ahimè son sola!
Alone, lost, abandoned, on a desolate plain! Horror! The sky
Darkens about me. Alas! Alone.

[OEDE] Orfeo: Più non resisto…smanio…tremo…deliro!
I cannot resist…I am raving…trembling…delirious!

[T] **Dido/Aeneas: Nuit d'ivresse et d'extase infinie! Blonde Phoebé, grands astres de sa cour, versez sur nous votre lueur bénie. Fleurs des cieux, souriez à l'immortel amour.**
Night of intoxication and infinite extasy. Blond Phoebus, the great stars of your train pour on us your beneficent light. Flowers of the heavens, smile upon immortal love.

La fleur que tu m'avais jetée…

Bit mozhet, eto vsyo pustoye, obman neopitnoi dushi…

O immoto cielo!

Salce! Salce!

De mon ami fleur endormie…

O Romeo

La haine est le berceau

Sombre et silencieux…

Addio…

Ya lyublyu…

Oui, entre nous…

Non, je l'ai pris. Laissez-le-moi… Oh de cette nuit d'amour…

Et les doux yeux…

Adieu…

O com'è dolce … te ne rammenti…

L'amour….

O tentatrice…

Est fascina d'amore…cedi

Son io che piango…

Où suis-je?

Je t'implore…rêve enchantée…

Je veux vivre!

Sa voix tender et sonore…

Ahhhh!…

Io che imploro… Io che piango…

Ein Schönes war….. Donna non vidi mai….

Endnotes

[1] All quoted comments by Dorothy Cross are from my taped interviews or correspondence with the artist unless otherwise noted.

[2] "[T]he surrealists do not cling obsessively to the relics of the nineteenth century. Rather [the surrealist gaze] uncovers them for purposes of resistance *through* reenchantment.... [T]he surrealist concept of history ... ruins in order to recover through an active return of the repressed" (Foster 1993, 166).

[3] Simon Morley was the first to recognize Cross's affinity with this category of artists of the "optical unconscious"(16).

[4] For an interesting discussion of this category of "artists of the trace" see Merewether.

[5] Works such as Juan Muñoz's "monument commemorating nothing but the act of public remembrance" or Rachel Whiteread's "[s]mall scale cenotaphs (literally 'a tomb without a body')" (Hilty 17) exemplify this paradoxical notion of art as "a reliquary without a relic" (Caygill 53).

[6] Cross also participated by invitation in the Edge Biennial in London and Madrid (1992), the Istanbul Biennial (1997), and the Liverpool Biennial (1999). Her work is in the permanent collections of the Tate Modern in London, the Irish Museum of Modern Art in Dublin, and other public collections in Ireland, the U.S., and Europe.

[7] She was included in the 1994 ICA London exhibition "Bad Girls."

[8] See Warner's *Alone of all her Sex: The Myth and the Cult of the Virgin Mary* (New York: Knopf, 1976).

[9] For further discussions of the "udder" works see MacGiolla Leith, Smythe, Anson, Hutchinson, Higgins, and Walker.

[10] For a review of *figure* see Rachel Ni Chuinn.

[11] Freud imagines how "for a long time perhaps, living substance was ... being constantly created afresh and easily dying," as inanimate matter was alternately irritated into animate form and compelled to return to the peace of the inorganic (32).

[12] Ironically, *Tilted Arc* was eventually removed from its "permanent" site after great controversy, and Smithson's *Partially Buried Woodshed*, which was intended to "disintegrate naturally," was "declared an eyesore ... [and] bulldozed" (Wallis 97). The remains of the installation were carefully excavated by artist Renée Green over twenty years later.

13 See especially Suderberg's and de Oliveira's edited collections, and works by Buren, Crimp, Foster (1996), Krauss (1985), Kwon, Lippard, and Meyer.

14 On the critique of the museum see Buren, Crimp, Krauss (1985), and Sherman and Rogoff.

15 For an analysis of the more critical treatment of the museum by Hans Haacke, see Rosalyn Deutsche.

16 See Deleuze and Guattari (351-423), and applications of their theories by Kwon (2002, 159 and 165) and Meyer (32).

17 "But there is no neutral site. Every context has its frame and its ideological overtones" (Serra 127).

18 Writing about contemporary Irish landscape artists, Liam Kelly describes them as engaged "no longer [in] a topographical journey but a subterranean quest" (19).

19 Among the contemporary artists who have explored the prison as site and as concept, Jonathan Borofsky, Willie Cole, James Casebere, Rebecca Horn, and Antony Gormley have produced particularly compelling work.

20 Garton-Smith criticizes the tendency of traditional heritage museums to freeze time, isolating the past from any relation to the present or future, and she is encouraged by the shift in several heritage institutions towards "hot interpretation" that is provocative rather than explanatory. Cooke has clearly steered the Kilmainham site in the direction of this new museology.

21 The *Prison Sentences* exhibit at Eastern State Penitentiary (see Courtney and Gillens) is a perfect example of the intervention of artists in a prison site as a transitional bridge between its abandonment as a functioning prison and its subsequent restoration as a heritage museum, a site of education or propaganda. While the museum mediates between visitors and the history of the site through an allegedly neutral and objective presentation of knowledge, subversive art installations cut through that mediation to open up a space for the return of a repressed and more direct encounter with the lived prison experience. For a discussion of the "New Museology" and its implications for prison museums in particular, see Garton-Smith.

22 The history of Philadelphia's Eastern State Penitentiary provides an example of the deep irony that often accompanies the renovation and transformation of prison facilities into cultural monuments. Although the original designers' blueprint for the moral rehabilitation of prisoners had limited success, the building itself has achieved a more certain salvation under the protection of Philadelphia's architectural "Standards for Rehabilitation" (Tyler 9).

23 See John Conway's insightful commentary on the relationship of the Bible to body, word, and absence in Cross's *Bible* (22).

24 See Lydenberg (1998–99).

25 Some feminists have read the survival of this "maternal genealogy" in the rich cult of the Virgin Mary. Cross pays homage to this tradition in *Stabat Mater* (2004), discussed in the Coda to this volume.

26 Once these chalices were removed from the convent site and context they "transformed themselves" from participation in this *First Supper* to their role in a new work as *The Twelve Apostles,* lined up in a row on a narrow wooden bench.

27 Joyce (162) and Moore (14-15).

28 I draw here from the brilliant account of the extension of this medieval carnivalesque tradition into the modern period in Mikhail Bakhtin's *Rabelais and His World* (1-58).

29 See Wood.

30 *Putting the Land on the Map* (1989); *Language, Mapping and Power* and *Maps Elsewhere* (1996); *Atlas Mapping* (1997); *Orbis Terrarum* (2000); and *Mapping: The Process* (2002) are just a few of these recent international exhibitions.

[31] This analogy is also put to work by Joshua Neustein in the 1970s in a work called *Territorial Imperative.* Irit Rogoff describes this piece in which "a dog urinates on various sites in the Golan Heights and a border line is drawn which connects these sites and superimposes them on all of the more official borderlines which criss-cross the area, drawing attention to the arbitrariness of borders and to the demagogy of the political rhetoric which has served to harden them into immutable facts" (98).

[32] The effect here is somewhat reminiscent of Marcel Duchamp's *Anemic Cinema.*

[33] For particularly cogent overviews of how literary critics, in particular, were theorizing desire during the period when Cross was creating these works see Goodheart and Belsey. I am grateful to Goodheart for the Brown reference cited above.

[34] Staten is quoting here from *The Seminar of Jacques Lacan: Book I* (122).

[35] See Dubinsky for a fascinating interdisciplinary study of the history of Niagara Falls as a sexually charged tourist site.

[36] See, for example, Freud's "On the Universal Tendency to Debasement in the Sphere of Love."

[37] For a particularly cogent analysis of Jung's libido theory in the larger context of myth, see Von Hendy (120-23).

[38] See, for example, *Bath* (*Ebb* 2), *Kitchen Table* (*Irish Art Now* 39), and *Passion Bed* (*Power House* 20).

[39] See Kristeva (1984, 72-85).

[40] Textual citations from *Romeo and Juliet* (R/J), *Manon Lescaut* (ML) *and Eugene Onegin* (EO) are taken from the program notes of *Chiasm*. The other operas used in *Chiasm* are: *Ariadne auf Naxos* (AN), Strauss (1912), *Dido and Aeneas* (D/A), Purcell (1689); *Orfeo ed Euridice* (OEDE), Gluck (1762); *Carmen* (C), Bizet (1875); *Les Troyens* (LT), Berlioz (1890); *L'Orfeo* (LO), Monteverdi (1607); *Pêcheurs de Perles* (PDEP); Bizet (1863); and *Otello* (O), Verdi (1887). Quotations from Cross's comments in the program notes of *Chiasm* will appear in the main text as PN; quotations from the artist's proposal for the project will appear as "*Chiasm*: AP." The full text of *Chiasm*'s libretto appears in the Appendix to this volume.

[41] See Foster on "Outmoded Spaces" (1993, 157-91).

[42] Tim O'Flaherty notes this absence of legends about the Worm's Hole, and invites storytellers to fill the gap (180); but Robinson finds the narrative silence around the Worm's Hole appropriate to its air of mystery (63).

[43] In an earlier work, *Teacup,* Cross addresses the myth of Aran life explicitly. From Robert Flaherty's 1934 "documentary" film *Man of Aran,* Cross extracts the scene in which several men being filmed in a curragh on very rough seas are nearly drowned. She then vignettes a three-minute film loop of this short dramatic sequence into a fine English china teacup. I refer to this work briefly here to point out that Cross is clearly aware of the ideological weight that the Aran land and seascape, its challenging way of life, and its relationship to English rule carry in the Irish imagination. She wittily takes up some of the historical and political ramifications of that mythology in *Teacup*. The Aran element in *Chiasm* seems less concerned with the Irish specificity of the place, and more with its peculiar geological structure and its geometric form. In her own working notes and drawings for the piece, Cross juxtaposes Poll na bPéist with a series of images from cultures all over the world where stone and water are similarly inverted and intertwined—stone surrounded by water, water contained within stone. The affinity here is formal, abstract, even spiritual.

[44] "To project the film of Poll na bPéist into the void of the alley is simply bringing the illusion of the constant movement of nature into the man-made structure" ("*Chiasm*: AP").

[45] For an interesting reading of the "vertiginous" topography of O'Dowd's *Uaimh* series, see Bourke.

[46] See Kristeva on "amatory codes" (1987, 281), and Barthes on "the morphology of the lover's features" (1985a, 292).

47 Recognizing the inevitable paradox of desire, Goodheart describes it as "at once a vitality, an extravagance and a lack or absence" (21).

48 Hal Foster has argued that conventional spectacle denies loss by projecting "fetishistic images" (1985, 83) that represent a comforting totality hiding the shattering of the subject by desire and death. See also Bersani (51-79) and Barthes (1985a, 302-3).

49 Koestenbaum's critical meditation on opera gradually dissolves into textual fragments that both express and enact the impossibility of the desire for unity and wholeness. His study of opera is also a brilliant theoretical and experiential exploration of homosexual identity and desire.

50 The romantic-sounding title of this piece recalls the singularly unromantic film (and novel) of the same name, in which a chance encounter leads to misunderstanding, betrayal, and murder.

51 For an interesting brief analysis of the relationship between sexual desire, train travel, dislocation, and loss in Freud's life and theoretical work, see Diane O'Donoghue.

52 This piece appears in the *even* catalog as *Untitled* (35).

53 See Hess for a detailed review of this P.P.O.W. exhibition.

54 A similar but more explicitly feminist work by Barbara Kruger highlights the deadening construction of gender in a full skeletal X-ray adorned with feminine accessories such as high heels and jewelry. See "Memory is your image of perfection" (Kruger 38). Because Cross's emphasis is not on gender differences but on the commonality of our inheritance of mortality, she leaves the gender and sex of her figure indeterminate.

55 *Teacup* is not without such cultural associations: the teacup is a piece of fine English china that belonged to Cross's mother, and the scene of threatened shipwreck is taken from *Man of Aran*, Robert Flaherty's 1934 documentary film about the arduous life off the Western coast of Ireland. The piece, then, has national and historical, as well as personal, resonances.

56 Bronfen and Goodwin make specific reference here to Sarah Kofman's *Mélancolie de l'art* (Paris: Galilée, 1979).

57 In his own meditations on mortality, Walter Benjamin tries to construct an alternative "representational mode" that could articulate "the semantic void of material violence and death" (Schleifer 316). Benjamin's technique has been described as a "nonhierarchical dialectic," a "constellation" of quotations, or "metonymic mosaic" of ideas in which materiality is never dissolved into abstraction or idealization (Schleifer 316, 323-24). The interaction of the disparate elements in *CRY* produces in a visual register something very close to Benjamin's alternative textual method.

58 Cross pursued her interest in the relationship between scientific and artistic ways of thinking in a collaborative project on jellyfish with her brother Tom Cross, Professor of Zoology. Their work, funded by the SciArt consortium in the UK, resulted in a piece called *Medusae.*

59 Although Cross knows this Duras text well, it doesn't figure directly in her work. She does make explicit use of another Duras text in a 1999 work entitled *lit-bed-leaba* for which she had a short erotic passage from Duras' *A Man Sitting in the Corridor* translated into Irish. This excerpt was then carved onto the wooden base of a bed. The explicit story of sexual desire remains obscured in its Irish translation.

60 See Donna Haraway for a brilliant discussion of the art, science, and politics of taxidermy in the dioramas of the Museum of Natural History. In the dioramas, the animals seems to have "transcended mortal life," a transformation "made possible only by their death and literal re-presentation" (30). See Wainwright on taxidermy in contemporary art and its relation to religious reliquary.

61 Several years ago Cross conceived of a work entitled *Hold*. In her vision of this project, an open barge is fitted with an interior plexiglass tank; inside the tank a figure seems to be sleeping in a bed as a

nearby bathtub slowly overflows and begins to fill the tank with clear water. As the man continues his peaceful sleep (breathing through an invisible tiny pipe), dirty water from the surrounding river is pumped into the hold around the plexiglass room. The audience witnesses, probably with growing anticipation and anxiety, the approaching and inevitable contamination of the interior chamber. The illuminated barge is plunged into darkness just before the crucial moment of overflow. The beautifully rusted barge that inspired this piece became unavailable, and *Hold* never happened.

62 For images and analysis of the "udder" works, see the catalogue of Cross's exhibition *even* (1996).

63 For images and discussion of Cross's use of snakes in her work, see the catalogue of Cross's exhibition *even* (1996).

64 Danby's source is *Book of Revelation* 6: 12-15: "And I beheld, when he had opened the sixth seal, and lo! There was a great earthquake; and the sun became black … and the moon became as blood. And the stars of heaven fell unto the earth…. And the heaven departed … and every mountain and island were moved out of their places."

65 Francis Greenacre quotes Danby's description of the painting's theme as "'a subject that I fear I ought to blush for venturing upon, but though it cannot be painted with entire truth, yet it is the grandest subject for a picture'" (99).

66 As Bourke and Bhreathnach-Lynch explain, "the picture is not solely a visual interpretation of the opening of the sixth seal, but is also a statement against slavery, the abolishment of which was a burning issue in the 1820s" (90).

67 See Benjamin.

68 The modern secular attitude toward death that viewers encounter in *CRY* is also at work in Marguerite Duras' texts, which have been described as exploring "the conniving, voluptuous, bewitching contemplation of death within us, of the wound's constancy" (Kristeva 1989, 236).

69 See Miller on this Lacanian concept.

70 Barthes defines "l'air" negatively as "not a schematic, intellectual datum…. Nor is the air a simple analogy … as is 'likeness' (1981, 109). "L'air" opens up an alternative mode of representation.

71 One also hears this language in the work of Marguerite Duras, who writes the silent cry that is our truest response to death and loss. Duras' language of loss has been described as an "opera" in which "[e]verything is stripped to the most obscene purity…. Scarcely a sound" (Forrester 27). One hears it, as well, in the "insomniac narrative voice that opens like a void … that speaks as one vast, continuous buzzing, a dull roar in the skull" in the work of Samuel Beckett (Critchley 175).

72 There are parallels here, of course, to the bureaucratic challenges faced by Christo and Jeanne-Claude in their site-specific projects.

73 Displayed in an art space, to which it returns for McMullen Museum's *GONE* exhibition, the *Ghost Ship* video and model ship invite a more intellectual engagement with problems of presentation and representation. In such a setting, viewers consider the problematic relationship between model and original, the impact of differences in medium and display, the effect of sequence and series, and the distinction between the iconic miniature replica and the indexical traces of the lightship's fading image on film. These conceptual challenges replace the communal experience available at the original spectacle in Dublin Bay. For an interesting review of the 2003 Boston showing, see Sherman.

74 Cross's video *Endarken* similarly dramatizes the disappearance of a certain Irish rural way of life, its beauties and its hardships. An image of a ruined famine cottage is slowly obliterated by an expanding black dot that eventually covers the entire screen. See Lydenberg 2003.

75 Virginia Woolf's *To The Lighthouse*, of course, gives readers a glimpse of the similar role played by light*houses* in the public and private imagination.

[76] "Often, for their amusement, sailors catch albatross, those vast birds of the seas.... No sooner have the sailors stretched them out on the deck than those kings of the azure, awkward and ashamed, let their long white wings trail painfully by their side.... How ungainly, how contemptible the winged traveler becomes, how laughable and graceless, he who but a moment ago was so full of beauty" [Prose translation of Baudelaire's "L'Albatros," by Francis Scarfe] (Baudelaire 8).

[77] Ryan distinguishes insightfully between Cross's site-specific piece and other contemporary monuments or postmodern works about memory that are often "prone to kitsch and overly personal or narcissistic." He finds in *Ghost Ship* an "unusually convincing synthesis of private themes and public symbolism" (24). *Ghost Ship* stages a "public viewing" of historical change, a "communal curtain call, a farewell to a piece of industrial era apparatus," as well as a more personal and poetic experience merging "the mechanical and the mnemonic"(Ryan 25).

Works Cited

Anson, Libby. “Cross Talk.” *Art Monthly* 203 (February 1997): 20-21.

Bakhtin, Mikhail. *Rabelais and His World*. Trans. Helene Iswolsky. Cambridge, Mass.: MIT Press, 1968.

Bal, Mieke. *Quoting Carravagio: Contemporary Art, Preposterous History*. Chicago: University of Chicago Press, 1999.

Barreca, Regina. “Writing as Voodoo: Sorcery, Hysteria, and Art.” *Death and Representation*. Eds. Sarah Webster Goodwin and Elisabeth Bronfen. Baltimore: Johns Hopkins University Press, 1993. 174-91.

Barthes, Roland. *Camera Lucida: Reflections on Photography*. Trans. Richard Howard. New York: Hill and Wang, 1981.

________. *Empire of Signs*. Trans. Richard Howard. New York: Hill and Wang, 1982.

________. *Grain of the Voice: interviews 1962-1980*. Trans. Linda Coverdale. New York: Hill and Wang, 1985a.

________. *The Responsibility of forms: critical essays on music, art, representation*. Trans. Richard Howard. New York: Hill and Wang, 1985b.

Baudelaire, Charles. *Baudelaire: Selected Verse*. London: Penguin Books, 1961.

Bazin, André. *What is Cinema? Vol. 1*. Trans. Hugh Gray. Berkeley: University of California Press, 1967.

Beckett, Samuel. *Waiting for Godot*. New York: Grove Press, 1954.

Belsey, Catherine. *Desire: Love Stories in Western Culture*. Oxford, UK: Blackwell, 1994.

Benjamin, Walter. “The Work of Art in the Age of Mechanical Reproduction.” *Illuminations*. Trans. Harry Zohn. Ed. Hannah Arendt. New York: Schocken Books, 1969. 219-53.

Bersani, Leo. *The Freudian Body: Psychoanalysis and Art*. New York: Columbia University Press, 1986.

Blake, William. *Selected Poetry and Prose of William Blake*. Ed. Northrop Frye. New York: Random House, 1938.

Bonaventura, Paul. “even: Dorothy Cross.” *even: recent work by Dorothy Cross*. Eds. Tessa Jackson and Josephine Lanyon. Bristol: Arnolfini, 1996. 13-20.

Bond, Anthony. “Introduction” and “TRACE: A Historical Contextualization.” *TRACE: 1st Liverpool Biennial of International Contemporary Art*. Curator Anthony Bond. Liverpool: Liverpool Biennial of Contemporary Art and Tate Gallery, Liverpool, 1999. 11-21.

Bourke, Angela. "Exploring the Darkness: Gwen O'Dowd's *Uaimh*." *Re/Dressing Cathleen: Contemporary Works from Irish Women Artists*. Eds. Jennifer Grinnell and Alston Conley. Boston: McMullen Museum of Art, Boston College, 1997. 69-73.

Bourke, Mary and Síghle Bhreathnach-Lynch. *Discover Irish Art at the National Gallery of Dublin: A Reference Book on Irish Art*. Dublin: National Gallery of Ireland, 1999.

Breton, André. *Mad Love*. Trans. Mary Ann Caws. Lincoln: University of Nebraska Press, 1987.

Bronfen, Elisabeth and Sarah Webster Goodwin. "Introduction." *Death and Representation*. Eds. Goodwin and Bronfen. Baltimore: Johns Hopkins University Press, 1993. 3-25.

Brooks, Peter. *Reading for the Plot: Design and Intention in Narrative*. New York: A.A. Knopf, 1984.

Brown, Norman O. *Life Against Death*. New York: Modern Library, 1959.

Bullfinch, Thomas. *Bulfinch's Mythology: The Age of Fable*. Garden City, NY: International Collections Library, 1968.

Buren, Daniel. "Function of the Museum." *Artforum* 12.1 (September 1973): 68.

Cavell, Stanley. *In quest of the ordinary: lines of skepticism and romanticism*. Chicago: University of Chicago Press, 1988.

Caygill, Howard. "Reliquary Art: Orlan's serial operation." *Time and the Image*. Ed. Carolyn Bailey Gill. Manchester, UK: Manchester University Press, 2000. 48-57.

Chuinn, Rachel Ni. "Review: Dublin 1." *Circa* 99 (Spring 2002): 50-51.

Clément, Catherine. *Opera, or, The Undoing of Women*. Trans. Betsy Wang. Minneapolis: University of Minnesota Press, 1988.

Colpitt, Frances. "An Interview with Dorothy Cross," *[Dorothy Cross 96.2]*. San Antonio: [ArtPace]: A Foundation for Contemporary Art, 1996.

Conway, John. [untitled]. *even: recent work by Dorothy Cross*. Eds. Tessa Jackson and Josephine Lanyon. Bristol: Arnolfini, 1996. 22.

Cotter, Holland. "Psychic Healing in the Uncanny." *New York Times* (17 April 1998): B44.

Courtney, Julie and Todd Gilens, eds. *Prison Sentences: The Prison as Site/The Prison as Subject*. Philadelphia: Moore College of Art and Design, 1995.

Crimp, Douglas. "Redefining Site-specificity." *Richard Serra*. Ed. Hal Foster with Gordon Hughes. Cambridge, Mass.: MIT Press, 2000. 147-74.

Critchley, Simon. *Very little—almost nothing: death, philosophy, literature*. London: Routledge, 1997.

Cross, Dorothy. *Dorothy Cross: Ebb*. Eds. Patrick T. Murphy and Tom Weir. Dublin: Douglas Hyde Gallery, 1988.

________. *Dorothy Cross: Power House*. Ed. Melissa Feldman. Philadelphia: Institute of Contemporary Art, University of Philadelphia, 1991.

________. *even: recent work by Dorothy Cross*. Eds. Tessa Jackson and Josephine Lanyon. Bristol: Arnolfini, 1996.

________."*Chiasm:* Artist's Proposal." unpublished.

________."*Chiasm:* Program Notes." unpublished.

________."*Ghost Ship:* Artist's Statement." unpublished.

Cross, Dorothy and Lewis de Soto. "Heat and Cold: Projects by Dorothy Cross and Lewis de Soto at ArtPace in San Antonio." *Tate: The Art Magazine* 10 (Winter 1996): 48-51.

Deleuze, Gilles and Félix Guattari. *A Thousand Plateaus: Capitalism and Schizophrenia*. Minneapolis: University of Minnesota Press, 1987.

De Oliveira, Nicolas. *Installation Art*. Washington, DC: Smithsonian Institution Press, 1994.

Deutsche, Rosalyn. "Property Values: Hans Haacke, Real Estate, and the Museum." *Hans Haacke: Unfinished Business*. Ed. Brian Wallis. New York: The New Museum Of Contemporary Art, 1987. 20-37.

Dollimore, Jonathan. *Death, Desire and Loss in Western Culture*. London: Routledge, 1998.
Donne, John. *John Donne's Poetry: authoritative texts, criticism*. Ed. Arthur L. Clements. New York: Norton, 1992.
Dubinsky, Karen. *The Second Greatest Disappointment: Honeymooning and Tourism at Niagara Falls*. New Brunswick, NJ: Rutgers University Press, 1999.
Duchamp, Marcel. *The Writings of Marcel Duchamp*. Eds. Michel Sanouillet and Elmer Peterson. New York: Da Capo Press, 1973.
Dunne, Aidan."Sting in the Tale." *The Irish Times* (12 April 2003): 55.
Duras, Marguerite. *The Malady of Death*. Trans. Barbara Bray. New York: Grove Press, 1986,
Forrester, Viviane. "Territories of the Cry." *Critical Essays on Marguerite Duras*. Ed. Bettina L. Knapp. London: G.K. Hall, 1998. 26-28.
Foster, Hal. *Compulsive Beauty*. Cambridge, Mass.: MIT Press, 1993.
________. "Death in America." *October* 75 (Winter 1996): 36-59.
________. *Recodings: Art, Spectacle, Cultural Politics*. Seattle: Bay Press, 1985.
________. *The Return of the Real: The Avant-Garde at the End of the Century*. Cambridge, Mass.: MIT Press, 1996.
________."The Un/making of Sculpture." *Richard Serra*. Ed. Hal Foster with Gordon Hughes. Cambridge, Mass.: MIT Press, 2000. 175-200.
Foucault, Michel. "The Eye of Power." *Foucault Live: Interviews, 1961-84*. Ed. Sylvère Lotringer. Trans. Lysa Hochroth and John Johnston. New York: Semiotexte, 1989. 226-40.
Fowler, Joan. "Voyages of Transformation." *Dorothy Cross: Ebb*. Eds. Patrick T. Murphy and Tom Weir. Dublin: Douglas Hyde Gallery, 1988. 3-21.
Freud, Sigmund. *Beyond the Pleasure Principle* (1920). New York: Norton, 1961.
________. "Femininity (1933)." *The Standard Edition of the Complete Psychological Works of Sigmund Freud*, vol. 22. Ed. and trans. James Strachey. London: Hogarth Press, 1953. 112-35.
________. "On the Universal Tendency to Debasement in the Sphere of Love (1912)." *SE,* vol.11. Ed. and trans. James Strachey. London: Hogarth Press, 1953. 179-80.
________. "The 'Uncanny' (1919)." *SE* vol. 17. Ed. and trans. James Strachey. London: Hogarth Press, 1953. 219-252.
Garton-Smith, Jennifer. "The Prison Wall: Interpretation Problems for Prison Museums." *Open Museum Journal* vol 2: 1-13.
"Ghostly Goings On." [anon. Review] *The Irish Times* (6 February 1999): 61.
Goodheart, Eugene. *Desire and Its Discontents.* New York: Columbia University Press, 1991.
Graham-Dixon, Andrew. "Darkness Visible." *The Independent Magazine* (11 February 1989): 36-42.
Greenacre, Francis. *Francis Danby, 1793-1861*. London: The Tate Gallery, 1988-89.
Hansen, Miriam. "Benjamin, Cinema and Experience: 'The Blue Flower' in the Land of Technology." *New German Critique* 40 (Winter l987): 179-224.
Haraway, Donna. "Teddy Bear Patriarchy: Taxidermy in the Garden of Eden, New York City 1908-1936." *Primate Visions: Gender, Race, and Nature in the World of Modern Science*. New York: Routledge, 1989. 26-58.
Healy, Paul. *Gaelic Games and the Gaelic Athletic Association.* Cork: Mercier Press, 1998.
Heaney, Seamus. *Death of a Naturalist.* London: Faber and Faber, 1966.
Hess, Elizabeth. "Cross Hatching." *The Village Voice* (16 May 1995): 86.
Higgins, Judith. "Report From Ireland: Art From The Edge (Part I)." *Art In America* 83 (December 1995): 37-43.

Hilty, Greg. "Thrown Voices." *Doubletake: Collective Memory & Current Art.* Eds. Lynne Cooke, Bice Curiger, Greg Hilty. London: The South Bank Center and Parkett, 1992. 14-19.

Irigaray, Luce. "The bodily encounter with the mother." Trans. David Macey. *The Irigaray Reader.* Ed. Margaret Whitford. Oxford: Blackwell, 1991. 34-46.

________. "The Invisible of the Flesh: A Reading of Merleau-Ponty, *The Visible and the Invisible." An Ethics of Sexual Difference.* Trans. Carolyn Burke and Gillian C. Gill. Ithaca: Cornell University Press, 1993. 151-84.

Isaak, JoAnna. *Laughter Ten Years After.* Geneva, NY: Hobart and William Smith Colleges Press, 1995.

Isaak, JoAnna and Dorothy Cross. "Dorothy Cross/JoAnna Isaak." *Circa* 75 (Spring 1996): 35-42.

Jacob, Mary Jane. "Making History in Charleston." *Places with a Past: New Site-Specific Art at Charleston's Spoleto Festival.* Curator, Mary Jane Jacob. New York: Rizzoli, 1991. 13-19.

Jarry, Alfred. *The Ubu Plays.* London: Methuen, 1968.

Jones, Rachel. "Transformations." *Hypatia* 15.2 (2000): 151-59.

Joyce, James. *Ulysses.* New York: Random House, 1961.

Kaye, Nick. *Site-specific Art: Performance, Place and Documentation.* London: Routledge, 2000.

Kelly, Liam. *Thinking Long: Contemporary Art in the North of Ireland.* Kinsale: Gandon Editions, 1996.

Koestenbaum, Wayne. *The Queen's Throat: Opera, Homosexuality, and the Mystery of Desire.* New York: Poseidon Press, 1993.

Krauss, Rosalind E. *The Optical Unconscious.* Cambridge, Mass.: MIT Press, 1993.

________. *The Originality of the Avant-Garde and Other Modernist Myths.* Cambridge, Mass.: MIT Press, 1985.

Kristeva, Julia. *Black Sun: Depression and Melancholy.* Trans. Leon S. Roudiez. New York: Columbia University Press, 1989.

________. "Interview with Julia Kristeva." *Women Analyze Women: In France, England and the United States.* Eds. Elaine Baruch and Lucienne Sarrano. New York: NYU Press, 1988. 129-45.

________. *Revolution in Poetic Language.* Trans. Margaret Waller. New York: Columbia University Press, 1984.

________. *Strangers to Ourselves.* Trans. Leon S. Roudiez. New York: Columbia University Press, 1991.

________. *Tales of Love.* Trans. Leon S. Roudiez. New York: Columbia University Press, 1987.

Kruger, Barbara. *Love for Sale: The Words and Pictures of Barbara Kruger.* New York: Abrams, 1990.

Kwon, Miwon. *One Place after Another: Site-specific Art and Locational Identity.* Cambridge, Mass.: MIT Press, 2002.

________. "The Wrong Place." *Art Journal* 59.1 (Spring 2000): 33-43.

Lacan, Jacques. "The agency of the letter in the unconscious or reason since Freud (1966)." *Ecrits: A Selection.* Trans. Alan Sheridan. New York: Norton, 1977. 146-78.

________. *Feminine Sexuality: Jacques Lacan and the école freudienne.* Eds. Juliet Mitchell and Jacqueline Rose. New York: Pantheon Books, 1982.

Lechte, John. "Art, Love and Melancholy in the Work of Julia Kristeva." *Abjection, Melancholia and Love: The Work of Julia Kristeva.* Eds. John Fletcher and Andrew Benjamin. New York: Routledge, 1990. 24-41.

Leith, Caoimhin MacGiolla. "Dorothy Cross: Model Arts Center." *Artforum* vol. 36 (October 1997): 109-10.

Lippard, Lucy R. *The Lure of the Local: Senses of Place in a Multicentered Society.* New York: New Press, 1997.

Lydenberg, Robin. "Dorothy Cross: Beyond Feminism." *Eire/Ireland* XXXIII 3 & 4; XXXIV.1 (Fall/Winter 1998 and Spring 1999): 212-26.

________. "From Icon to Index: Some Contemporary Visions of the Irish Stone Cottage." *Eire/Land.* Ed. Vera Kreilkamp. Boston: McMullen Museum of Art, Boston College, 2003. 127-33.

________. "Ways of Seeing: Recent work by Dorothy Cross." *Contemporary* (January 2002): 26-31.

Macritchie, Lynn. "Report from London: Uneasy Rooms." *Art in America* 81 (October 1993): 60-61.

Malbert, Roger. "Fetishism and Form in Contemporary Art." *Fetishism: Visualizing Power and Desire.* Ed. Anthony Shelton. London: South Bank Center, 1995. 89-124.

Maxton, Hugh. "In a State." *Circa* 58 (July/August 1991): 45-6.

McGonagle, Declan. "Renegotiating the Given." *Irish Art Now: From the Poetic to the Political.* Eds. Declan McGonagle, Fintan O'Toole, Kim Levin. London: Merrell Holberton Publishers Ltd., 1999. 9-20.

Melchionne, Kevin. "Rethinking Site-specificity." *Art Criticism* 12.2 (1997): 36-49.

Merewether, Charles. "A Lasting Impression." *TRACE: 1st Liverpool Biennial of International Contemporary Art.* Curator Anthony Bond. Liverpool: Liverpool Biennial of Contemporary Art and Tate Gallery, Liverpool, 1999. 167-70.

Merleau-Ponty, Maurice. "The Intertwining—The Chiasm." *The Visible and the Invisible, followed by working notes.* Trans. Alphonso Lingis. Ed. Claude Lefort. Evanston, Ill.: Northwestern University Press, 1968. 130-55.

________. "Eye and Mind." *The Primacy of Perception and Other Essays in Phenomenological Psychology, the Philosophy of Art, History and Politics.* Trans. Carleton Dallery. Evanston, Ill.: Northwestern University Press, 1964. 159-90.

Meyer, James. "The Functional Site: or, The Transformation of Site-specificity." *Space, Site, Intervention: Situating Installation Art.* Ed. Erika Suderberg. Minneapolis: University of Minnesota Press, 2000. 23-37.

Miller, Jacques-Alain. "Microscopie." *Ornicar* 47 (1988): 46-64.

Moore, Thomas. *Selections from Moore's Irish Melodies.* Cork: Ossian Publications, 1986.

Morley, Simon. "Irish Art International." *Art Monthly* 196 (May 1996): 13-16.

Muller, John P. and William J. Richardson. *Lacan and Language: A Reader's Guide to "Ecrits."* Madison: International Universities Press, 1982.

Murphy, Patrick. "Foreword." *Dorothy Cross: Power House.* Ed. Melissa Feldman. Philadelphia: Institute of Contemporary Art, University of Pennsylvania, 1991. 5.

Nolan, J.C.M. "Regarding Danby's Apocalyptic Art." (article on file at the National Gallery of Ireland): 1-8.

O'Connor, Patrick J. *Some Guides to the Irish Scene.* (*Irish Landscape Series,* no.2). Newcastle West: Oireacht na Mumhan Books, 1992.

O'Donoghue, Diane. "On the Train(ing)." *Journal for the Psychoanalysis of Culture and Society* (Fall 2001): 313-15.

O'Flaherty, Tom. "Coming Home." [excerpt from *Aranmen All* (1934)]. *An Aran Reader.* Eds. Breandan and Ruairi Ó hEithir. Dublin: Lilliput Press, 1991. 176-83.

Oliver, Kelly. "The Look of Love." *Hypatia* 16.3 (2001): 56-78.

________. *Reading Kristeva: Unraveling the Double-bind.* Bloomington: Indiana University Press, 1993.

O'Toole, Fintan. "In a State." *In a State: An exhibition in Kilmainham Gaol on National Identity.* Dublin: Project Arts Centre, 1991. 11-14.

Owens, Craig. *Beyond Recognition: Representation, Power, and Culture.* Berkeley: University of California Press, 1992.

Phelan, Peggy. *Mourning Sex: Performing Public Memories.* New York: Routledge, 1997.

Rabelais, François. *The Histories of Gargantua and Pantagruel.* Trans. J.M. Cohen. London: Penguin Classics, 1955.

Ragland, Ellie. "Lacan, the Death Drive, and the Dream of the Burning Child." *Death and Representation*. Eds. Sarah Webster Goodwin and Elisabeth Bronfen. Baltimore: Johns Hopkins University Press, 1993. 80-102.

Robinson, Hilary. "Beauty, the Universal, the Divine: Irigaray's Re-valuings." *Women Artists and Modernism*. Ed. Katy Deepwell. Manchester, UK: Manchester University Press, 1998. 159-74.

Robinson, Tim. *Stones of Aran: pilgrimage*. London: Viking, 1986.

Rogoff, Irit. *Terra Infirma: Geography's Visual Culture*. London: Routledge, 2000.

Rose, Jacqueline. "Introduction-II." *Feminine Sexuality: Jacques Lacan and the école freudienne*. Eds. Juliet Mitchell and Jacqueline Rose. New York: Pantheon Books, 1982. 27-57.

Ryan, Raymond. "Memory Vessel." *Blueprint* 158 (February 1999): 24-5.

Scarry, Elaine. *The Body in Pain*. New York: Oxford University Press, 1985.

Schleifer, Ronald. "Walter Benjamin and the Crisis of Representation: Multiplicity, Meaning, and Athematic Death." *Death and Representation*. Eds. Sarah Webster Goodwin and Elisabeth Bronfen. Baltimore: Johns Hopkins University Press, 1993. 312-33.

Serra, Richard. *Writings/Interviews*. Chicago: University of Chicago Press, 1994.

Sherman, Daniel and Irit Rogoff, eds. *Museum Culture: Histories, Discourses, Spectacles*. Minneapolis: University of Minnesota Press, 1994.

Sherman, Mary. "'Mystic' embraces haunting images." *Boston Herald* (9 February 2003): 65.

Smyth, Cherry and Laura Cottingham. *Bad Girls*. London: Institute of Contemporary Art, 1993.

Staten, Henry. *Eros in Mourning: Homer to Lacan*. Baltimore: Johns Hopkins University Press, 1995.

Suderberg, Erika. "Introduction: On Installation and Site-specificity." *Space, Site, Intervention: Situating Installation Art*. Ed. Erika Suderberg. Minneapolis: University of Minnesota Press, 2000. 1-22.

Tomkins, Calvin. *Duchamp: A Biography*. New York: Henry Holt, 1996.

Tyler, Richard. "Eastern State Penitentiary: From Closure to 'Prison Sentences.'" *Prison Sentences: The Prison as Site/The Prison as Subject*. Eds. Julie Courtney and Todd Gilens. Philadelphia: Moore College of Art and Design, 1995. 8-11.

Von Hendy, Andrew. *The Modern Construction of Myth*. Bloomington: Indiana University Press, 2002.

Wainwright, Lisa. "From Norman Bates to Annette Messager: Taxidermy for a Reason." *The New Art Examiner* (May 1966): 19-22, 37.

Walker, Dorothy. *Modern Art in Ireland*. Dublin: Lilliput Press, 1997.

Wallis, Brian. "Excavating the 1970s." *Art in America* (September 1997): 97-99, 122.

Wood, Dennis. *The Power of Maps*. New York and London: Guilford Press and Cooper Hewitt Museum of Art, 1992.

Acknowledgements

I am grateful to Boston College, colleagues, friends, and family for their support of this project. I am most indebted to the earliest readers of the manuscript, Steven Lydenberg and Anne Ferry, and Susannah Hollister, for their invaluable insights and encouragement. This project was begun under the influence of Prof. Adele Dalsimer, who first introduced me to Cross's work, and has been brought to fruition by the creative vision of Nancy Netzer and Alston Conley. Without their commitment to supporting faculty research, promoting interdisciplinary pedagogy, and recognizing important work by contemporary artists, *GONE* would never have appeared. Stephen Vedder's talent and professionalism made possible the high quality of the images reproduced in this volume and in the exhibition. Special thanks to Prof. Vera Kreilkamp for her always astute suggestions for manuscript revisions, and for her creation of a course in contemporary Irish culture built around the Cross exhibition at the McMullen Museum. Naomi Blumberg lent her sharp eye to copyediting the manuscript, helped me with image selection, and co-coordinated the exhibition with Alston Conley. Thanks to Keith Ake for the refined eye that created this beautiful catalogue design. Ultimately, my warmest thanks go to the artist, Dorothy Cross, who has been remarkably generous in sharing her time, her thoughts, and her work.

— ROBIN LYDENBERG

March 11, 2005. Dublin

I have just come out of a recording session of Pergolesi's *Stabat Mater,* with singers and players re-recording the beautiful music that got obliterated by wild weather in the cave during the live performance. It reminds me how complex all these projects are and how reliant on the multiple talents and passions of others. None of these works could have happened without the support, talent, and effort of many people, all of whom I thank. I would especially like to thank Robin Lydenberg for finding the work and making such a wonderful excavation of it with her mind. Also Nancy Netzer and the staff at McMullen Museum for taking on a strange show and beautiful book.

— DOROTHY CROSS